DATA WITH SEMANTICS

Data Models and Data Management

DATA WITH SEMANTICS

Data Models and Data Management

J. Patrick Thompson

VNR Van Nostrand Reinhold
New York

Library of Congress Catalog Card Number 88-27920
ISBN 0-442-31838-3

Printed in the United States of America

Van Nostrand Reinhold
115 Fifth Avenue
New York, NY 10003

Van Nostrand Reinhold International Company Limited
11 New Fetter Lane
London EC4P 4EE, England

Van Nostrand Reinhold
480 La Trobe Street
Melbourne, Victoria 3000, Australia

Macmillan of Canada
Division of Canada Publishing Corporation
164 Commander Boulevard
Agincourt, Ontario M1S 3C7, Canada

16 15 14 13 12 11 10 9 8 7 6 5 4 3 2 1

Library of Congress Cataloging-in-Publication Data

Thompson, J. Patrick
  Data with semantics: data models and data management

Includes index.
  1. Data base design.   2. Data structures (Computer science)
  I. Title.
QA76.9.D26T47   1989   005.7'3   88-27920
ISBN 0-442-31838-3

Dedicated to:

Diddums
Schelum
Bryan-e-bee
and Guy-Guy

In Broken Images

He is quick, thinking in clear images;
I am slow, thinking in broken images.

He becomes dull, trusting to his clear images;
I become sharp, mistrusting my broken images.

Trusting his images, he assumes their relevance;
Mistrusting my images, I question their relevance.

Assuming their relevance, he assumes the fact;
Questioning their relevance, I question the fact.

When the fact fails him, he questions his senses;
When the fact fails me, I approve my senses.

He continues quick and dull in his clear images;
I continue slow and sharp in my broken images.

He in a new confusion of his understanding;
I in a new understanding of my confusion.

Robert Graves

Contents

Preface

The principal objective in writing this book was to produce something that deals with the real world—the world as it is. The book has to accommodate two major aspects of data processing and data management: First, a data processing environment must provide a level of inzformation that is detailed enough to be useful. The information should be broad enough to cover a wide range of requirements, including those of an organization's data processing department and of anyone who has to deal with that department on a regular basis.

The second major aspect concerns the processed data. The viability and stability of organizations depend on having data processed correctly. The data should accurately describe the real world because it will be used in guiding and determining the behavior of individuals and objects in the real world. But because the data represent a *hypothetical* description of the real world, the correctness, completeness, adequacy, or even reasonableness of the data can only be assessed by using the tools that are applied to hypothetical descriptions, in the context of scientific research. There is no other basis for a confrontation between our understanding and the object we seek to understand. Attempting to deal with databases and database design without addressing this issue is like teaching motor mechanics without mentioning the internal combustion engine.

After discussing the ways in which databases correctly or incorrectly describe the real world, the book deals with traditional database-related topics, such as files, indexes, keys, records, and so on. It also deals with the implications of the match between the data in the database and the world being modeled. To cover the practicalities of the day-to-day management of data, the book describes performance, integrity, and security.

As the book involves some fairly deep philosophical issues, it was necessary to find a vehicle for the presentation of the issues—hence, the dialogues. The underlying theme of the dialogues can be summarized as follows: Cartesian dualism and the triumph of mathematics and Newtonian mechanics has led to an excessive trust in the efficacy of formal systems. Hume and the problem of induction have completely undermined the Cartesian system and left us playing a guessing game with reality. Opinions, individual perceptions, and broad moral issues are as essential as observation in understanding the world around us. This is true in science, in data processing, and in our personal lives.

There is a pervasive awareness—one might almost say uneasiness—centered on the potential of data processing systems. It is a potential that may either materially and aesthetically enrich our lives or, for many,lead to a situation in which the very instruments that could enhance our understanding become an additional source of confusion and loss of faith. This book and the systems it describes are an attempt to tip the scales toward openness and clarity, versus the prevailing technical parochialism and general confusion.

The Characters in
the Dialogues

These characters appear in fabricated dialogues throughout the book. All of the voices (with the possible exception of *Auth*) are also caricatures of the aspects of the data processing environment.

Auth   (author)
myself.

Meph   (Mephisto)
cynic and Devil's advocate.

Dasd   (A Short Dark Lady)
a practical viewpoint, a lady who means business.

Ivle   (I. V. Lenin)
an idiot with peculiar political leanings and a genius for interrupting things, given to expressions of inappropriate enthusiasm.

Desc   (Rene Descartes)
mathematical extremism. He thinks the whole world is a mechanism, and everything can be reduced to an algorithm.

Pscl   (Blaise Pascal)
mathematics restrained (but not too much). He believes that

"knowledge provided by our hearts and minds is necessarily the basis on which our reasoning has to build its conclusions."

Gola   (Good Old Liebniz)
logic gone wild. He tends to have a boundless faith in the ability of science to penetrate the secrets of nature.

Cmmn   (Sir Isaac—call me mister—Newton)
logic troubled by formalisms. He is dazzled by the results of science but always acutely aware that his mechanics depended upon the very doubtful concept of gravity.

On the Book

Techniques	Content	Applications	Contents
Data Processing and Data Models	Why anyone would bother with data models and data management systems (presumably they have some data to manage). What is a data model? Some models worth knowing about	ServiceDB	An application servicing system that keeps track of customers and of visits by engineers to service their appliances. The system illustrates some of the problems of a record-based approach to database design
Problems with Records	Records in filing systems, be they steel cabinets, magnetic tape, or direct access storage devices	PalaeoDB	Some of the most complex systems of classification are used by biology; the database is concerned with storing information not only about data, but also about classifications of data, and even about classifications of classifications of data; but these issues are not unique to paleontology; even the humble ServiceDB encounters them
Description of the Data Model	A description of the semantic data model—what you can do with it and what it looks like		
Database Design	How the semantic data model can be used in designing databases		
Semantic Data Model Implementation	More on the semantic data model—approximately how it works and how you might use it		
Performance	The kinds of things that might make it all go a bit faster, and some reasons why systems are sometimes very slow.	CamDB	A database built around a computer aided manufacturing (CAM) application. The database is sufficiently complicated to make a sophisticated data model essential
Integrity	Making sure the data does not get lost or scrambled	SapperDB	Illustrating some of the pitfalls of moving data from one database to another, especially where the type of the data may vary.
Security and Control	Protecting data against malicious or illegal access		

Auth.   What's it really all about? You have before you a single source for a basic but useful level of knowledge about designing, accessing, tuning, and maintaining databases. Although the book is mainly concerned with data management, it occasionally does wander a little.

Ivle.   What was that?

Auth.   Allow me to introduce I. V. Lenin—a personage of peculiar political leanings, with a genius for interrupting things. He, along with a number of other characters, participates in the various discussions that punctuate the book and provide an entertaining backdrop to the more technical aspect of the text.

The material in the book is presented in three different styles—namely, techniques, discussions, and applications.

The book is aimed specifically at persons who have to design or to use databases that must function well in a commercial business environment. It is not aimed at persons (a) who are going to build data management systems, (b) who have to write examination papers about data management systems, or (for that matter) (c) who are going to lecture about data management systems—which is not to say that these other individuals might not find the book of some interest—simply that it is not aimed at them.

As a result of the target audience for the book, there is a heavy emphasis on dealing with things as they are. The working environment, the personnel, the programs and data, and the data management and file systems are all assumed to exist before being encountered by any one individual who may need to deal with them.

Some parts of the book are difficult to read, but all of the techniques and applications should be read. Anyone who is going to design, maintain, or program a database should know this book from cover to cover. If they do not, they can rely on messing things up sooner or later. If you read the book you will probably still mess things up, but you might at least understand both why you messed them up, and even—who knows—how to fix them.

Incidentally, even if you do not have to design, maintain, or program a database, reading this book is probably also helpful if you have to be able to determine whether a database is reasonable, correct, adequate, uncorrupt, or uncorruptable (if you are, for example, an auditor or a manager).

Before we carry on, I must offer an apology (and a warning) about the style of the book. I have tried to present a coherent and complete approach to database design and database management. In some cases I have skated over an issue, giving a rather superficial discussion where more detail might be desirable. At times, I must confess, the book might reasonably be accused of being "slick." But it does have to cover a lot of ground so the odd skid here and there is inevitable. For the most part I must leave the spotting of the "slick" bits as an exercise for the reader!

Further, subjects such as logic, the relational data model, the functional data model, and object-oriented languages are very complicated. A number of data modeling approaches that are not described in the book have a sound formal basis and either have been or may become extremely influential—for example, the Artificial Intelligence-related (e.g., Prolog- or Lisp-related) models using semantic nets. So far as logic is concerned, *modal logics* (i.e., systems of logic that allow such things as *true*, *false*, and *maybe*) are not discussed. In the areas of performance, integrity, and security and control, the presentations are reasonably comprehensive but some approaches are omitted in order to follow a single thread through the subject at hand. For example, a large performance-related literature on optimization is hardly mentioned. What amounts to a single approach to integrity is described—a number of other approaches, especially schemes associated with temporal data models, are also hardly mentioned. So consider yourself warned. Is there anything else?

Ivle.   Yes, the acknowledgments and the references to women.

Auth.   I have generally used the epithet "him" rather than "him or her"; the former I find easier to read. I hope that it will not offend too many readers.

As to the acknowledgments, it would be impossible to enumerate all of the people who helped, intentionally or unwittingly, in the production of this book. Some may recognize themselves in the dialogues; I hope no one takes these as too much of a back-handed compliment; no offense is intended (usually!). I must say a particular "thank you" though to Hamid Mirza, the manager of the section responsible for the development of the Semantic Information Manager, who was an inspiration and a stimulus to us all. I also extend particular thanks to Doug Tolbert, Hamid's former supervisor, who has been unstinting in his assistance in the process of producing this book. Thanks, Doug!

1

Data Processing and Data Models

INTRODUCTION

Why would anyone bother with data models and data management systems? Presumably, they have some data to manage, but a lot more is involved than just that. This chapter (a) looks at what a data model is and (b) talks about some data models that are important because they form the logical foundation for the semantic data model. This chapter is intended to introduce and/or clarify these topics. Later chapters assume this knowledge and focus on more advanced concepts of database design and use.

The first portion of this chapter, up to the discussion of the entity–relationship model, is a general description of data processing and data models. You may skip the first few sections of this chapter, up to the "entity–relationship (E–R) model," if you have a good understanding of what the fundamental problems of data processing are, and you know what a data model is, or you prefer to absorb this information from the rest of the text. The second portion of this chapter describes the relational, functional, and entity–relationship models. Understanding these models is useful but not essential for understanding the rest of the book, so the sections on these topics may also be skipped, at least on first reading.

COMPUTERS *AS* SYSTEMS AND *IN* SYSTEMS

The concepts underlying a computer form a useful starting point. Most persons are now familiar, in general outline, with what a computer does. Yet it is easy enough to forget why it is that computers are unique —what it is that distinguishes computers from almost every other artifact produced to date by the human race—computers are essentially concerned with the manipulation of information. Specifically, they allow data to be transformed from one state to another; at a certain level of abstraction, it is possible to view all operations on a computer as state transformations. The transformation can be thought of as follows:

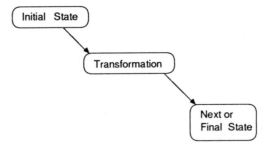

But this could also characterize almost any operation (digging a ditch, for example!). The details that characterize a computer must at least include the following:

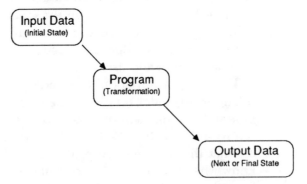

Yet this description is also not specific enough to characterize the computer as a modern stored-program device; one of the calculating engines built by Pascal or Leibniz would fit the data input–program–output model. The modern stored-program computer repre-sents a major departure because of the stored-program concept. This feature may be represented as follows:

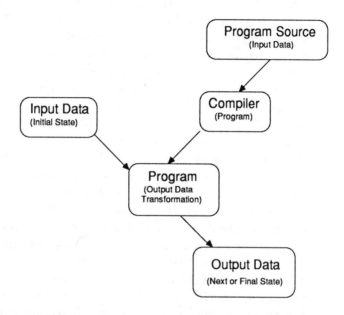

Here, a program is no more than the output of another program— a compiler. The *input to* the compiler is a series of language statements (or whatever), which are stored in a data file. The *output from* the com-piler is a code stream, representing the compiled program, which also is stored in a data file (hence, the term *stored program*).

The input to the program produced by the compiler might itself be a code file, assuming that the program was either a link editor or a code-file analyzer of some sort. The program produced by the compiler might itself be a compiler, it being usual for systems to be able to compile their own compilers. In this way, the system can be used to edit and modify its own operating system and compilers. The system can be used to extend itself. This is the fundamental feature of a computer and offers great power and flexibility.

Data management generally, and database design in particular, should be primarily concerned then with the business of describing states and transformations or, to put it slightly differently, data and programs. It should always be borne in mind that a data processing system is essentially a formal system with certain acceptable states and acceptable transformations. The system itself is utterly unforgiving in this respect; it does not recognize any uncertain states or fuzzy transformations. Data management (and database design) have to be concerned with a precise description of states and transformations if the system is to work with any degree of reliability. Database design, as presented here, is primarily concerned with a precise and complete description of states, which is half the battle!

There is a caveat: Avoid precision for its own sake. Precision, where it is possible and achieves some end, is highly desirable, but if the precision achieves nothing, forget it. Take, for example, a management information system that is to include addresses; the address information in the system is not going to be accessed other than as an entire unit; individual elements of the address will not be accessed by the program. In designing such a system, what would be the point of breaking down the address into house number, street name, street number, city name, zip code, and so on? It merely irritates the poor soul who has to use it, passing through all of those fields all the time, and provides almost no advantage over a simple alphanumeric item.

Unfortunately, the demon of precision has a ready audience in the world of data processing. The business of specifying and producing the system software for a data management system lives or dies by the precision with which it is performed. Therefore, the person writing the code to access and maintain someone else's data must be obsessed with precision and correctness. This attitude inevitably tends to filter through to areas where it is not as appropriate.

The power of extremely simple computational systems based on states and transformations was established by Alan Turing in the form of the Turing machine. A Turing machine is a very simple formalism for describing computations that breaks down the computation into excruciatingly small steps. Doing arithmetic with Turing machines is rather like building a picture of an elephant one square centimeter at a time—perfectly feasible so long as you are very methodical and do not lose your place. The analogy is a good one because looking at an elephant that way may be a very useful thing to do if, for example, you wanted to encode the picture of the elephant in a form suitable for storage in a computer. In a similar sort of way, Turing machines are helpful in the business of analyzing the fundamental components and limitations of computational processes.

Turing basically established that all of the known forms of logic are expressible using Turing machines. Logic can be expressed using

Turing machines, and Turing machines can be expressed as states and transformations. There is, then, a complete and proven equivalence between what can be done using logic and what can be done using a computer. This vision of the computer as a fundamentally infallible device may underlie much of the mystique of "artificial intelligence." This must surely be the most optimistic vision that we have ever possessed based on an artifact made by ourselves. But there is another side to all this.

The equivalence of logic and computation as expressed by Turing was new, and the formality of the approach was new, but an understanding of the process of acquiring knowledge expressed as states and transformations is actually very old. The state–transformation approach to the manipulation of information is closely related to the concept of a dialectic. A *dialectic* is an argument form that consists of The following:

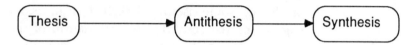

This argument form was recognized by the Greeks, and it conforms to the commonsense notion of the development of an understanding of a complex situation. This will usually (some would say always) take the following form:

1. *Thesis*—an initial understanding, which may be regarded as a more or less crude approximation

2. *Antithesis*—some contradictory information, which does not fit in with the initial understanding, and which throws some doubt on the initial understanding

3. *Synthesis*—a new and presumably better understanding that incorporates and accounts for both the original understanding and the contradiction.

This should not, incidentally, be confused with the Marxist or Hegelian idea of a dialectic. In these systems, the argument form has been perverted to the purposes of a historicist pseudologic. Such a system is of no interest at all to someone concerned with the business of handling data.

This dialectical approach to the development and improvement of systems may be seen in a variety of different contexts. The situation is often characterized by a systematic feedback process—a process that is an integral part of the system as a whole.

Take, for example, a steam engine with a regulator. The regulator ensures that the steam pressure and speed of operation of the engine do not exceed certain limits, thereby maintaining the state of the engine across time. The system is continually monitoring and correcting itself.

Another example is Newton's method for finding approximate solutions to an equation. The method involves repeated iterations, taking the value produced by the nth iteration and using it as input to the iteration $n + 1$, the process being repeated until some desired degree of accuracy is achieved.

The essential features of the systems are the following:

- Repeated execution of a process, with the repetitions either (a) producing some useful side effect (e.g., usable energy from an engine) or (b) resulting in termination of the process at some desired state, such as the root of an equation, to some desired degree of accuracy

- The process is assumed to be stable, in the case of Newton's method, successive values must converge; in the case of the steam regulator, the engine's speed and pressure must not exceed certain limits.

Two different types of systems have been distinguished on the basis of the techniques that the systems use in order to maintain a stable state. They are closed systems and open systems.

Closed systems are systems in which the feedback mechanism derives all information from within the system itself. The system ignores changes in the state of the environment. *Open systems* are systems in which feedback takes account of both the state of the environment and the state of the system itself.

There are any number of mechanisms and processes that represent examples of closed systems, the steam engine being an obvious one. An example (some would say the only example) of open systems is an intelligent organism. The steam engine can take account ("knows") of alterations in the steam pressure; it will, however, not hesitate to go over a cliff. But a human being is aware of being hungry or overfed and will not, ordinarily, walk over the edge of a cliff. The person takes account of the surrounding environment; the steam engine only does so to an extremely limited extent.

Feedback, then, is essential to the stability and survival of a large class of systems. These systems can often be described in terms of the dialectic or some similar state-change model.

One of the problems with a data processing system is that it is inherently a closed system. It has no built-in capacity for reacting to certain types of changes in the environment. These types of changes are usually changes to circumstances that were one of the original design assumptions. How many systems, for example, were put together in the 1960s and 1970s, based on the assumption that two characters were enough to represent the year?

So we have come full circle, from (a) the idea of a data processing system as the ultimate flexible tool, because it may be used to modify itself and encompasses the whole of logic, to (b) the idea of a data processing system as a member of a class of closed systems, which take no account of cliffs or other external obstacles. Both visions are valid: Computers represent both a challenge and an opportunity, providing a powerful enhancement to our ability to deal with and manipulate the world; the corollary, of course, is that they also enhance our ability to make a mess of things—and therein lies the challenge.

Karl Popper (Popper, 1965) has proposed a way of viewing the world that is useful in this context. It involves splitting the world into three realms:

1. World 1 is the world of real things, of things in and of themselves, as they exist independent of any particular observer.

2. World 2 is the subjective world of the individual. It represents World 1 as experienced by any particular individual, and it is peculiar to that individual.

3. World 3 contains all systems that have some ordering logic in terms of which the system may be understood. As such, it contains logic and all systems that aim to be logical. It contains science; it also contains the arts, assuming one grants the existence of criteria for evaluating and understanding individual works of art.

Worlds 1 and 2 may interact, and Worlds 2 and 3 may interact; however, no mechanism exists that allows direct interaction between World 1 and World 3. World 2 is fragmented; each individual exists in isolation, having no direct access to the World 2 of some other individual.

People can communicate essentially only through World 3; most forms of language belong to World 3.

Any system established by people to serve some goal (such as making a profit) will have to operate within the limits implied by Popper's three worlds. The goals must be established and understood as World 3 objects. The system itself must be depicted and understood as a World 3 object (assuming it is to have more than one manager), and the model of the system must continually be reviewed and altered to accommodate any discrepancies that arise between the system, as it exists in World 1, and the model of the system, which exists in World 3. This always presupposes understanding of the model, and contact with the system by some individual (in World 2), as World 3 and World 1 cannot interact.

THE REALM OF THE DATA ADMINISTRATOR

The place of database design in such a system should be obvious. The database must represent, at least in part, a World 3 object, a tool that may be used by our innocent selves, isolated and adrift in our World 2s, struggling to come to terms with, and control, an intractable World 1.

This view of the data processing world is compelling if the typical problems experienced in running and administering an installation are considered. Much of the data processing system actually exists outside of the machine itself and is dependent on the knowledge and expertise of the individuals using the computer. The information in the machine, on its own, is never an adequate basis for understanding the use of the computer. The typical data processing department could be represented as follows:

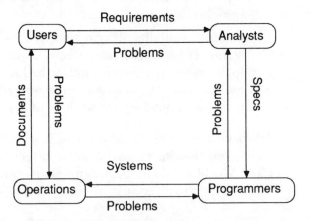

From this diagram, it should be quite obvious why it is so often the case that users do not get what they want. There are so many components to the system, and so many of the components are poorly defined, or poorly motivated, that it is inevitable that discrepancies should arise between one part of the system and another.

Database systems have a key role to play here. A well-designed, well-understood database will provide a sound basis for the elimination of inaccuracies and inconsistencies within the system. With sufficient thought, the data management system can even be used to shortcut some of the circuitous routes of the typical system development life cycle.

Most data processing departments have neither the time nor the expertise to provide for any more than a superficial degree of control over both the data they process and the programs they use to process it. How then do they survive? The answer is that they do not. This may seem preposterous, but in terms of the degree of control being considered here, it is almost certainly true.

Most data processing departments do not have systems that are written or documented to a standard whereby they can be readily taken over or understood by others. This is evident in the curious and all-pervasive phenomenon of the "indispensable" expert. The species has several distinct subspecies:

The autochthonous expert (*Autochtone* = original inhabitant) was one of the team that originally developed the system. This person is happy to stay put after everyone else goes, secure in the knowledge that this indispensability leads to absolute freedom.

The latecomer, through months of searching through program listings and system dumps, has come to an understanding of the system. Useful, but somewhat unreliable, the latecomer may go off and do the same thing somewhere else.

The contractor, exercising a grip like iron, and employed precisely because of unequalled expertise, is essential because the systems are so badly documented and difficult to understand.

There have been attempts to institutionalize the indispensable expert. Approaches to project management have been suggested that would recognize and attempt to capitalize on this person's existence. These suggestions revolve around developing programs in teams. Only one person, the lead programmer, does all the work; the rest of the team provides various supportive roles. It is no exaggeration to say that this approach is entirely a result of a failure to depict, in World 3, what is going on in the lead programmer's private World 2.

If everyone has equal and adequate knowledge of the system being developed, there is no real problem about having several people working on it at once. Sadly, this is not the case. Largely due to the lack of good data models, systems remain undocumented, understood only by specialists and only in fragments—that is, no one person understands the whole thing. This leads to a defeatist attitude toward systems that people are not directly involved in.

A black-box mentality becomes common: Users assume that if the system does not do what they want it to, it must be broken. This attitude can turn a sensible, intelligent individual into one of Skinner's rats, blindly pushing the button in the hope that this time, it will produce the goods.

The Somebody Somewhere Syndrome is a more subtle version of the black-box mentality. The assumption is that Somebody Somewhere understands how it works, can fix it if it goes wrong, and knows why you have to put that incomprehensible code in that stupid field every time you use the system even though it has no apparent purpose. This syndrome leads to a blind and unreasoning acceptance of the system as it is.

This, then, is how a Luddite's ideal becomes manifest. The machine makes work for the chosen few. As long as it remains the perquisite of a minority, it is a passport to the select fraternity of the machine minders—all others are denied intelligent usage of the system's labor-saving capabilities. If the situation changes, however, the latter-day Luddite may not destroy the machinery with hammers though certainly no incentive is felt to publicize and popularize the machine minder's work.

DATA MODELS

Why bother? One answer lies in the aforementioned logistical complexities of the data management environment. Given that the data is to be accessed by a variety of different people, over a potentially very long period of time, it is vital that some structuring mechanism be available to allow these different people to come to some common understanding of how the data is to be interpreted.

Another answer is derivable from the characteristics of the computer itself. Computers are not nearly as good at storing data as is a human brain. It is necessary to resort to all sorts of subterfuges and devices in order to get the computer to accept data in the first place, and particularly to do so in such a way that it is subsequently possible to get the data out again. To do so, it has proven desirable to structure these various techniques in a variety of ways, and this is very much what certain forms of data modeling are all about, notably the relational and functional models.

Yet another answer can be derived from another set of limitations inherent in the currently available computers: not only are they not very good at storing data, they are also not very powerful. They have finite memories; the number of I/Os and the number of operations that they can perform per second is limited. This provides additional reason to try and impose some order on the bag of tricks at the disposal of the database programmer facing these problems. This also gives rise to a rash of data models, such as the hierarchical and network models.

A data model usually comes in two parts:

1.   A method of describing and storing data
2.   A method of accessing and manipulating the data.

This is a straightforward reflection of the state–transformation approach to understanding a data processing system; in fact the state–transformation approach is itself a very abstract data model.

Logic is a kind of data model. As we shall see, data modeling is now going back to basics and building very directly on the realm of logic. In fact, it is fair to say that data modeling grew out of the application of logic to the business of managing data. The term *data modeling* was first popularized by E. F. Codd (Codd, 1970) who was trying to use ideas drawn from logic to understand data.

Background

The original model of data used in the implementation of computers was the architecture proposed by John Von Neumann during the very early stages of the design and development of electronic data processing systems. This architecture was proposed in the 1940s and became known as the Von Neumann architecture. The Von Neumann architecture is just a very simple data model, which may be represented as follows:

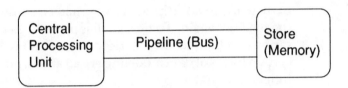

The model consists of an addressable store of data that may be accessed by the central processing unit (CPU), using a *fetch operation* that specifies the address at which to find the word to be fetched from the store. The CPU can perform operations on fetched words using a limited set of storage locations present in the CPU itself (called "registers"), and it ultimately can store data back into memory (at some specified location), using a *store operation*.

This model of the system has had a profound influence on the general development of data processing, and especially on the development of programming languages. This is most readily seen in a language such as COBOL, which divides the program into two parts: the *working storage section*, which is a description of the memory used by the program; and the *procedure division*, which is a description of the series of actions to be carried out by the CPU in processing the program. The Von Neumann architecture clearly illustrates the two aspects of a data model—namely, a data storage mechanism and a data manipulation mechanism.

The Von Neumann model obviously relates very closely to the state–transformation model of data processing, with the major (very major) exception that it adds the concept of the pipeline. The pipeline is limited to transferring information one word at a time, from the CPU to the store, or from the store to the CPU. This is in contrast to the state–transformation model, which does not limit the amount of data that can be affected by a single transformation.

This word-at-a-time limitation is what dictates most of the characteristics of the languages based on the Von Neumann architecture; it has become known as the "Von Neumann Bottleneck." It is the source of the contemporary emphasis on what are known as procedural languages, and it is regarded by many as the ultimate reason for the lack of useful formal characteristics in most of the currently used programming languages (a topic outside the scope of the current discussion).

Incidentally, there seems to be a law associated with bottlenecks:

> The usual result of the elimination of one bottleneck is the discovery of another one.

Most systems are thick with bottlenecks of one kind or another. Given that it invariably takes a long time to find and fix any particular bottleneck, most system tuning must either be very modest in its aims, or must accept a high probability of failure.

Beyond Von Neumann, the data models developed have mainly taken the form of ad hoc solutions to the problem of how to represent and manipulate data in a machine based on the Von Neumann architecture. These models (notably the hierarchical and network models) do not have many useful formal characteristics and are only of interest when considering the question of how a database might be implemented, as opposed to the far more important question of how it might be logically represented or described.

A considerable number of data models have been designed on an explicit formal basis, and there are two contrasting approaches evident in these data models: a network approach and a record approach. Both approaches have made some important contributions to the ways that we can think about data. The relational data model exemplifies the record approach; the functional data model illustrates the network approach. These are discussed in some detail, as concepts drawn from both are useful in understanding the semantic data model. The entity–relationship model is considered first, as it provides a convenient means of describing data in a manner that makes sense in the context of a variety of different models.

The Entity–Relationship (E–R) Model

The E–R model is not an entirely suitable basis for a working database management system. It is intended to be a mechanism for providing a unified view of data generally, and, as such, in some respects, it is too generalized for use in designing a database management system. But it is extremely useful in understanding or designing a particular database. The generality of the model is actually only a problem when a data manipulation language (DML) has to be specified. As this is not at issue here, it does not pose a problem.

One way of viewing some of the current developments in data modeling theory is in terms of the restrictions on the E–R model necessary to make a DML possible. To be fair, many of the ideas that have subsequently surfaced, particularly in the various models that have been labeled "semantic," are present in some form in the entity–relationship model. Its major significance, though, seems to have been its break with the concept of a record.

In this discussion of the model, the emphasis is on a basic understanding of entities and relationships. The subtleties of the model (e.g., the subtleties of handling different types of relationships) are disregarded here because similar ideas are covered in more detail in the description of the semantic data model.

COMPONENTS OF THE E–R MODEL

In an E–R model, the world is viewed in a commonsense way as composed of *entities*, or things. The entities may have *relationships* to each other, and the entities and relationships may have attributes. An *attribute* is just some characteristic of an entity or relationship, such as a name, or an age, or a date of birth.

People naturally tend to think of the world in terms of things, particularly in terms of different types of things. A particular thing, Mr. Newton for example, may be said to be of a particular type, as a result of its having particular characteristics.

Assuming that the thing, Mr. Newton, is the historical character Sir Isaac Newton, we can ascribe to it a gender (i.e., male) and legitimately refer to it as him. He has any number of other characteristics, such as height (at some particular time), father's name, color of eyes, and so on. The type of the thing, Mr. Newton, is *Homo sapiens*. It is the very fact that he is a *Homo sapiens* that allows him to have all of these characteristics.

If, on the other hand, Mr. Newton is a neutered cat, then poor Mr. Newton cannot be referred to as him, but remains an it. We can console Mr. Newton by allowing him to be a Fat Cat, a Tabby Cat, and any other appropriate characteristics. Again, the type is important. Mr. Newton, as indicated, is here a neutered cat. It is this which dictates what characteristics "he" can and cannot have.

A data model must live or die by the ease with which it may be understood. The network model was one of the first to popularize the use of diagrams for depicting data. The E–R model introduced the E–R diagram, which is a very convenient method of portraying the structure of a database. Following a standard notation, entities may be represented as rectangles:

Relationships are represented as diamonds:

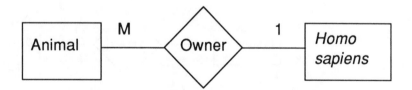

Relationships are assumed to be bidirectional, and the cardinality of the relationship (that is, how many things you can have on either end of the relationship) is indicated along with the relationship ("M" is for many"). For example,

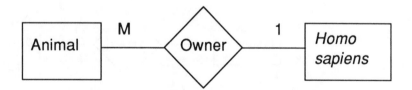

There is some confusion here over the use of the term *entity*. Both *Homo sapiens* and Mr. Newton have been referred to using the term *entity*. In fact, *Homo sapiens* is a collection of entities, whereas Mr. Newton is assumed to be, in this case, a single entity. Properly speaking, we should be talking about a entity–relationship–collection diagram.

But entity–relationship diagram is quite enough of a mouthful, and the dual use of the term *entity* is continued throughout this volume. When we look at the semantic data model, the fact that the object Mr. Newton is different from the object *Homo sapiens* is not as obvious as it might at first seem. So, if you find yourself confused by the term *entity*, this is entirely reasonable; it is going to take a good deal of discussion to sort it all out.

A very similar problem arises in distinguishing between the relationship father, and the entity *Homo sapiens*. It is not at all obvious why a father is a relationship and not an entity. Surely, a father is at least as much of a thing as a cat is? This again is a problem tackled by the semantic data model, and it is deferred for the time being. For the moment, determining whether a thing is (a) a thing, (b) a collection of things, or (c) a relationship among things is left as an exercise for the reader!

E–R EXAMPLE

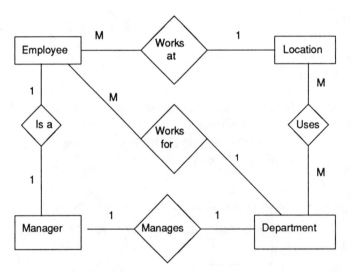

E-R Model Example

This example illustrates a simple database containing the entities, employee, location, department, and manager. An employee may only work for one department and may only work at one location. An employee may be a manager, and a manager may manage a department. Departments may only have a single manager, may use multiple locations, and may have multiple employees working for them. All of these entities may have any number of attributes, and in practice, a database like this could be expected to have many more relationships in it.

SOME OBSERVATIONS ON THE MODEL

The E–R model was one of the first to represent a real break with the record-based model. Many of the ideas that later crystallized in the semantic data model are present in the E–R model. Many of the problems that the semantic data model solves could not even be adequately expressed until the E–R model had been proposed.

For example, the question of when a thing is an entity and when it is a relationship cannot be described using records because records do not explicitly recognize either entities or relationships. However, it is not uncommon to find an entity being thought of as a record, which is not a useful attitude. Peter Chen, the original designer of the E–R model, cites the following example:

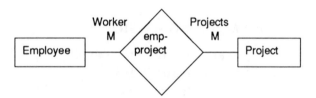

Here, employee has the role, "worker," so far as "project" is concerned. The concept of a role here is a means of indicating what the significance is of a relationship so far as some participant in the relationship is concerned. In a sense, an employee as a worker has some characteristics that an employee alone does not have. The employee as a worker may, for example, have an attribute indicating the amount of time spent on the project he or she is assigned to. An employee who is not a worker (i.e., has not been assigned to a project) does not have such a characteristic, and as such, she or he is something different. Remember that entities are distinguished according to the different attributes that they have; if they have different attributes, they are necessarily different types of entities. What the E–R model is allowing here is for a single thing—that is a single entity—to be of more than one type simultaneously. At this point, records go out the window.

This cannot be emphasized too strongly. An entity cannot be equated to a record, nor can a record be equated to an entity. There are many facets to this inequality. It should always be borne in mind when thinking about data in a computer because the data ultimately will be *represented* as a collection of records. The data ultimately, however, must be *interpreted* as a set of entities.

(Note also the continuing confusion over the term *entity*. The foregoing paragraphs can be read by interpreting *entity* to mean either a single thing or a collection of things.)

It has been extremely difficult for the programming community to make the break with the record-based model. Most people accustomed to writing or deciphering programs can only think in terms of records and data, and they find it extremely difficult to use entities and relationships instead. For an adequate approach to the logical side of database design, records are quite useless, while entities and relationships are a promising beginning. It is essential, then, to grasp entities and relationships. It is also sensible, in coming to terms with the semantic data model, to start with the E–R model, as so much of the one grew out of the other.

SOME MODELING MILESTONES

The general area of data modeling has evolved enormously over the period from the early 1970s to the mid-1980s. The evolution of the subject has been marked by the publication of a series of articles. Virtually all of these have been published in one of the journals produced by the Association for Computing Machinery (ACM), mostly either in the *Communications of the ACM*, known as CACM, or in the *Transactions on Database Systems*, affectionately known as ACM TODS. The milestones, then, are as follows:

Author	Title	Date
E. F. Codd	*The Relational Model of Data for Shared Data Banks*	June 1970
P. P-S. Chen	*The Entity–Relationship Model: Towards a Unified View of Data*	March 1976
J. M. Smith and D. C. P. Smith	*Database Abstraction: Aggregation and Generalization*	June 1977
W. Kent	*Data and Reality: Basic Assumptions in Data Processing Reconsidered*	1978
M. M. Hammer and D. J. McLeod	*The Semantic Data Model: A Modeling Mechanism for Database Applications*	1978
J. Backus	*Can Programming be Liberated from the Von Neumann Style? A Functional Style and Its Algebra of Programs*	1978
W. Kent	*Limitations of Record-Based Information Models*	March 1979
D. Shipman	*The Functional Data Model and the Data Language DAPLEX*	1979
O. P. Buneman and R. E. Frankel	*FQL—A Functional Query Language*	1979
E. F. Codd	*Extending the Database Relational Model to Capture one Meaning*	December 1979

Modeling Milestones

DATA MODELS AND LOGIC

The relational model was first proposed by E. F. Codd (Codd, 1970) and was based on an attempt to use results drawn from the theory of logic, particularly from first-order predicate calculus. It is therefore necessary to give a brief outline of what predicate calculus consists of. And to explain predicate calculus, it is necessary first to describe the propositional calculus on which it is based.

Propositions and the Laws of Thought

The logic of propositions, or propositional calculus, was proposed by George Boole in his book, the *Laws of Thought*. The proposals put forward by Boole form the basis for the Boolean algebra. Boolean algebra consists of a set of rules that indicate how certain types of statements may be transformed in various ways (the parentheses indicate precedence in the usual way). For example, given the following statement,

$$(P \text{ OR } Q) \text{ AND } P,$$

it is possible to derive the statement

$$(P \text{ AND } P) \text{ OR } (Q \text{ AND } P),$$

which in turn may be used as the basis for

$$P \text{ OR } (Q \text{ AND } P).$$

The expression "derive the statement" means that there are rules that allow other statements to be substituted for the original statement, which are guaranteed to be equivalent to the original statement. That is, the derived statement will always be true when the original is true and always false when the original is false.

This is very similar to what a compiler does; it take a series of source language statements (e.g., a COBOL program) and translates them into another equivalent set of statements (most likely machine language or code, but it may also be microcode or another programming language).

Propositional calculus aims to allow us to take any propositional form, substitute particular values for all of the propositions in the form, and then derive, in a systematic way, whether the resulting proposition is true or not. It also allows us to take such propositional forms as the following:

$$P \text{ OR } (Q \text{ AND } P)$$

and determine whether it is possible for any set of things to be true of the propositional form. The calculus allows us to take the propositional form and manipulate it, as a form, deriving other equivalent forms that may be easier to handle or more convenient to deal with in some way.

For example, "Horn clauses" are propositional forms in which the proposition is broken down into fragments, each of which consists only of parts connected by ORs, with a single part negated. For example,

P OR Q OR NOT P

There are certain well understood algorithms for analyzing propositions expressed as Horn clauses. As a result, they are fundamental to logic-based programming languages such as prolog. The following are examples of propositions:

> the animal went left
> the animal went right
> the animal did not go left

Propositional calculus is concerned with the relations between such propositions. Truth tables make use of propositional variables and plot the possible values of various combinations of propositions. For example,

P	Q	P OR Q
T	T	T
T	F	T
F	T	T
F	F	F

is a truth table; it lists every combination of the possible values of P and Q. For each combination, the value of the expression (in this case P OR Q) is provided. The truth table is a way of describing how OR is to be interpreted in a proposition. The same may be done for the other logical operators. The fundamental logical operators are NOT, AND, and OR. All of the other operators of the propositional calculus can be derived from these three.

The argument forms of the propositional calculus do not say anything about the internal form of the statements involved. The only thing at issue is whether the individual propositions are true or false. If for P, we substitute

> the animal went left

for Q, we substitute

> the animal went right

and if we are also given the information P OR Q—that is, *either* the animal went left *or* the animal went right, and if we are further given that Q is false, we can read from Line 2 in the table that P is true.

A variety of argument forms have been tabulated; for example,

Modus ponens	NOT P OR Q
	P
	therefore Q
Modus tolens	NOT P OR Q
	NOT P
	therefore Q
Hypothetical syllogism	NOT P OR Q
	NOT Q OR R
	therefore NOT P OR R
Disjunctive syllogism	P OR Q
	NOT P
	therefore Q
Conjunction	P
	Q
	therefore P AND Q
Addition	P
	therefore P OR Q

In considering the direction in which the animal went, we were using a disjunctive syllogism. The argument forms then are just different things that can be derived from truth tables.

Various propositional forms also play a major role in propositional calculus. They are a set of propositional forms that are necessarily true, such as the following:

Law of noncontradiction:	NOT (P AND NOT P)
Law of the excluded middle:	P OR NOT P
Law of double negation:	P is equivalent to NOT NOT P

and so on.

The hope was that by identifying and formalizing all of the rules that govern the propositions we use in describing and solving problems, the problem-solving process itself could be reduced to a formalism. Logic, in this scenario, becomes the universal answer to all possible questions.

George Boole was doomed to disappointment in his assumption that *The Laws of Thought* would become a closed book once he had finished it. Any number of important developments have followed his work—notably, the idea of predicate calculus.

Predicates and Quantifiers

Predicate calculus deals with argument forms in which the validity of the argument form depends not just on the external relations of the propositions involved, but also on the internal construction of the propositions themselves. It is always the case with a proposition that something is stated about something else. For example, the proposition

the animal went right

states something ("went right") about something else ("the animal"). In this case, the *subject* of the proposition is the animal, the thing stated about the proposition (went right) is the *predicate*. Whether the proposition is true depends on whether the predicate is true for the given subject. Argument forms such as *modus ponens* or the disjunctive syllogism are indifferent to the relations between the subjects and the predicates of the propositions involved in the arguments. But there are argument forms in which these relations are important. It is best to explain this idea with an example. The following argument cannot be rendered in the propositional calculus:

all men are mammals

all mammals are animals

therefore, all men are animals

Apart from the "therefore," this argument is simply three separate propositions. What makes the argument sensible is the fact that the predicates and subjects of the constituent propositions are repeated through the argument. These types of statements ("all mammals are animals," for example) are referred to as propositional functions or predicates.

There is a rather unfortunate dual use of the term "predicate" here; it can refer either to a statement in a particular form or to something asserted about a subject. From here on in this book, "predicate" is only used in the first sense.

Predicate calculus is concerned with propositional functions or predicates. Predicates themselves are propositions containing terms that can stand for any one of a class of objects, not just for some single definite object. When all these types of terms in a predicate are replaced by some definite instance of the class involved, the predicate becomes a proposition. In programming terms, a predicate is a proposition containing variables.

For example,

$$x < 100$$

(or "x is less than 100") is a predicate, where x may stand for any integer whatsoever (x being any integer, by the way, is a rule I just made up about x). Now if some definite value is substituted for x, such as 99, then we have the proposition,

$$99 < 100$$

(or "99 is less than 100"), which happens to be true. Each of the x's in the proposition are usually referred to as "terms," or "variables."

Predicate calculus assumes that the terms in a proposition each have a potential range of values, known as the *domain* of the term. A predicate is just a proposition that has at least one term for which the actual value of the term is not specified, but the range of permissible values is. If each term in a predicate has some specific value substituted for it, the predicate becomes a proposition, which may be either true or false and may be evaluated using Boolean algebra.

A predicate is not restricted to just one term; it may have as many terms as necessary. Predicate calculus places no restrictions in this respect. A predicate such as

$$x < y \text{ and } x > z$$

has three terms to it, x, y, and z; and as such is known as a 3-place predicate. The previous example of "$x < 100$" was a 1-place predicate. Generally, predicates may be described as n-place predicates, where the n is some integer value indicating the number of distinct variables contained by the predicate. It should be noted that the x, y, z predicate is not a 4-place predicate because x is only counted once, even though it appears in the predicate twice.

Quantifiers are another important idea of predicate calculus. There are two quantifiers: the universal quantifier and the existential quantifier. The universal quantifier is often represented by an upside-down A, and the existential quantifier is represented by a back-to-front E. This text will stick to the use of the terms "there exists" for the existential quantifier (meaning that there is *at least* one to which the predicate applies) and "for all" for the universal quantifier (meaning that the predicate applies to *every* one).

The quantifiers are used are follows: Assuming we wanted to render the conclusion to the preceding argument about humans being animals:

(for all x) (x is a human AND x is an animal)

Or to express the idea that there is at least one honest human among us

(there exists x) (x is a human AND x is honest)

This merely says that there is at least one such x, where x is human and to be trusted. It does not, of course, say that there is more than one.

It is interesting to note that universal predicates can be disproven by a single counterinstance. Existential predicates, however, can only be disproven by examining every possible instance, which is often virtually impossible. The moral: Beware of prophets proclaiming existential predicates!

This has implications, for example, so far as query processing is concerned. Compare the following two queries:

Give me the name of those departments that employ at least one person over the age of 60

Give me the name of those departments all of whose employees are over 60

To satisfy the first query, for any department not returned, every single person working for the department will have to be examined.

For the second query, the first counterinstance will terminate the query. Given that ordinarily small subsets of the information in the database will be returned for queries, this means a dramatic difference in the impact of the type of query used on the system.

If the query resembles an existential statement, then the only way to refute it is to search the entire database. If, however, the query is a universal one, the first counterinstance will terminate it.

Universally or existentially quantified predicates then are predicates in which one or more of the terms is bound to a quantifier—either a universal or an existential quantifier. Any term that is not bound to a quantifier is a free term. A predicate in which all of the terms are quantified cannot be turned into a proposition in the ordinary way. It is necessary to have at least one free term to be able to turn a predicate into a proposition. If all the variables are bound, the predicate will be either true or false and as such, it can be treated as a proposition anyway.

There is a substitution that is at least apparently possible for universally and existentially quantified variables, though it is not very practical. Consider the variable x, where x is a dinosaur, in the following predicate:

(for all x) (x is extinct)

This would almost be equivalent to the proposition

ankylosaurs and plesiosaurs and thecodonts and . . . are extinct

It would be necessary to list all of the possible x's in order to produce a proposition equivalent to a predicate containing x as a universally quantified variable.

For an existentially quantified variable, the ANDs would be changed into ORs. For example

(there exists x) (x is a common ancestor)

says that there is an x that is a common ancestor of the dinosaurs. This might be turned into a proposition such as the following,

ankylosaurs or plesiosaurs or thecodonts or . . . were the common ancestor of the dinosaurs

For various reasons, neither of these propositions are very satisfactory as representations of their equivalent predicates. But they do serve to illustrate the point that it is not possible to substitute a single instance for a quantified variable. The quantified variable either stands for one of a whole class of things, as in the case of the existential variable, or for every member of a whole class of things, as in the case of the universal variable.

Turning predicates into propositions is also allowed, however, in an effort to refute or establish a predicate. The idea here is that a single counterinstance of a universally quantified variable may be used to refute the predicate containing the variable. Similarly, a single positive instance of an existentially quantified variable will establish the predicate containing the variable (in both cases, of course, assuming that there are no other clauses contained in the predicate that may also require evaluation).

To summarize, then, the formalisms that arise in logic may be classified as follows.

Propositions: ordinary everyday statements that may be true or false

Propositional forms: ways of organizing propositions without regard to their internal form; uses the normal operators of Boolean algebra—NOT, OR, AND

Predicates: propositions that contain variables; propositions derived from the predicates consist of the predicate with all of the variables replaced by concrete instances (referred to as *instantiation*)

n-place predicates: predicates having *n* variables (or terms) in them.

Universally or existentially quantified predicates: predicates in which one or more of the terms is "bound" to either a universal or an existential quantifier. Any term that is not bound to a quantifier is a free term. A predicate in which all of the terms are quantified cannot be turned into a proposition in the ordinary way.

The comparison between predicates and queries against a database is not an idle one. A query in a properly formulated language must be expressible as a predicate. Logic is absolutely fundamental to a proper understanding of the process of retrieving data from a database.

THE RELATIONAL MODEL

The relational approach to data management consists of providing a set of operations that are a special case of predicate calculus. Generally speaking, any operation in a relational database management system should be expressible in predicate calculus and should have a comparable meaning. As a result, a relational database management system will inherit all of the rules of predicate calculus. For example, the following four rules (from Gray, 1984) are specified as a part of the semantics of predicate calculus:

1. A variable in an expression can only be quantified once, so

    $$(\text{there exists } x) \ (\text{for all } x) \ P(x)$$

    is illegal.

2. Wherever a predicate is used, it must always take the same number of parameters.

3. The values of all constants and variables, and the arguments of predicates and functions, must be taken from a predefined universe (or domain of discourse) over which they are defined.

4. A statement in the calculus is a formula, all variables of which are quantified.

All of these rules are then inherited by a relational system. Consider, for example, the implications of the third condition; it amounts to the idea that only finite collections of data can be dealt with by the model.

Predicate calculus has been used as the basis of other languages, such as Prolog. In Prolog, programming is regarded as proving a theorem based on "horn" clauses. The relational model is extremely simple and may be described in terms of tables and operations on tables.

Tables

The basic data structure used by the relational data model is the table. A table is considered to be a two-dimensional object, consisting of a collection of rows, collectively making one dimension, each row having the same number and type of columns, which make the second dimension.

One of the attractive features of the model is that everything can be considered to be some form of table: The database, the data extracted from the database, and the data applied to the database may all be thought of as tabular in form. This is sometimes referred to as *closure*; that is, a relational system is a closed system with respect to tables. Whatever you do, you will always be dealing with tables.

Tables are usually presented in a format such as the following:

| Employee ◄─────────────────────────────── Table Name |

Employee Number	Employee Name	Employee Department	◄─ Column Names
			◄─ First Row

Returning to predicate calculus, an n-place predicate is a proposition with n terms or variables in it. A proposition is a predicate in which each of the terms has been replaced by some actual individual.

So—a table can be seen as a predicate in which each row of the table represents a true proposition that is derived from, or an instance of, the predicate. The employee table, for example, may be taken as the following predicate:

The individual with EMPLOYEE NUMBER x, EMPLOYEE NAME y, and EMPLOYEE DEPARTMENT z is an employee.

Each row of the table represents a proposition, inasmuch as it provides a set of values that may be substituted for the various terms in the predicate; such as the following:

The individual with EMPLOYEE NUMBER 1234, EMPLOYEE NAME ISAAC NEWTON, and EMPLOYEE DEPARTMENT 1001 is an employee.

Operations on Tables

There are three basic operations on the model:

1. The **select** operation applies a condition to each row of a table, returning those rows that satisfy the condition.

2. The **project** operation makes a new table, consisting of a subset of the columns present in the original table.

3. The **join** operation makes one table out of two tables. There are a variety of different types of **join**; for example, the natural **join** forms a new row by taking two tables and joining rows in the one table to rows in the other table, where any columns in the two tables with the same name have the same value.

The following is an example of a **join** operation involving two tables. One table represents information about employees, the other about the departments for which the employees work.

Employee

Employee Number	Employee Name	Employee Department
1234	I.Newton	1001
2341	B.Pascal	1001
4321	D.Mephisto	1002
3211	G.Leibniz	1000

Department

Department Number	Department Name
1001	Pragmatists
1000	Idealists
1002	Advocates

Taking a **join** of DEPARTMENT and EMPLOYEE produces the following:

Department–Employee

Department Number	Department Name	Employee Number	Employee Name	Employee Department
1001	Pragmatists	1234	I.Newton	1001
1001	Pragmatists	2341	B.Pascal	1001
1001	Pragmatists	4321	D.Mephisto	1002
1001	Pragmatists	3211	G.Leibniz	1000
1000	Idealists	1234	I.Newton	1001
1000	Idealists	2341	B.Pascal	1001
1000	Idealists	4321	D.Mephisto	1002
1000	Idealists	3211	G.Leibniz	1000
1002	Advocates	1234	I.Newton	1001
1002	Advocates	2341	B.Pascal	1001
1002	Advocates	4321	D.Mephisto	1002
1002	Advocates	3211	G.Leibniz	1000

Restricting attention for the moment to a two-table **join**, note that the **join** has the effect of taking every row in one table and combining it with every row in the other table, thereby giving a new table consisting of every possible combination of the rows in the original two tables. This type of **join** is sometimes referred to as a crossproduct. It is illustrated by the DEPARTMENT and EMPLOYEE tables, which, when joined, give the DEPARTMENT–EMPLOYEE table. The process can be extrapolated to any number of tables, simply by taking the tables two at a time and doing a series of two-table **joins**.

Obviously, the information in the DEPARTMENT–EMPLOYEE table does not make much sense. This is where the **select** and **project** operations come in. Assuming that ultimately we are interested in a table consisting of people and the departments they work for, the first thing to do is to take the DEPARTMENT–EMPLOYEE table and **select** those rows where the EMPLOYEE–DEPARTMENT is equal to the DEPARTMENT–NUMBER, giving the following:

Department–Employee

Department Number	Department Name	Employee Number	Employee Name	Employee Department
1001	Pragmatists	1234	I.Newton	1001
1001	Pragmatists	2341	B.Pascal	1001
1002	Idealists	3211	G.Leibniz	1002
1000	Advocates	1234	Mephisto	1000

The only columns of interest are DEPARTMENT NAME and EM-PLOYEE NAME so **project** may be used to produce a table that excludes all of the other columns:

Department–Employee

Department Name	Employee Name
Pragmatists	I.Newton
Pragmatists	B.Pascal
Idealists	G.Leibniz
Advocates	Mephisto

The combination of **join**, **select**, and **project** has produced a single table that combines information from the two original tables. It should be noted that there is a major assumption here: the DEPARTMENT NUMBER and EMPLOYEE DEPARTMENT columns contain comparable values. There is, of course, no guarantee of this, and there is nothing specified about the **select** operation (so far) that would disallow a **join**, **select**, and **project** sequence based on any two columns—for example, DEPARTMENT NUMBER and EMPLOYEE NUMBER.

Relational Model Example

This example uses the same database as that used for the E–R model example. The database consists of a series of tables. The tables may be used in **join** operations in which some value from one table is matched with a value from another table. The existence of a matching value is taken to imply the existence of a relationship between the two table rows involved. Establishing the relationship involves extracting a value from one table row and placing it in another. Assuming that it is just these two table rows that are to be related to each other, the extracted value must be unique. The extracted value is usually referred to as a "key." The item that receives the extracted value is usually called a "foreign key."

In the following, only foreign keys and table keys are provided. Key names are the table name, suffixed with the word *number.* Each table is represented by the name of the table, followed by the table's column names, which are enclosed in parentheses:

```
Employee(
   employee-number,
   employed-by-dept,
   works-at-location)

Manager(
   employee-number,
   manages-dept)

Department(
   department-number)

Location(
   location-number)

location-usage(
   location-number,
   department-number)
```

Some Observations on the Model

The relational model is based on predicate calculus, with the added limitation of not having NOTs. This, in turn, is derived from limiting the operations of the model to producing or using tables that have a finite, limited, storable number of rows.

In order to make the model usable as a basis for a database management system, a variety of features and caveats have had to be added. Many of these have either complicated the model considerably or brought in a number of limitations of their own. Notable in this respect is normalization.

Relational systems are very much tied to the idea of an n-place predicate, or record. This is at some point an unavoidable view; for example, when it comes to the storage of data in a data processing system, records are the only technique available. If what you want to do is store data onto disk or tape, a system that deals with records is inescapable.

A very similar argument may be applied to machine code. Ultimately, the machine must be dealt with in terms of machine code, so machine code too is unavoidable. The fallacy is obvious: Although machine code is unavoidable so far as the machine is concerned, it is not unavoidable so far as the end user is concerned, and the same applies to records.

There is no reason to believe that people think in terms of n-place predicates any more than that they formulate algorithms in terms of machine code. There is every reason to believe that there are other methods of expressing information that is more meaningful to the end user, and that ultimately can be translated into a form that the machine can understand. In much the same way, a compiler can translate a (more or less) human-readable program into machine-executable code.

It is, apart from anything else, a question of an appropriate level of detail. For example,

$$
\begin{aligned}
& 24 \\
\times \;\; & 3 \\
= \;\; & 72
\end{aligned}
$$

is essentially an abbreviation of

$$
\begin{aligned}
24 \times 3 &= (2 \times 10 + 4) \times 3 \\
&= (2 \times 10) \times 3 + 4 \times 3 \\
&= (2 \times 10) \times 3 + 12 \\
&= (2 \times 10) \times 3 + (1 \times 10 + 2) \\
&= 2 \times (10 \times 3) + (1 \times 10 + 2) \\
&= 2 \times (3 \times 10) + (1 \times 10 + 2) \\
&= (2 \times 3) \times 10 + (1 \times 10 + 2) \\
&= 6 \times 10 + (1 \times 10 + 2) \\
&= (6 \times 10 + 1 \times 10) + 2 \\
&= (6 + 1) \times 10 + 2 \\
&= 7 \times 10 + 2 \\
&= 72.
\end{aligned}
$$

Two points follow then:

1. It is not always necessary or desirable to work with a lot of detail.

2. It is often possible to add layers onto a more fundamental layer without detracting from the importance of the functions performed by the lower layer. The propositional and predicate calculus are excellent examples of this. There are arguments that can be expressed in predicate calculus that cannot be expressed in propositional calculus, yet predicate calculus assumes propositional calculus as a basis.

In a similar way, it is to be expected that any data models subsequent to the relational model will have to assume the relational model in some sense. It seems likely that the relational model will always be of use either to the person building the system software for a data management system or to the person concerned with an accurate and precise description of the physical level of the system.

THE FUNCTIONAL DATA MODEL

The functional data model is ultimately derived from both Alonzo Church's work on lambda calculus and related work by Curry. Lambda calculus, as a basis for a programming language, was popularized by McCarthy and Landin in the 1960s, with McCarthy proposing an early version of LISP, and Landin describing a method of implementing an interpreter for lambda expressions. A detailed description of LISP and lambda calculus is, however (fortunately), not required by the current discussion. Much of the current work on the functional approach can be traced to the paper by John Backus, "Can Programming Be Liberated from the Von Neumann Style?"

A *function* is a mapping that describes a relationship between two sets of objects. For example, the function SQR (*x*) (in Pascal) maps integers to their squares. The function can be represented as a table:

x	SQR (x)
0	0
1	1
2	4
3	9
4	16
5	25
. . .	. . .
n	n^2

It is usual to write a function as

$$F(x),$$

where F is the name of the function, and x is the argument or parameter to the function. It is also usual to allow $F(x)$ to appear (in suitable contexts) as an expression, and to take the expression $F(x)$, where x has some definite value, as denoting the result of applying F to x. If, for example, F is the function SQR, as just defined, and $x = 4$, $F(x) = 16$.

So the expression

$$F(4) + 1$$

is equal to 17.

Functions may have more than one parameter. Generally, a function with one parameter (like SQR) is known as a *unary function*, two parameters gives a *binary function*, n parameters gives an *n-ary* function (**note**: A *binary relationship* is not the same as a *binary function*; a *binary relationship* maps one set to another set—hence, it is a *unary function*).

Functions are defined as having a *domain of values* (i.e., the values are the x's on which the function acts), which are the values the function accepts as arguments, and a corresponding *range of values,* which are the values produced by evaluating the function. *Evaluating* the function means returning a value in the range, given a value in the domain. The function is said to map from the domain to the range.

Functions are always 1:1 (one to one) or M:1 (many to one) relationships between the function domain and the range. It is not acceptable for a function to map a particular object in its domain to more than one object in its range (i.e., a 1:M [one to many] or an M:M [many to many] relationship).

Composition of functions is allowed where the range of some function is the domain of another function. This is usually expressed by embedding functions inside each other:

$$(\text{for all } x)\ (\text{SQR}\ (\text{CUBE}(x)) = x^6.$$

Where the same function is composed with itself more than once, the resulting *composite function* is sometimes referred to as a *transitive function.*

Where a function represents a 1:1 relationship, it is possible to define an *inverse function,* which represents a mapping from the range to the domain. Given that F' is the inverse of F, it follows that:

$$(\text{for all } x)\ (F'\ [F(x)]) = x)$$

There are two common methods of writing functions: infix and prefix notation. The following are examples of *infix notation:*

Parameters	Function	Expression
1,2	+	$1 + 2$
1	−	-1
2,3	/	$2/3$
3,4,5,TRUE	+,=,AND	$((3+4) = 5)$ AND TRUE

The following are equivalent examples in *prefix notation:*

Parameters	Function	Expression
1,2	PLUS	PLUS (1,2)
1	NEGATIVE	NEGATIVE (1)
2,3	DIVIDE	DIVIDE (2,3)
3,4,5,TRUE	PLUS,EQL,AND	
		AND (EQL (PLUS (3.4) ,5),TRUE)

The main advantage of expressions in prefix notation is that it is always clear how many parameters a function has and the order in which the functions are to be evaluated. Or (what amounts to the same thing), it is easy to express the composition of functions using prefix notation. Throughout this document, wherever appropriate, prefix forms are used in preference to infix, but the two are occasionally mixed.

Database as Stored Functions

The functional data model, using the foregoing concept of a function, views a database as a collection of stored functions. Recall that a function is a mapping from one set of objects to another. The domain of the function then may be taken as the record (for the moment anyway), and one function may be defined for each field in the record. So, given a record r, with attributes $a_1, a_2, \ldots a_n$, there are the functions

$$Fa_1(r), Fa_2(r), \ldots Fa_n(r)$$

Each function, given a record as a parameter, returns the value of the appropriate attribute.

The model gives a very neat definition of an index (for example, an alphabetically arranged set of employee names) that is a function:

$$Fa_n'(a)$$

This function maps attribute values to records. This is as opposed to the function $Fa_n(r)$, which maps records to attribute values. $Fa_n'(a)$ is, of course, the inverse of $Fa_n(r)$.

The model also allows a very tidy representation of relationships. Recall that a function maps a domain (D) to a range (R); assume that a database exists with record types $R_1, R_2, \ldots R_n$. A relationship between R_1 and R_2 is represented in functional notation as a function:

$$Fa_n(R_1)$$

such that the function Fa_n returns a record of type R_2.

Functional Data Model Example

Using the same example as that used for the E–R model, in functional terms, the database is presented as a series of functions with associated domains and ranges. The notation is based on the notation used by

Buneman (see Gray, 1984), the form X → Y can be read as "maps X to Y."

Function			Type
department			Department
employee			Employee
employed-by	Employee	→	Department
works-at	Employee	→	Location
Managed-by	Department	→	Employee
Manager	Employee	→	Employee
Name	Employee	→	String

The disjoint structures "department" and "employee" are simply associated with a type and are considered to return a series of values. A number of primitive types are recognized as a part of the system, such as "string," with the obvious interpretation as a character string.

Most implementations of the functional data model allow M:M and 1:M relationships. Because these, properly speaking, are disallowed by the underlying formalism, they tend to look somewhat awkward in some circumstances.

CONCLUSION

This chapter has looked at data models in some detail. In particular, the place of data models in the working environment has been described as having three major current data models: The E–R model provides a good introduction to the subject of entities and relationships, the relational model underlines the very close connection between data models and logic, and the functional model introduces the idea of a mapping between one set of objects and another. All of these concepts are essential to an understanding of the semantic data model.

On Things

Oh Soc-ra-tes Oh Soc-ra-tes I think you know the an - swer

Scene: A maze in which Mephisto is singing.

Ivle.   What is it you want, Comrade?

Meph.   Who in Hades are you?

Ivle.   I. V. Lenin, of Revolutionary fame.

Meph.   Author! Author! I protest! I had a question for Socrates, and something revolting turns up.

The author speaks.

Auth.   I'm sorry. I wasn't really paying attention. I thought I heard someone singing "The Red Flag." What kind of question was it?

Meph.   I had it in mind to get Socrates to explain these new-fangled function things to me. You can't pick up a piece of paper these days with out finding "F" this or "→ that".

Auth.   By "→ that," I assume you mean "arrow that."

Meph.   No. Actually, I meant mapping. Although how you get from arrows to mappings is beyond me; I had hoped that old Socrates might be of some assistance.

Auth.   I don't know why you picked on Socrates. He had other rather more important things on his mind. I expect that if you started talking about arrows, maps, and F's to him, he wouldn't see the point of it at all. Besides, functions weren't really invented 'til the seventeenth century. Why not try and whistle up someone like Descartes?

Author disappears. Mephisto whistles.

Desc.   Diable! Estoie en train de fère des complôts coordinés et maintenant je me truis . . . je ne siu où! Qui estas, ce biau Sire?

Meph.   First a gibbering agitator, now agitated gibberish.

Desc.   Evidemment nos ne nos comprenons. Qui estez-vous?

Meph.   Author! Hey you, Author, either translate or get rid of this individual.

Meph.   Are you René Descartes?

Desc.   Ah yes! That's better. Indeed I am.

Meph.   Allow me to introduce myself. Mephisto's the name, D. Mephisto. This is V. I. Lenin . . .

Ivle.   I. V. I said, not V. I.

Meph.   Really? I thought it was V. I. Well, as I was saying, Mephisto's the name. Among other talents, I have this knack of whistling things up—your own good self being an example, if you will excuse the liberty. Now it seems to me that a good deal of disorder and confusion has gone out of the world of late. I sought an explanation. People are the same as they have always been, so what, I ask myself, has changed?

Ivle.   Well you may ask, Brother.

Meph.   As I was saying, what has changed? I was most struck by all this theorizing that goes on these days. Looking into this, I came to realize that there is a whole class of ideas current that were not around in the good old days. A prime example of this class is this idea of "functions."

Ivle.   The function of a class is to seek the fulfillment of its sociohistorical role in the unfolding dialectic of world history! Many have come to an untimely end through a misunderstanding of the Leninist–Marxist doctrine of the function of classes.

Desc.   I only know classes as collections of schoolboys. I am familiar with functions, although I am ordinarily not very sociable. You must explain yourself.

Meph.   A class of schoolboys is merely an example of a Class— "Class," that is, with a capital "c." Class in this sense refers to any old collection of things.

Desc.   And what do we take as being the point of such a collection?

Meph.   Precisely. The point is that there is no point, except perhaps in the sense that if you can point at it, it's a class. If there are some things that are in it and others that are not, it's a class.

Ivle.   For someone who wants to know about functions you certainly seem to know a lot about classes.

After an unexpected interruption, Descartes will express some concerns and introduce some of the groundwork for an explanation of Cartesian Dualism using functions (or, rather, provoked by functions).

Ivle.   And don't forget historical materialism!

Descends a short dark lady.

Ivle.   Oh! Ah! You gave me a fright!

Dasd.   Sorry guys—I must be in the wrong meeting. Now, where's that corridor gone? I know we keep changing this place, but this is ridiculous.

Meph.   Was I whistling "Shortnin' Bread"?

Dasd.   O.K. guys, no short jokes please.

Meph.   Who's joking?

Dasd.   Hey, buster, if you keep chewing on your thumb like that, no one'll have to ask what's eating you, you'll have eaten yourself!

Desc.   Pardon, Madam. I was considering the matter of a function. The extension of the idea beyond mathematics concerns me. Most especially, how is one to extend the set of functions without losing the immediacy of one's understanding?

Ivle.   What's the problem? Historical materialism teaches us to respect the realities of the historical process. If you don't believe in the power of classes, brother, come with me and I'll show you the dictatorship of the proletariat.

Desc.   You miss the point. One has to be very careful in dealing with very broad ideas and in any attempt to extrapolate them beyond the original intuition that gave rise to them. Take, for example, a square in the plane—thus.

He draws a square.

Desc.   Consider the position of any creature inside the square. It cannot stay in the plane and leave the square without crossing the line that marks the edge of the square. Is this not so? But if we allow the creature to fly out of the plane— that is, to move in three dimensions not just two—then it is a simple matter to leave the square without crossing the edge. Just fly over it. Now, consider a creature similarly inside a cube. If we allow the creature movement in a fourth dimension, then it can leave the cube without going through the surface of the cube. By extrapolation from the first case, this appears to be plausible. But I do not think it is reasonable, and I fear the same fate awaits classes and

	functions when extrapolated beyond the realms of methematics.
Meph.	You mean mathematics.
Desc.	I beg your pardon. As I was saying, I had myself hoped that algebra combined with geometry would provide a universal basis for human reason, but when faced with the practicalities of the thing. . . . one grows older, and perhaps a little wiser.
Dasd.	Well . . . some people have come up with this idea of an object-oriented language.
Meph.	Good, very good.
Ivle.	But Karl Marx has successfully extended the idea of dialectical materialism to an account of history that incorporates a complete description of the effects of the conditions of production on the objective state of the classes present in any socioeconomic epoch.
Dasd.	Seems to me someone around here's got a screw loose.
Desc.	Allow me to expand on my method. The basis of knowledge must be intuition. Intuition is not the fluctuating testimony of the senses, nor is it the misleading judgment that proceeds from the blundering constructions of the imagination. Instead, it is the conception that an unclouded and attentive mind gives us so readily and distinctly that we are wholly freed from doubt about that which we understand. Or what comes to the same thing, intuition is the undoubting conception of an unclouded and attentive mind, and it springs from the light of reason alone; it is more certain than deduction itself in that it is simpler, though deduction cannot by us be erroneously conducted.
Auth.	(Aside: *Speak for yourself boyo!*)
	Thus, each individual can mentally have intuition of the fact that he exists and that he thinks, that the triangle is bounded by three lines only, the sphere by a single superficies, and so on. Facts of such a kind are far more numerous than many people think, disdaining as they do to direct their attention upon such simple matters. You may find all this, and more, in my *Discourse on Method*.

Dasd. I'm a little confused here, how did we get to all that from functions?

Desc. There must be some basis for the process of deduction. In this scheme, it is reduced to the manipulation of intuitions. We are not concerned with the objective significance of things, only with the way that they are presented to the intuition. So we may take as given such a conclusion as "I think, therefore I am," and draw conclusions from there.

Dasd. Wow! Heavy stuff. What if there's no thinking agent involved? What happens to your intuition then?

Auth. (Aside: *Desc is here presented with a real problem. After all, when he formulated his method, no one had even thought about thinking machines or, more accurately, machines that reason—or at least that manipulate symbols. At the least they can add up. Or can they? Let's see what they have to say.*)

Desc. It does not seem to me that there can be intuition without a thinking agent. You may be able to manipulate symbols in various ways. But ultimately it must be the interpretation of the symbols that counts. This interpretation can only be performed by a thinking agent. A person must be involved somewhere. If the process is a purely mechanical one, the devising of the mechanism can be accounted for in a similar fashion. This allows the whole system to be understood in terms of my method.

Dasd. So processes for solving problems can be understood in the same way as the problem solutions themselves?

Desc. Precisely.

Meph. We seem to have lost track of the object-oriented languages. You were concerned about algebra not permitting the extension of its ideas beyond the realm of mathematics.

Desc. Yes, as I said I have some doubts, if only from a practical point of view. Please describe how these object-oriented languages work.

Dasd. O.K., let me think about this a minute.

Meph. Psst! Reader, are you listening to all this? Did you see what he just did? Such a religious man too! It is a huge, monumental joke—he has made himself a god! Who but God Himself can know, purely by intuition, enough to make a world? We humbler sorts may glean the odd fact from intuition, but to know everything intuitively—this is truly divine. Delicious! I love it! Let's see what Dasd can do.

Dasd.　Object-oriented languages—let's call them OOLs—have three basic parts to them. I'll tell you about those first, then we can have a look at how these correspond to functions. The parts are messages, objects, and methods. Let's say that this square is an object.

Dasd writes "OBJECT" over the square.

As an object, the square will contain methods; these are the things that the object can do. Messages can be sent to the object, and they will have the effect of triggering a method; that is, given a message, the object will look up and execute an appropriate method. The method will result in some sort of response being returned to the message.

Dasd writes "METHOD" and "MESSAGE" and arrows labeled "sent to," "responds to," "looks up," and "executed by."

Desc.　What is the connection between a method and a message?

Dasd.　When an object receives a message, it takes the message as referring to some particular method; the name of the message will be the same as the name of some method. Either that or there must be some way of translating message names into method names so that it's just a straightforward correspondence.

Desc.　Explain then please, what the function of a message is. I assume that being a "message," it contains some sort of information.

Dasd.　You got it. Associated with a message, there is always some kind of information that the object's method acts on. So for example, for the object *number.* . . .

Desc.　The object *number* may have a method *square-root* and a message *square-root*. When the message *square-root* provides a numeric value, the method *square-root* returns the square root of the numeric value. Excellent, so all arithmetic functions can be similarly defined. What about algebraic functions?

Dasd.   The same applies. Objects may send messages to other objects. Objects may even send messages to themselves. Most OOLs.

Ivle.   OOLs? What's an OOL?

Dasd.   Object-Oriented Language—remember? That is what we're talking about, isn't it?

Meph.   Never mind. Please, carry on.

Dasd.   As I was saying, most OOLs allow one object to be contained in another object. Let's say that the square is for the integers. I can draw another square for the real numbers, like this. Anything that is an integer is also a real number. So any method you can use on a real number, you can also use on an integer.

Desc.   The integers can, of course, be broken down into primes, squares, perfect numbers, and so on, each with its appropriate set of methods. Wonderful!

Ivle.   I'm ecstatic.

Dasd.   The idea, then, is to build up a set of objects, and associated methods that are adequate to whatever it is you want to do. The objects, of course, can be of any type.

Desc.   Now let us return to functions. I think I understand the matter well enough to be able to establish the correspondence between OOLs and functions, you may correct me where necessary. A message then corresponds to a function, the function parameters correspond to the information associated with the message, objects correspond to the domain of the function, the response corresponds to the range; and methods are simply computational techniques. Am I right?

Dasd.   That's about my understanding of it.

Desc.   This is most excellent. One can then be assured of the validity of each object and its associated methods. And beginning from simple and immediate intuitions, one can proceed to a system of arbitrary complexity. I am reassured. I am in your debt.

Dasd. Oh don't thank me. It's just another OOL as far as I'm concerned.

Desc. No, no, don't belittle this; we may use this OOL to dispel a great fog, allowing the human mind to rise triumphant like the sun, bathing the world around us in the glorious light of reason!

Dasd. Is Mephisto laughing? What's he laughing at?

Ivle. I don't know, whatever it is it must be monumentally funny.

Desc and Ivle disappear.

Meph. This is too much, what a day. Well, bye bye, see you again.

Meph disappears.

Dasd. I don't believe this, what the heck is going on here?

Auth. I don't know, you tell me. What was Mephisto laughing at?

Dasd. Desi getting so enthusiastic about OOLs, I suppose. Well, he has a point perhaps. There's really no difference to speak of between an F and an OOL. Anyway, time I was off to that meeting.

Auth. Well, what next? Oh by the way, if you were wondering what on earth old Desi was going on about, have a look at his *Discourse on Method*; it's all in there. If you couldn't be bothered to plow through all that, there's a very good article written by Herbert Read in his *Essays on Literary Criticism*, that summarizes it all very well. Not that you'll find that in your neighborhood bookstore.

Especially important is understanding what an impact old Desi has had. He's made the world believe in mathematics and formal systems. Finding a formalism is the only thing that counts. What Meph found so funny is how Desi manages to ignore the weakness of intuition as a basis for understanding the world. It's truly remarkable how all his intellectual descendants do the same.

As to OOLs, I think Dasd was actually describing LittleSpeak fourscore. This was produced of course by Exrox, at Exrox Carp. There is an endless supply of diabolically expensive books describing the system.

If you were wondering what that diagram looked like, here it is:

Reals

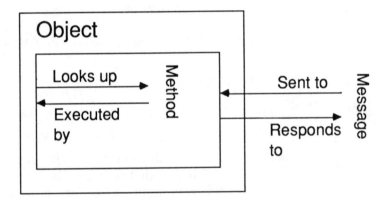

3

Service Database (ServiceDB)

INTRODUCTION

This section describes a system designed for an organization that services appliances. As applications go, the system is quite simple. All the same, it is full of problems both for the user and for the designer of the system. A description of a condensed form of Pascal, PSL (pretty small language) is given at the end of this chapter. PSL appears both in ServiceDB and elsewhere in the book where concepts drawn from programming languages are used or have to be illustrated.

In the description of the appliance servicing system, only the section of the system that deals with engineer service calls is described. Other parts of the system (such as payroll or inventory) are not considered. In the business for which the system was designed, engineers make visits to mend appliances. An engineer has a name, address, and telephone number. An engineer may already be trained on a particular appliance, or an engineer may be a trainee. Both the actual time and date and a scheduled time and date are recorded for each visit. More than one engineer may be on a visit if one of the engineers is a trainee. Duration of the visit and costs of spare parts are noted by the engineer. For any given visit, there must be at least one engineer trained on the appliance involved. Engineers should not make visits to service appliances on which they are not trained.

Clerks keep track of customer billing and booking. Engineers may make inquiries on previous visits, and they use the system as an appointment book.

THE ENTITIES AND RELATIONSHIPS

In terms of entities and relationships, the database will look as follows:

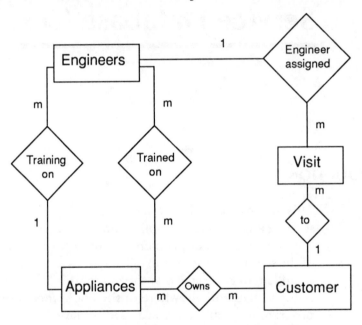

THE RECORDS

The record layouts for the entities in the appliance servicing system are described using records with record pointers (signified by an "@" symbol preceding the name of the type of the record). For example, an item declared as "@rec-id" is a pointer to a record of the type "rec-id," and it may have any record of that type associated with it in an assignment statement (see the description of PSL for more details). The record pointer is a way of representing a relationship. The record layouts are as follows:

```
Type
     Employee        =   Record
                         Name             :  String[1..50];
                         Status           :  {engineer,
                                              trainee,
                                              clerk};
                         Trained-on       :  Array[1..30]
                                             of @appliance;
                         Training-on      :  Array[1..30]
                                             of @appliance;
                         Telephone        :  1..9999999999
                         End;


     Customer        =   Record
                         Name             :  String[1..50];
                         Address          :  String[1..150];
                         Owns             :  Array[1..10]
                                             of @appliance;
                         End;


     Visit           =   Record
                         Engineer-assigned :
                                       @employee;
                         Trainee-assigned  :
                                       @employee;
                         Sched-date       :  1..999999;
                         Sched-time       :  1..9999;
                         Actual-date      :  1..999999;
                         Actual-time      :  1..9999;
                         Elapsed-time     :  1..9999;
                         Spares-costs     :  1..999999;
                         End;


     Appliance       =   Record
                         Name             :  String[1..50];
                         End;
```

Some comments on the records are in order at this point:

- Having engineers trained on an array of appliances does not quite capture the intention of the original system description. There was nothing there specifying some maximum or minimum number of appliances. Nor was there anything to say that the order in which the training took place was significant, yet the array presumably, unintentionally represents such an order.

- There was nothing in the specification of the system about date or time formats, but obviously one has been assumed. Like just about everyone else, we shall try and forget about the year 2000.

- How many trainees can go on a visit? The record layout assumes one, the specification does not really say. Can a person be training on more than one appliance type at the same time?

- Is the spares-cost really the same kind of thing as a date? Or the elapsed-time the same kind of thing as the sched-time and actual-time? They all have the same format.

- What is there to guarantee that a trainee does not get booked to go on a visit to an appliance he is not training on? For that matter, what is there to guarantee that an engineer is appropriately trained for the appliance he is supposed to service?

- How will the system cope if it becomes necessary to keep track of different versions of an appliance type (i.e., if engineers have to be trained not just on appliance types, but also on versions)?

- Or what if it becomes necessary to keep track of which particular machine a customer purchased?

- What is the implication of adding and deleting appliance types? Does deleting an appliance mean it is no longer supported, so we are no longer interested in whether a customer has one or whether some engineer is trained on one?

- What is there to guarantee that in the visit record, a record would not be stored with values in the actual time and date but not in the scheduled time and date?

These issues are typical of the kinds of problems that tend to arise in attempting to construct records to represent information.

For any relational database buffs it is worth noting that none of these problems are addressed by normalization. To really get into normalization problems, it would be necessary to start putting in extra record types. This would require one extra record type for each relationship type where the relationship happened to be many to many (M:M), which they all are, with the exception of ENGINEER-ASSIGNED. The establishment of these new record types, far from solving any problems, would only introduce a whole horde more. For example:

- Who is to guarantee that the record representing the relationship gets deleted when a record on either end disappears?
- How does the record represent a minimum or maximum value for the number of things on either end of the relationship?
- In what sense can a record be said to represent a relationship anyway?

A further crop of problems are encountered when attempting to deal with the external interface.

THE SCREENS

Clearly, the complete system would need many more screens than just the ones presented here, but these two illustrate some of the problems facing the screen designer.

The first area is concerned with the question, "How is one to tie in what the user sees with what is in the database?" In particular, the database stores relationships between things (e.g., between engineers and visits), so how is the existence of such a relationship to be presented to the user? For that matter, how is the user to represent to the system the fact that he or she wants to change some relationship?

The approach that has been taken in designing these screens is to use both names and other external characteristics of the entities that are stored in the database. These characteristics are "external" in the sense that they have meaning outside the database; they are produced by some process that is outside of the database. This is in contrast to such internally generated values as, for example, the absolute memory address of some region of memory, or the location on disk of some record. Provided, of course, that the record never moves, the disk location of a record would probably be an excellent way of identifying the record, from the point of view of a program that has to access the record as efficiently as possible. But pity the poor end user! The user cannot be expected to remember some large, incomprehensible, arbitrary number just in order to book some engineer out on a visit. So in this system, ENGINEER, CUSTOMER, and APPLIANCE records are addressed by names.

But just look at the problems this causes:

- If an engineer gets married and changes name in the process, the system falls apart.

- If the clerk making the booking misspells the engineer's name, the system fails. Or if an engineer gets into the system twice with two slightly different spellings, the system fails.

- If there is more than one engineer with the same name, some poor unfortunate may become known as John Jones the Ninth (or J. Jones 9th or J Jones 9 ad nauseam)

All the same problems arise with customer names and with appliance names. If anything, matters are even worse so far as the visit record is concerned. It does not even have a name associated with it, except indirectly. For the visit record, one has to resort to using combinations of dates, times, and names in the fond hope that they are all entered and interpreted correctly.

In trying to understand the implementation of a system, this problem of identifying things becomes a double-headed monster:

1. As discussed previously, it is difficult to know how to identify things to the user.

2. There is the question, "How are things to be identified inside the machine?" This one is dealt with (along with many more) in the next chapter, "Problems with Records."

There is no simple answer to the question of how to identify things to the user. A complete answer would be equivalent to an answer to the question "How can I describe things in such a way that the description will not be misunderstood?" To this question there is not now, nor will there ever be, a complete answer.

PSL (PRETTY SMALL LANGUAGE)

PSL is a condensed form of Pascal. It is used both with ServiceDB and elsewhere in this book to illustrate ideas drawn from modern, block-structured programming languages.

The PSL syntax is presented using *railroad diagrams*. A railroad diagram is a mechanism for describing the syntax of a language. Briefly, valid statements in the language correspond to valid paths through the diagram. A valid path through a railroad diagram follows the lines from left to right and top to bottom, picking up things on the way. It is only permissible to go backward (that is, from right to left or bottom to top) where there is an arrow on the path pointing upward or to the left. The end of a diagram is indicated by a vertical bar; a continuation is indicated by a right arrow. **Note:** Things in angle brackets (that is, "<" and ">") stand for something else—usually another railroad diagram.

The syntax begins with <PSL program>:

<PSL Program>

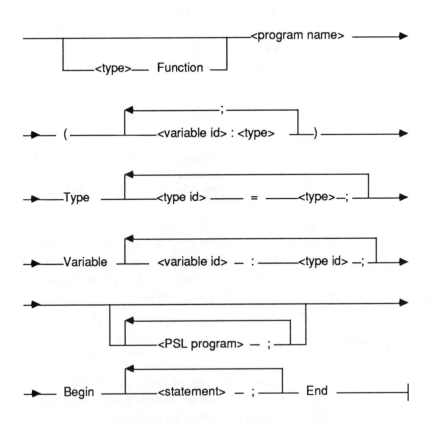

The syntax implies that parameters, types and variables are required; in fact, they are all optional.

The <type> after the program parameters indicates the type of the program if the program is a function. Anything with "id" in the name is just an identifier.

Statements are used to manipulate variables. Variables may be input to the program, output from the program, or assigned to other variables. A number of operations on variables are possible. For a given variable, which operations are possible is largely dependent on the variable's type.

<Type>

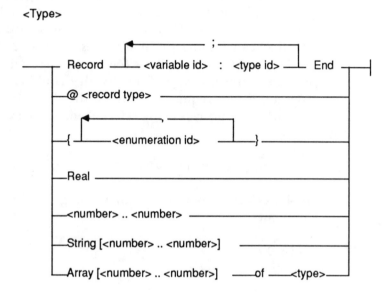

The @<record type> declares a variable that can be used to point at a record of the specified type. This can be used, for example, to declare a list of related items, as follows:

```
Type
      Employee-record = Record
                        Name  :  string [1..50];
                        Manager  :  @Employee-record;
                        end;
```

The <enumeration id> list is a series of values that may be assumed by any variable of the associated type. For example

```
Type
     Grade = {Good, Bad, Ugly};
Variable
     His-grade  :  Grade;
```

In the preceding example, the variable His-grade may take any of the values Good, Bad, or Ugly, and it may have more than one at the same time. For example, His-grade could be both Good and Ugly.

The <number> .. <number> declares an integer type, the minimum value of which is the first number, the maximum value of which is the second number. "Real" provides a floating point number—That is a type that can assume decimal values such as 2.7182 or 3.141593. "String" is a type that allows for the storage and manipulation of character strings, such as "How I wish I could calculate pie." In the program, arrays require subscripts, the subscript indicating which element of the array is being referenced. An array declared as

```
Type
     Song = Poem [1..100] Of String[1..80];
```

can have information stored in it using a subscripted assignment statement.

```
Variable
     Pi  :  Poem;

Begin
Pi[1]  := "How I wish I";
Pi[2]  := "Could calculate pie";
```

The second row of the array contains the second line of the poem. The third and subsequent rows are empty, or null.

PSL Statements

The statements supported by PSL are

```
Assignment statements
Compound statements
Procedure/Function invocation
```

```
Do <statement> Until <condition>
For <variable>  := <initial value>
    Downto/Upto <final value> Do
    <statement>
If <condition> Then <statement> Else <statement>
While <condition> Do <statement>
```

A compound statement is a series of statements bracketed by "Begin" and "End."

4

Problems with Records

INTRODUCTION

This chapter describes the problems associated with record-based information models. It is not essential to an understanding of the semantic data model, and it may be skipped on first reading. It is worth bearing in mind, though, that much of the motivation for the semantic data model is derived from the problems associated with the record-based model. To properly understand the semantic data model, it is advisable to also understand the limitations of the record-based model.

Although computers tend to depend heavily on records, the same may be said generally of information storage and retrieval systems. The concept of a record, as stored by a computer, is really no different from the records to be found in a manual, paper-based, filing system. Any form, be it a tax form, a student enrollment form, or a company purchase order, is just a record. All of the problems discussed in this chapter then apply to these systems as much as to electronic data processing systems. Much of the bureaucracy typically surrounding taxation, student administration, and company spending is directly a result of the inadequacies of the record model.

Therefore, it is not to be expected that either records or the problems associated with them are simply going to disappear. In certain contexts, such as a semantic database system, a great deal can be done to ameliorate the problems, but outside of that context, the problems still remain.

To a large extent, the problems can be hidden so far as the internal layers of the database system are concerned, although it is unlikely that they will ever entirely disappear. But so far as the interfaces to the database are concerned, they will always be a live issue. So long as we have to deal with the world using reports, forms, screens, and other essentially record-based data presentation techniques, both system users and system designers will have to have some awareness of the problems discussed in this chapter.

PROBLEMS WITH RECORD-BASED INFORMATION MODELS

Records are adequate for representing information that fits into a certain pattern. Basically, the record data model assumes that all information can be arranged in two-dimensional tables, each row of the table being a record and having the same layout as other rows. Most information does not fit the pattern, so while some information cannot be represented at all using records, other kinds of information can be represented in so many different ways that any one representation becomes ambiguous.

A further problem with records is that what can be done with the record is not evident from the record itself. The record is not an abstract type and says nothing about how it can be manipulated.

Data models that use records (such as the hierarchical, network, and relational models) may overcome some of these limitations, but they never overcome all of them. As the models are built on records, they inherit all of the difficulties that records have. In some cases, the models simply add yet more ways of doing things that can already be accomplished using records.

So far as the record itself is concerned, a record may be taken as a fixed sequence of fields. Ordinarily, records may be thought of as formalized records (in the relational sense)—that is, a record without occurring items.

To summarize:

- Record-based models work fine so long as the data fits into a certain very limited pattern.

- Generally, either there are too many ways of doing things, or there is no way at all.

- The record says nothing about what can be done with it.

- Some record-based data models overcome some of the problems; none overcome all (or even most) of them. Many models just make matters worse by adding yet more ways of doing things.

- It is important to appreciate that the model assumes normalized records. Even an occurring item within a record must be understood as no more than a set of records embedded inside another record.

Some examples:

Car parts in a CAD/CAM database	Different types, sizes, components, units of measurement, versions, contexts
Animals in an ecology database	Movements in an ecological space, food types, association patterns
Furniture in a decor database	Usage, weight, size, shape (e.g., pianos, carpets, stools are all furniture).

Please note that these examples include no accounting databases and no parts-supplier databases. The three databases described here are associated with application areas, where the data to be stored is based on complex interlocking sets of things. And things are never as simple as they seem.

BASIC ASSUMPTIONS

The record-based information model assumes both

1. *Horizontal homogeneity*–that is, everyone has the same kinds of attributes, and

2. *Vertical homogeneity*–that is, all attributes are to be interpreted the same way.

If these assumptions are not valid for the underlying data, a variety of difficulties are likely to crop up.

Horizontal Homogeneity of Relevant Facts

A record-based approach is likely to be most appropriate where the entire population has the same kinds of attributes; the existence of exceptions inevitably represents a problem.

Consider clothing, for example; there are many fields that are not relevant to all types of clothing or have differing meaning depending on context—for example, clothing sizes:

> waist size
> neck size
> sleeve length
> 3/4, full, short sleeve.

There are a number of techniques for dealing with variability, including:

- Define a record format to include a union of all the possible field items.

- Allow the same field to have different meanings in different records.

Both approaches have any number of attendant drawbacks.

Lack of homogeneity is especially a problem when the attribute needs to be used as an identifier (for example, Social Security Number, employee number, International Standard Book Number, Library of Congress Catalog Number). If the identifier happens to be absent or duplicated or unknown, the system does not work properly.

Vertical Homogeneity within Fact Type

The previous section dealt with situations where not every record has the same field; here, the issue is situations where some field involves (potentially) references to several different types of objects.

For example, one might have a database that must represent the fact that cars can be assigned either to employees or to departments. Any solution to the representation of the relationship "assigned-to" is going to cause problems. Some examples:

- The car record could have a type field indicating the type of the assignee.

- The record could contain a different field for each assignee type. (This may be necessary if the foreign keys are of fundamentally different types.)

- Assuming the assignees have disjoint identifiers (employee numbers and department numbers are never the same), the record may contain a single item that may be either an employee number or a department number.

- Assignee records may be in a separate file.

- Everyone and everything may be given an assignee number.

The basic modeling concept is quite simple, merely involving

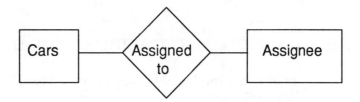

The problem is that an assignee can be any one of a number of different things. Anyone interested in the assigned-to relationship probably wants to be able to consider the assignees as a single collection of objects. The record model is inherently unable to do this.

All of these approaches, at a minimum,

- Present difficulties from an access point of view—it is not possible to come up with a simple algorithm that will return the names and types of all assignees for any car

- May become inconsistent unless correctly handled

- Will be difficult to extend. If it becomes necessary to assign cars to locations, as well as to employees and departments, the whole structure will probably have to be revamped; worse yet, all the programs that access it will probably have to be recoded.

This is, of course, assuming lack of homogeneity on only one side of the relationship. The problems are compounded if the relationship is complex on both ends; if, for example, the relationship is between assignees and tools.

Similar problems may arise with object identifiers. A classic example is provided by the use of ISBNs (international standard book numbers) versus Library of Congress Catalog Numbers. If a library attempts to use both numbers as identifiers, situations may arise where a single field may reference data of different types from one record to the next.

Alternatively, consider a database that has to represent information about owners of stock, in which the owners may be either companies or persons. Persons may be citizens or foreigners. In the European Economic Community (EEC), foreigners may be either EEC foreigners or others, all with implications as to how the individuals involved may be identified, contacted, paid dividends, taxed, exercise voting rights, and so on. And this is only half of it; a similar set of issues arises, of course, with the companies.

PRESUMPTIONS UNDERLYING TRADITIONAL IMPLEMENTATIONS

Traditional implementations of record-based systems tend to have difficulties with

- The separation of descriptions and data
- Minimal requirements for descriptions
- Resistance to changing descriptions.

Separation of Descriptions and Data

The issues in this area are associated with the impossibility of giving sensible answers to certain types of queries, even though the information is in the system. The trouble is that the information is a part of the system description, not a part of the data. For example consider the following queries:

What relationship is there between Joe Bloggs and the accounting department?

How is the accounting department managed?

Who handles personnel matters for the accounting department?

Or in a slightly different vein:

How many employees are there in the accounting department?

What is the maximum number of employees permitted in a department?

How many more employees can be recruited into the accounting department?

One obvious answer is to make the system description a part of the database. But will this really help? If the system description consists of a set of low-level record descriptions, with perhaps item-level dependency information, or uniqueness constraints, or lists of required items, will this really help in understanding what the data in the database means? Will it help in answering the preceding kinds of questions?

Minimal Requirements for Descriptions

Record-based systems tend to provide descriptions that are oriented toward the needs of the system. As a result, the descriptions often either provide information that is irrelevant (such as compaction-related data) or do not provide information that is necessary to an understanding of the data.

The problem is, of course, that it is simply not possible to describe, in an easily manageable way, what the data means when the description has to be provided in the form of a set of record descriptions.

Resistance to Changing Descriptions

Even assuming that an explicit description of the system does exist, because of the fact that much of the system description is concerned with physical rather than the logical aspects of the system, and much of the system description is inevitably nonexplicit, changes to the system will be difficult. Every time the system is changed, the physical and logical impact of the change will have to be dealt with. Whenever the system is changed, any programs or related systems that "know" about the internal structure of the system will have to be examined to determine what the impact of the change will be.

Record-based systems have difficulties where facts are unstable (they vary from time to time and may or may not be present), where descriptions of facts are unstable, and where descriptions of facts are not precise. Frequently, in a record-based system, it is necessary to resort to a text or comment field when the data simply defies normal types of classification.

INFORMATION CONCEPTS

Record-based information models have difficulties with the basic concepts involved in the analysis and manipulation of information. In dealing with information, it is necessary to be able to cope with the following:

- Entities
- Entity types
- Relationships
- Attributes
- Naming (entity identifiers)

Entities and Entity Types

It is frequently impossible to represent the information about an entity in a single record. There are a number of different aspects to this problem. It is often true that a single record cannot contain all of the facts (occurring items being a particular problem). Very large amounts of information may, in some cases, have to be maintained, while other records of the same type may only hold quite small amounts of information. Some families have many children, some have none. It is impossible to devise a scheme that does not deal awkwardly with one extreme or the other.

Entities are not always single types. For example, a person may be an employee, a stockholder, or an instructor. It may be possible to represent the information about a person by using a single record, but it is doubtful that the record will have a clear relationship to the type of person it is supposed to represent.

A single entity may even be multityped. In this figure, it is possible for a vehicle to be a land vehicle, a water vehicle, or both, an amphibious vehicle. Entities may have many records. Entities may be made up of many things. How, for example, could a car be represented? It is an entity, but it is made up of thousands of constituent parts.

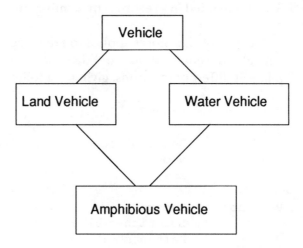

Also, records may exist without any entities. A record may represent a whole range of different things—relationships, for example. A single record can contain multiple entities. There is nothing about a record that requires the record to represent just one thing. With the family example, it could be argued that the record containing information about families and their children, actually contains information about multiple entities. This harks back to the confusion over what is and is not an entity.

Relationships

In the entity–relationship model, there is one reasonably clear concept of a relationship. But in the record model, one of the problems with relationships is that there are many different representations of this one concept.

Binary relationships are a fairly simple concept, but there are about half a dozen different ways of representing them. Most approaches involve pairing the identifiers of the two entities into one record, which may be any of the following:

1. In the record representing one entity or the other, or both

2. In a separate (intersection) record representing the relationship itself

3. Embedded in a record representing some other entity altogether.

An example is a Stores application that keeps track of parts. Parts are kept at different locations, and they may be supplied by different suppliers at different locations, giving the following kinds of records:

```
Part       = Record
             Name                String(20);
             Description         String(100);
             Number              1..99999;
             End;


Part-loc   = Record
             Location-number     1..99999;
             Part-number         1..99999;
             Supplier-number     1..99999;
             Responsible-clerk   1..999;
             End;


Location   = Record
             Number              1..99999;
             Name                String(20);
             Address             String(100);
             End;


Supplier   = Record
             Number              1..99999;
             Name                String(20);
             Address             String(100);
             End;
```

```
Clerks     = Record
             Number              1..999;
             Name                String(20);
             End;
```

RESPONSIBLE-CLERK is an example of relationship type 1, the entire record PART-LOC is an example of relationship type 2. The three-cornered relationship, SUPPLIES-PART-TO, represented by Part-loc, is an example of 3.

This all makes the assumption that a single, simple key item is used for both identifiers involved. Whereas it may be the case that

- One identifier or the other may be a subset of a key
- The identifiers together may be a part of the key
- It is effectively required that the identifiers both be record keys, and this in turn implies a variety of update problems, as the key values are scattered around all over the place but must all be kept consistent.

Relationships may be implied by other relationships. A may be related to B and B to C, with the system assuming that A then has some specific relationship to C.

In systems that provide file structure as well as record structure, such as CODASYL (Conference on Data and System Languages) system, relationships may be represented by file order (e.g., seniority in a list of captains) or by a hierarchy.

Normalized systems do reduce the number of alternatives; however there are still problems at least so far as 1:1, 1:M, and M:M relationships are concerned, as they all may be represented differently. For example,

- The ISBN contains a code for the language of the book, the country of origin, and the publisher of the book. The ISBN may be taken as representing a relationship between the book, the country of origin, and the publisher.
- A part number may contain a vehicle code and a factory code, so it may represent a relationship between the vehicle and the factory. That is, this factory makes part of this vehicle.
- In a system that codes employees by region in which they work, an

employee who keeps getting transferred between regions gets a new employee number each time. His employee file becomes a complete mess. The key keeps changing.

Naming and describing records introduces a whole new problem area. In the record model, relationships are neither described nor named effectively. Record descriptions rarely provide clear evidence of the presence of a relationship.

- Multifield keys may represent relationships, or they may be a qualified name. For example, EMPLOYEE-NUMBER and RE-GION-NUMBER may just represent the region that first hired the employee; it may, for example, be necessary to keep track of the region that first hired the employee in order to ensure that the employee number is always unique. Or EMPLOYEE-NUMBER and REGION-NUMBER may represent the region that the employee currently works in.
- If a record, or a pair of records, happen to contain fields that represent relationships in which neither field is a key, there may be no indication of a relationship at all.

The naming of relationships is very important if the system is to be understandable and manageable. In the record model, relationships cannot be effectively named:

- The name of the relationship may be a record-type name (intersection record). For example, in a system that has a customer file, an order file, and a parts file; the order record represents the relationship.
- The name may be a field name.
- The name may be only implied (by a **join**, for example). Effectively, then, it has no name.
- A (CODASYL) set name could be used.
- If something like a hierarchical structure is used, there may be no named object actually associated with the relationship.

The names themselves (where they are present) are unlikely to be very meaningful anyway.

The user has no reliable way to examine the system description and find a clear account of what relationships exist in the system. In any case, there are a great many things that have to be said about a relationship before its significance is likely to become apparent—far more than could be suggested by a mere name.

Attributes

The common distinction between relationships and attributes ("fields" in the context of the record model) is largely a result of the limitations of the record model. The distinction is neither clear nor helpful, and it has more to do with the implementation of the system than with the information being represented.

Relationships and attributes are merely mappings between two or more sets of objects; as such, there is no obvious reason why the two should be distinguished. In practice, the distinction between them is often quite arbitrary. Get away from records and the attribute–relationship distinction goes away.

The arbitrary nature of the distinction becomes most apparent in the entity–relationship (E–R) model. The E–R model comes in two varieties, the E–R model and the E–R–A or entity–relationship–attribute model. In the E–R–A model, in addition to squares and diamonds, the E–R diagrams have circles to indicate attributes.

It is a fact that any E–R–A diagram can be turned into an E–R diagram simply by replacing the circle with a square and a diamond. For example,

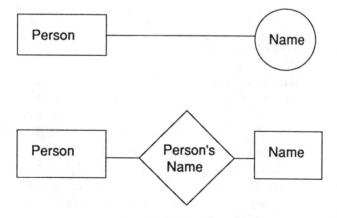

In the second diagram, names becomes a set of entities or things instead of a set of attribute values, as in the first diagram. From a data modeling point of view, there is very little difference between the two. If there is a difference, it is one concerned with implementation and programming rather than with the meaning of the thing.

NAMING

Naming, or symbolic reference, is the process of establishing some way of referring to a thing. This is usually evident in an application system in the form of numerous record items called "[something]-number." The values contained by the item are names or symbolic identifiers that can be used to find the associated record. Typical examples are such things as EMPLOYEE-NUMBER, International Standard Book Number (ISBN), PART-NUMBER, and so on.

In the record model, most facts are represented by the inclusion, in one record, of the symbolic identifiers of two or more things; for example, EMPLOYEE-NUMBER and DEPARTMENT-NUMBER, EMPLOYEE-NUMBER and SALARY. Symbolic references have a number of unfortunate characteristics:

- They allow reference to nonexistent entities.

- They lead to undesirable interactions between entity identifiers and entity types.

- They have problems with synonyms, changeable names, and complex (compound) names.

Naming and Simple Identifiers

To the extent that a record represents an entity, symbolic reference allows reference to nonexistent entities. In record model terms, wherever a relationship is to be expressed, there is always the possibility that the "thing" on the other end of the relationship is not present. The system offers no guarantees in this respect.

Using facts as labels, which is what is usually meant by "symbolic reference," is acceptable until some exceptional circumstance arises that invalidates the fact as a label. In a Presidential elections database, where elections are identified by year, two elections occurring in 1 year cannot be handled.

At best, symbolic identifiers will be unique within entity type; as a result, it is necessary to know both field and type if the data is to mean anything. In most cases, the type information is not available. If there are several simple identifiers (Social Security Number, employee number, etc.), it is necessary both to know which is being used in any particular context and to be able to translate from one to another.

The entity type will affect the perception of entity identifiers. In the elections database, if U.S. Presidential elections only are considered, year is good enough; if other elections are involved, the symbolic reference will have to be further qualified—by office, for example.

The converse may also, unfortunately, be true: The existence of identifiers may adversely affect the perception of entity types, causing an entity to be included in the database description simply because there is a convenient range of values available to use as a key item. This is the appalling consequence of some approaches to normalization. Consider, for example, the ISBN idea of a *book* versus the Library of Congress Catalog Number idea of a *publication*, which can include films. Is the ISBN book attribute location the same as the Library of Congress publication attribute location? Normalization could easily make the answer "no."

There are any number of issues in this area; for example,

- Names may be abbreviated or punctuated differently, so symbolic reference implies some method of standardizing or checking the reference before using it

- Something has to be selected as a primary identifier (for normalization if nothing else); inevitably the choice is arbitrary and colors the perception of the underlying entity.

Consider the following list of items. There can be no doubt as to what is to be taken as entity identifiers. Given such a list of items, the question as to how to arrange the items has been rendered unnecessary by the existence of the supplier number and the part number.

1 Supplier name	5 Part name
2 Supplier number	6 Part number
3 Supplier location	7 Part size
4 Supplier delivery time	8 Supplier's quantity of a part

In order to understand the data, the question to ask would be "why do only suppliers and parts have numbers?" It is unlikely that this will be evident from any information associated with the database itself. Such a database design is quite arbitrary, and therefore meaningless.

The ServiceDB system illustrates some aspects of these issues. As indicated in the discussion of ServiceDB, there are two broad issues involved in dealing with identifiers in a database:

1. how to identify things inside of the system

2. how to identify them outside of the system.

The first problem is not very difficult to solve (provided expense is no object). It is the subject of much of the rest of this book. The second problem is the more intractable of the two. It is an interfacing issue, coming in two forms:

2.a. When the data management system involved has to interface to and pass data to other separate data management systems, which gets into the realms of distributed systems

2.b. When the system has to be understandable to human users.

The human interface problem revolves around the question, "How is a user supposed to identify things in the database?"

Consider, for example, an interactive interface to a data dictionary. It is necessary to be able to establish relationships among the following elements:

Programs	Files
Records	Items
Databases	Screens
Processes	Users

This implies that all of these should have some uniform method of identification. This in itself is unlikely to be simple and will probably consist, at a minimum, of each element having a version and status, as well as a name.

Precisely the same problem is apparent in ServiceDB. How are customers to be identified, how are engineers to be identified? What if someone frequently misspells a name?

Note: All of these are unavoidable interfacing problems, as opposed to avoidable implementation problems. The implementation problems can safely be put aside for the time being; provided one is prepared to pay a sufficient cost, they are ultimately soluble.

Naming and Compound Identifiers

All of the issues relevant to simple identifiers apply equally to compound identifiers, which have a number of problems all their own. Consider, for example, a dependents database, holding information about the dependents of a company's employees. The dependent is taken as related to some employee, known as the "sponsor." How is the dependent to be identified?

- If the dependent is qualified by sponsor (giving a compound identifier consisting of sponsor-plus-dependent name), what if a dependent has more than one sponsor?
- What if the sponsor gets deleted?
- What if a sponsor has two dependents with the same name?
- If two sponsors have a dependent named Joe, how do we know whether there are two Joes or just one?
- Given multiple sponsors of a dependent, it would be possible to designate one sponsor as primary. What if the primary sponsor leaves the company—how can we be sure that the dependent is transferred to the formerly secondary (now primary) sponsor?
- What if it should come about that dependents have to be allowed without a sponsor?

Composite names used as identifiers almost always convey additional information, and as such, they are not precisely equivalent to simple names as identifiers, and they give rise to differences in the techniques used to manipulate them.

SEMANTIC STRUCTURE AND THIRD NORMAL FORM

Third normal form signifies that all the items in a record are directly dependent on the key. The value in any one key item for a third-normal-form record will be unique across the whole file. And there will not be any other item present in the whole file from which it would be possible to build another file that had the other item as its key but did not include all of the records in the original file. This is actually a Boyce–Codd normal form, which is a slight refinement of the third normal form. As an example, consider the following file:

```
Part  =   Record
          Part-Name            String(20);
          Part-Description     String(100);
          Part-Number          1..99999;
          Factory-number       1..99999;
          Factory-location     String(100);
          End;
```

Assume that a factory may make many different parts, and a particular factory location will always be associated with a particular factory code (factories do not move about), the FACTORY-LOCATION item will have many duplicate values in it. The record is not in third normal form because FACTORY-LOCATION is dependent on FACTORY-NUMBER and only indirectly dependent on PART-NUMBER, which is the record key. Third normal form would require an additional record, giving the following:

```
Part  =   Record
          Part-Name            String(20);
          Part-Description     String(100);
          Part-Number          1..99999;
          Factory-number       1..99999;
          End;

Factory  =                     Record
          Factory-number       1..99999;
          Factory-location     String(100);
          End;
```

While third normal form is intended to prevent a number of undesirable side effects of the record model (particularly such things as update anomalies), it has a number of unfortunate side effects of its own:

- Functional dependencies used in deriving the third normal form are not reflected in the record description; most of the record is then, by definition, meaningless. A record in third normal form will consist of a primary key plus a number of items that are directly dependent on the primary key. For example, the type of dependency might be that no employee number may be associated with more than one location number at the same time. That is, an employee can only work in one place. This is represented in the employee record by the presence of a single location-number item. The existence of the original dependency rule is not precluded by the presence of the location-number item, but it is by no means implied by it either. The user has to guess what it might mean.

- Records in third normal form can include many relationships that are not suggested at all in the record description, even in the form of (unstated) functional dependencies. It is, of course, possible to see all attributes as relationships.

- Attributes of relationships tend to be lost. Except with M:M relationships in which the attributes can be placed in the intersection record, there is no obvious location for the attributes of a relationship. As a result, someone looking for data about a relationship may easily look in the wrong place.

- Duplication of information, particularly in compound foreign keys, is positively required by third normal form. This clearly violates the spirit, if not the letter, of the form, by giving rise to duplicated data. Most systems legislate the problem away by disallowing key changes.

In any case, normalization is not an optimal technique for describing the semantics of data. Consider, for example, the complications of fifth and fourth normal forms, especially when expressed formally, using dependency relations. It is not reasonable to use this type of approach in presenting the meaning of data to the end user, or even to the programmer who has to maintain it.

SUMMARY

The problems with record-based information models are difficult to summarize. As a whole, they are extremely diverse and do not really fit into any particular pattern; this is especially true so far as the offered solutions are concerned. Each of the areas covered may be summarized as follows:

- Issues related to entity identifiers and to naming and symbolic reference
  - Uniqueness
  - Existence
  - Synonyms
  - Scope
  - Changeability
- Relationship issues
  - Come in too many different shapes and sizes
  - No uniform method of describing relationships
- Entities issues
  - Entities are not explicitly described
  - Complex entity types are not adequately handled.

Generally, the issues revolve around the fact that the model is unable to deal with either the description of data or the data itself, plus the fact that the data simply does not fit the model.

One of the reasons why the issues are so complex and difficult to come to grips with (which is a normal by-product of ad hoc solutions) is that record-based systems usually represent an attempt to solve too many problems at once. Records are used to solve navigational problems, while simultaneously being expected to capture semantics; records are expected to provide for space and key management while simultaneously providing a solution to the entity identifier problem.

An answer can then be found to many of the issues posed in this section by simply separating the logical layers from the physical layers. Given a reasonable logical model, divorced from the concept of a record (or any other implementation-related idea), it becomes possible sensibly to tackle the problem of how to provide a physical representation of such a model.

Chapter 6, "Semantic Data-Model—Description" deals with the description of the logical model; Chapter 11, "Semantic Data Model—Implementation" covers approaches to the implementation of the model.

5

On Definitions

Scene: The maze again. Dasd is trying to explain the idea of a transaction to Pascal.

Pscl.　My reading of the word *transaction* differs very considerably from yours.

Dasd.　Yes, but you must remember that we are dealing with a very specialized context here. There are many words that have a specialized meaning within this context, there are some that even have no meaning outside of it.

Pscl.　Well then, you take on an onerous burden.

Dasd.　Onerous?

Pscl.　A heavy burden, or a difficult task.

Dasd.　Oh. Why?

Pscl.　Well, if you start to change the accepted meanings of words, then you must be prepared to state what the new meanings are. Not an easy task. The problem is that each definition of a word cannot itself use the word that it is defining. If it were to do so, the definition would be circular and therefore useless. If each definition cannot use a word that

	it is defining (either directly or indirectly), it must use some new words. These words in turn will have to be defined, and so on. Therefore, your use of the term *transaction* cannot, ultimately, be defined.
Dasd.	I didn't notice you having any trouble defining *onerous.*
Pscl.	Yes, but there we were dealing with a common language and common usages of words, in which we were happy to assume a mutual understanding of what the words "heavy" and "burden" mean. A very similar problem arises with any type of reasoning. If we have A is implied by B, and we assume that B is proven, then we may take it that A is proven. But how do we prove B? Why, we must assume that some C implies B. If C is proven then B is proven. And so on. Any conclusion must be based on some kind of premise. The premise itself, if it is to be proven, must be the conclusion in some argument. So nothing can ever be proven, in much the same way that nothing can ever be defined.
Dasd.	But you don't really believe that, do you?
Pscl.	There are some ways to escape. Statements can be of two kinds: Analytic and Synthetic. Analytic statements are statements that are logically either true or false. For example, the statement, "I am here or I am somewhere else," is necessarily true because of the rules of logic; it is then an analytic statement. All analytic statements may be proven or disproven by deriving them from other statements, which in turn are known to be true. Synthetic statements, on the other hand, cannot be proven by unaided logic, and they are either true or not true depending on some sort of external considerations—typically, correspondence with the real world.
Dasd.	Getting back to the problem of definition then: What you are saying is that we ultimately have to appeal to synthetic statements, statements about the real world, if our definitions are not to be vacuous?
Pscl.	Vacuous?
Dasd.	Empty, meaningless, without content.
Pscl.	Oh. Why look, here's Good Old Leibniz, Aristotle incarnate—just the man for a discussion on definitions.

Gola. Hi Blaise, who's your friend?

Pscl. A lady with an interest in definitions and meaning.

Gola. Oh, ho! How to define a term without using undefined terms. A pretty problem.

Dasd. Downright ugly, I'd say. All this synthetic–analytic business doesn't help much when it comes to looking at information that has to be stored in a database. It has to be possible for someone to retrieve the information and understand it. Now from what Blaise here has been saying, it seems as though any such information is only going to be meaningful to those people who know how to tie it into the real world. It's only going to be meaningful to people who know what the synthetic significance of the data is. Anyone who can't make that tie-up, might as well not bother looking at the stuff.

Gola. Yes, yes, that seems reasonable. But there are realms beyond the synthetic and analytic, you know.

Dasd. No I don't.

Gola. Allow me to explain then. The analytic–synthetic distinction applies to the logical status of two different types of statement. Using logic, analytic statements may be demonstrated to be either true or false. Synthetic statements may not; they are usually assertions about the "real world" and independent of logic, at least as far as proof goes. Now, it is possible to further distinguish statements as "a posteriori."

Dasd. Posterior?

Gola. A posteriori, I said. If a statement is *a posteriori*, then it is dependent on experience. By contrast, statements may be *a priori*, which implies that they are independent of experience. They may be known to be true regardless of any actual events or circumstances. Wait a minute, what's going on here? Author, Author, I protest.

Auth. What's the problem?

Gola. I never said anything like this. This doesn't sound like me at all.

Auth. Yes you did.

Gola.   No I did not. Kant might have, but I certainly did not.

Auth.   Well, he was German, wasn't he? Go on. Be a good fellow and tell them all about it.

Gola.   I think it's pretty shoddy. I'll tell Kant next time I see him. Where was I? . . . Analytic statements are all a priori; synthetic statements are generally a posteriori. What I am (supposed to be) saying is that there may also be a priori synthetic statements. Herein lies the solution to the problem of defining terms without using undefined terms.

Dasd.   The devil it does!

Gola.   And here comes Mephisto. Who's this he has with him?

Meph.   Hello, everyone. Allow me to introduce Sir Isaac Newton.

Cmmn.   Please—call Me Mister Newton.

Meph.   What's going on then? These continentals spinning more yarn, are they?

Gola.   I was just explaining the difference between a priori analytic, a posteriori synthetic, and a priori synthetic statements. I was about to point out the importance of the a priori synthetic. As I was about to say—given that there are statements about the world around us that can be taken as true—that is, immediately and obviously true—it is possible to escape from the cycle of proof and still say useful things about the world around us.

Pscl.   So we may have truths about the real world on the basis of these a priori synthetic statements. These truths are as valid and compelling as the truths of logic.

Gola.   Exactly!

Dasd.   Wait a minute, I need to see all this written down.

Gola.   Happy to oblige.

Gola scribbles the following:

Synthetic	→	about the real world; i.e., factual
Analytic	→	about the logical world
A posteriori	→	possibly true
A priori	→	necessarily true
Analytic a priori	→	necessarily true logical statements
Synthetic a posteriori	→	possibly true factual statements
Synthetic a priori	→	necessarily true factual statements

Gola. It is generally considered that there is no such thing as analytic a posteriori statements. That is, there are no statements concerned with the logical world that are not necessarily either true or not true.

Dasd. So why use a priori synthetic? What's the matter with the good old synthetic posterior statements?

Gola. A posteriori, please. The problem with these statements is that they cannot be proven. Unless of course, one is prepared to take Bacon seriously.

Cmmn. Bacon proposed the experimental method as a means whereby truth could be grounded in the real world. Observation is used as a source for generalizations, which, being based on the facts, will be true. It is a persuasive approach.

Gola. Persuasive, but flawed. Apart from anything else, unless we know all possible instances of a fact, how can we be sure we will never see a contradiction? Perhaps all possible swans are not white; perhaps there are people with six toes. No, observation is not a sufficient basis for generalization.

Cmmn. What then is the basis for your synthetic a priori statements?

Gola. Why, intelligence, what else? Given a mind of sufficient intelligence, of sufficient powers of inner perception, the a priori synthetic statements will flow.

Meph. [*aside*] What little angels they are!

Dasd. What?

Pscl. Getting back to the problem of definition. The truly intelligent individual will be able to resolve all questions of definition, or chains of argument, on an a priori synthetic basis where

> necessary. This seems to be somewhat akin to my friend Descarte's concept of intuition as a basis for knowledge.

Gola.   Yes, there are clear parallels. Meine Dame, are you satisfied?

Dasd.   No, you seem to be telling me that the super smart will have no trouble understanding the database, but what about everyone else?

Gola.   Oh, people manage. They can always rely on someone to explain to them what is going on.

Dasd.   Hey Isaac, what do you think? You've told us about this Bacon character, but what do you think?

Cmmn.   If you really want to know: I think that we have an almost unlimited capacity for making sense out of the things that we see around us. It is this faculty that the storyteller relies on—our ability to make a whole personality out of a few words, a whole figure out of a few lines. We have a complete sense of what a world should be like. As soon as we know that what we are looking at or listening to is a representation of a world, we can fill in the gaps, we know what the rest of it is like without being told.

Dasd.   Good, I like it. So where does meaning come from?

Cmmn.   From the shoulders of others! From your predecessors, from antecedents, from those who have worked and thought before you.

Dasd.   Sounds good. I'm not sure it helps, but it sounds good. What are you looking so glum about, Mephisto?

6

Description of the Semantic Data Model (SDM)

INTRODUCTION

This part of the book describes the semantic data model (SDM). Previous sections of the book have outlined the reasons why an SDM is necessary; subsequent sections go over some of the things that are needed to actually make use of an SDM and how the model might be used in designing a database.

This chapter consists of various descriptions of the model. The descriptions each take a different view of how the model might be used and understood. There are five different descriptions, each of which could probably be read on its own. Particularly for someone unfamiliar with databases and with data models, reading them in sequence is a good idea, as each description is both reinforced by and reinforces each of the descriptions that precede it. The descriptions, briefly, are the following:

1. **The concepts of the model**—the basic ideas underlying the model—namely, entities, classes, subclasses, and attributes

2. **SDM diagrams**—a diagramming technique for representing databases and the objects they contain

3. **Data description language (DDL) syntax**—DDL is a language that can be used to describe a database; this section gives the syntax for a language that can be used to describe a semantic database.

4. **The metaschema**—these days, it is often the case that a database will contain a database that describes the database as a whole; the data in the database that describes the database as a whole is called *metadata*; the schema of such a database is referred to as *metaschema*, and it amounts to a generalized and potentially very formal description of the data model.

5. **Operations on the model**—how data in a semantic database can be manipulated; this section describes a data manipulation language (DML) for an SDM.

Many of the ideas in both the DDL and the DML are based on the Unisys Corporation's Semantic Information Manager (SIM) database management system. The concepts of the model and the metaschema are common to a number of systems currently in the public domain. The SDM diagrams were devised specifically for this book.

Before proceeding, an issue that needs to be put out of the way is the implication of the term *semantic* in "semantic data model." In what sense can a data model be semantic?

Taking some liberties with the English language, two possible meanings could be applied to the term *semantic*: a strong one and a weak one—strong-semantics and weak-semantics.

Strong-semantics refers to the meaning or significance of the sentences that may be generated by a grammar. The grammar provides a mechanism that allows legal sequences to be distinguished from illegal sequences, but the grammar does not, and cannot indicate how the sentences are to be interpreted. Strong-semantics deals with interpretation.

Weak-semantics may be used in describing a programming language. In this context, the grammar (or syntax) merely specifies what is possible, the weak-semantics indicate what is reasonable. The syntax can easily be enforced by the compiler, although the compiler will happily generate code for a program that is, weak-semantically, absolute gibberish. Formal techniques for proving the correctness of programs, and languages such as Modula-2 and Ada, can be considered to be attempts to extend the weak-semantics of the program.

Weak-semantics then is still concerned with the formal characteristics of the system. Strong-semantics is concerned with meaning and significance. With a little effort, weak-semantics can be transformed into syntax; this is partially what has happened in going from assemblers to COBOL, and from COBOL to Modula-2. Strong-semantics will always be more of interest to the users of the system than of interest directly to the system itself, although one of the primary characteristics of a computer is that it is a system that can use itself.

Strong-semantics implies an observer of some sort; this is because ultimately, meaning is in the mind of the beholder. As such, a database cannot store meaning. Its contents can only be meaningful given a context of some kind. Meaning or significance (in the sense of the implication or meaning of a sign) can be looked at in terms of interpretation within a context. A red flag being waved by a man at a railway station is not the same as a red flag being waved by a man at a May Day Parade. The first man is probably a railway employee, the second is probably a communist; the first flag signifies danger, the second signifies political affiliation.

In a similar way, to be able to attribute meaning to data in a database, it is necessary not only to have a beholder, but also to have a context within which the beholder can work. Essentially, it is the business of semantic databases to provide such a context. A semantic database does not, and cannot, provide meaning, or strong-semantics, but it provides contexts within which it is possible for data to be meaningful.

Programming languages in which more of the weak-semantics of the language are incorporated into the syntax can be compared to semantic databases. With programming languages, the weak-semantics are being moved out of the execution environment (in which the programs runs) and into the compiler, allowing invalid code to be detected at the time of compilation rather than at run time (time of execution). With semantic databases, the weak-semantics are being moved out of the applications that access the database and into the database itself.

The term *semantic* in "semantic database" then can be taken in both these senses. Semantic databases provide a context within which it is possible for the data to be meaningful. They also provide for the migration of the weak-semantics of the system out of the application programs and into the database.

FIRST DESCRIPTION: THE CONCEPTS OF THE MODEL

The semantic data model is defined in terms of classes and attributes. Briefly, an *attribute* is a characteristic of an object, and *classes* are collections of objects that happen to share the same set of attributes. The SDM then follows the entity–relationship model in describing the world in terms of collections of things and their associated characteristics.

Class

A *class* is a collection of objects. The objects may be of any type, so long as they have some characteristic in common. It is possible for one object to participate in many different classes—in some cases, very diverse classes. Isaac Newton is a member of the class *Homo sapiens*; he is also a member of the class of partially pink objects.

A class is defined when, given an object, it is possible to determine whether the object belongs to the class or not. There are two possible approaches to the business of defining classes:

1. A list of the members of the class may be provided
2. Some condition may be stated that applies to all of the members of the class; it must also be the case that the condition does not apply to any object that is not a member of the class.

The first type of definition, defining the class by providing a list of its members, is known as *definition by extension*. The second type of definition is known as *definition by intension*.

Intensional definitions are regarded as being more fundamental than extensional ones. If some object is in a list, one may always ask "Why is it in the list?" Assuming that the list is not just a random selection of objects, whatever is the rationale for the list, is also the intensional definition of the class. The following are some examples of classes:

1. Musical instruments
2. String instruments
3. Wind instruments

4. Wooden instruments

5. Woodwinds

6. Brass instruments

7. {french horn, trumpet, trombone, tuba}

8. {violin, viola, cello, double bass}

Classes 1, 2, 3, 4, 5, and 6 are all definitions by intension, 7 and 8 are defined by extension. Class 7 is an extensional version of 6; 8 is an extensional version of 2.

It may be noted that extensional definitions are inherently unsatisfactory. This is because it is, in practice, extremely difficult always to enumerate all of the possible members of a class of real world objects. What, for example, happened to the cornet? What if someone goes and invents a new instrument and chooses to classify it as a "brass instrument"?

Subclass

Subclasses are a natural extension to the idea of a class. Where all the members of a class are also members of some other class, the first class may be taken as a subclass of the second. For example, "wind instruments" are a subclass of "musical instruments." Anything that is a "wind instrument" (a recorder for example) is also necessarily a "musical instrument."

A class that has subclasses may itself be a subclass of some other class. It is also possible for a class to be a subclass of more than one other class. Consider "woodwinds," for example. Any "woodwind instrument," such as a recorder, is both a "wind instrument" and a "wooden instrument."

This may be represented diagrammatically.

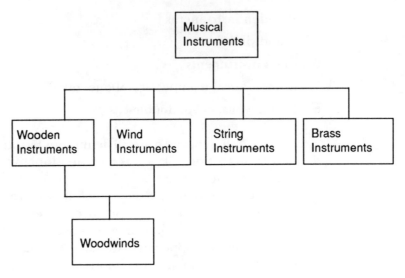

This is a part of an items database for the great Auction House of Northerbees's, more of which is described later.

Attributes

Things have attributes. The attributes provide a mechanism for describing the thing. If the thing in question happens to be some particular violin for example, it may have a weight attribute, indicating how much it weighs, and it may have a maker attribute, indicating who made it. In entity–relationship terms, this may be depicted as follows:

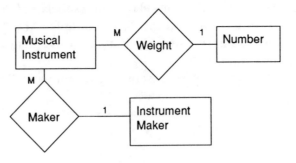

The crucial thing about the attributes is that they are mappings or relationships between one class and another.

It is tempting to regard the class "instrument maker" as somehow different from the class "number (2,2)." "Instrument maker" may have a whole host of attributes of its own (e.g., "name," "country of origin," "date of birth," "specialty," whereas "number (2,2)" is, in a sense, atomic; it stands for itself. This is all very true but quite irrelevant from a data modeling point of view.

Attributes then are to be understood as mappings from one class to some other class. While the implementation of the database is not at issue, it is extremely important not to distinguish one attribute from another on the basis of the method of representing the objects that the attribute maps to. The type of the object is extremely important, but how it is represented is not important at all.

A particular attribute value for a particular member of a class may be taken as pointing to some member of the class that the attribute ranges over, or points to. For example, some particular violin then has an attribute maker, which points to the particular instrument maker who made the violin, he or she in turn has an attribute name, which in this case points to the string "Stradivarius."

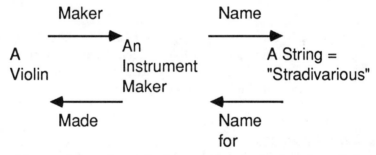

Looking at things from the instrument maker's point of view, the other end of the "maker" relationship is a "made" relationship. The relationship "made" indicates which instruments were made by some instrument maker. Though a particular violin could only be made by one maker, a particular instrument maker may have made many violins.

In terms of the entity–relationship model, this could be diagrammed as follows:

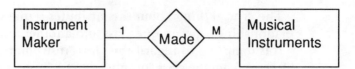

With the usual interpretation of the M:1 relationship, in SDM, the attribute "made" is known as a *multivalued attribute.*

The main difference here from the entity–relationship approach is that there are two different attributes involved, "maker" and "made," or

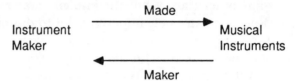

These two attributes are coordinated inasmuch as

1. If a musical instrument is made by an instrument maker, it must be the case that

2. The maker of the musical instrument is the same instrument maker.

In functional terms, "made" and "maker" are inverses of each other. In the SDM, it is possible to declare explicitly the inverse of an attribute. Also in the SDM, it always assumed that each attribute has an inverse, whether the inverse is declared or not.

Classes and Attributes

Classes are characterized by attributes. Attributes represent mappings between classes. Membership in a class is decided on the basis of the entity involved having a particular characteristic. Membership in a class is itself a characteristic.

Attributes will be appropriate to entities of a particular type (or class). For example, it would not be appropriate to ask the Northerbees's database how many strings a trumpet has. Trumpets simply do not have strings. Nor would it be appropriate to ask what kind of wood a brass instrument was made of. Brass instruments, by definition, are not made of wood. It may, however, be very relevant to some prospective purchaser to know that a particular recorder was made from pearwood because this has a direct bearing on the appearance and value of the piece.

Attributes then are associated with some owning class. For an attribute to be applicable to an entity, it must first be a member of the right class.

The class of "musical instruments" now has some added attributes:

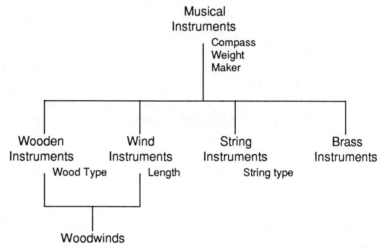

All instruments have a *compass*—that is the highest and lowest notes they can play; similarly, all instruments have a weight and a maker. Only wooden instruments have a wood type. One has to be a string instrument to have a string type.

All string instruments are also musical instruments. String instruments are a subclass of musical instruments; therefore, all string instruments must have the attributes of "compass," "weight," and "maker." In the SDM, the subclass is said to inherit all of the attributes of the superclass. All this means is that if you know that B is a subclass of A, because every B is an A, every B must also have all of the characteristics or attributes of an A.

A collection of subclasses and superclasses, such as the musical instruments class, is known as a *generalization hierarchy*. Somewhere at the top of the hierarchy is a single class. All the attributes of all of its superclasses are inherited by any class in the hierarchy.

Considering woodwinds in isolation, it has the following attributes:

```
Woodwinds
    Compass
    Weight
    Maker
    Wood Type
    Length
```

Woodwinds has all of the attributes of all of its superclasses, regardless of how far away the superclass is or whether there is more than one superclass at a particular level of the generalization hierarchy.

Note also that an entity can not only participate in many different classes at different levels of the hierarchy; it may also participate in multiple classes at the same level of the hierarchy. For example, it is possible for something to be both a wooden instrument and a wind instrument.

It is easy enough to go wrong in constructing class hierarchies. Consider the following diagram:

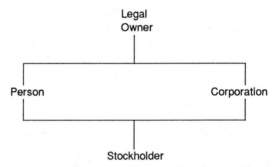

It is tempting to take the attitude that "stockholders" are a subclass of both "person" and "corporation." That is, all "stockholders" are either "persons" or "corporations," and therefore, it is permissible to model the situation with "stockholder" as a subclass of both "person" and "corporation." This is quite wrong.

It is not possible for something to be simultaneously both a "person" and a "corporation." But this is what is implied by the preceding diagram. Where an entity participates in a subclass, it must also participate in *all* of the superclasses of the subclass at the same time. A more reasonable representation of the "stockholder" class would be the following (if all legal owners are stockholders):

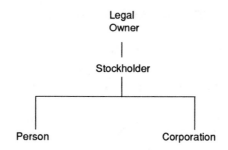

Or it could be the following (if some legal owners are not stockholders):

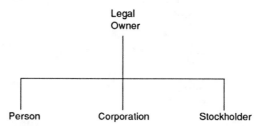

(with the constraint that something may not be both a "corporation" and a "person").

There is a very simple test for the validity of a hierarchy, which goes like this:

- For each class in the hierarchy, select an entity that clearly belongs to the class.

- For each of the superclasses of that class ask the question: Is it reasonable for this entity to be a member of this superclass?" If the answer is "no," the hierarchy is wrong.

The use of the hierarchy has several beneficial side effects:

- By locating any entity in the hierarchy, a number of possibilities are explicitly excluded.

- An entity will be placed in a context in the hierarchy that indicates which characteristics it shares with other entities.

- It is not necessary to look at the lowest level of the hierarchy all the time; someone wanting information from the database can focus attention on a level of the hierarchy that is relevant to the information desired.

SECOND DESCRIPTION: SDM DIAGRAMS

Conventions for Describing a System

The usual convention used in describing a database schema is a formalism based on a series of language elements, each language element consisting of a production in a grammar. All of the productions of the grammar taken together are assumed to describe the language as a whole.

Various formalisms have been devised for this purpose—notably BNF (Backus Naur Form), railroad diagrams, and the COBOL meta-language of dots, ellipses, and braces.

The choice of an approach to the description of a language is typically based on the approach's ability to assist in

- The verification of the completeness and consistency of the language
- The implementation of a compiler based on the language.

The formalisms are not generally aimed at aiding the users of the system the language describes. The user is likely to be interested in formulating a subjectively based understanding of the system and is unlikely to be aided in this by either a grammar aimed essentially at compilers or one concerned with completeness and correctness.

The approach appears especially inappropriate in the context of a semantic data model. In an SDM, the intention of the system is to communicate as much meaning as possible to the users of the system. Though a formalism is still essential, one based on diagrams seems far more likely to be remembered and understood. The alternatives are as follows:

- Terms or symbols especially devised for the language (these may have the advantage of being free of spurious connotations, they will also probably be difficult to understand and remember)
- Formalisms based on terms that are given a formal definition when used as a part of the system but that have a similar meaning in everyday use; inevitably, such terms do not quite fit, giving rise to a variety of anomalies and difficulties.

The intention of this section is to provide a formalism for describing semantic databases, derived from Venn diagrams. Venn diagrams may be extended to allow both a description of a semantic database and a description of a query against a semantic database, without violating the spirit or the interpretation of the diagrams.

Classes and Types

As mentioned previously, classes are collections of objects having some set of characteristics in common. It is the usual assumption that the entities in the class will have some common range of values for a common set of attributes, although the actual values of the attributes for individual entities will generally not be the same. The class is then an attempt to impose some order onto diversity, to characterize a varying set of individuals as belonging to some identifiable group, in such way that a given individual may be classified both as belonging to the group and as distinguished from other members of the group.

A type is the same concept viewed in a slightly different way. A *type* is a set of possible values that may be used to characterize the members of a class. It is still a collection of individuals, the individuals still have enough in common to be both identifiable as belonging to the type and distinguishable from each other. The main difference between a type and a class, in the context of an SDM, is that a *type* is an "outputtable" object. It can be printed or displayed on a screen.

For example, it is not possible to print the attribute "department" of the class "employee," but it is possible to print the attribute "age." It is also possible to print the attribute "name of department of employee," but this is obviously not the same as the department itself. Nor is it good enough to print all of the attributes of department; among other things, where do you stop? "Department name" is obviously a department attribute, but what about "name of manager of department," or "name of spouse of manager of department," or "name of secretary of manager of department"? It is very difficult when representing an entity to know what attributes really characterize the entity. As we shall see one of the principal features of the SDM is that it allows almost the whole of the rest of the database to be viewed as characterizing any particular entity.

Subclasses and Subtypes

Classes may be related to other classes in a variety of different ways. One kind of relationship between classes is that all or some of the members of a class are also members of some other class.

When all of the members of a class are also members of another class, the one class is said to be a subclass of the other. When some of the members of a class are members of another class, a third class is defined, which is a subclass of both classes.

The subclass–superclass relationship provides a generalization hierarchy that allows the database to be approached through a subclass appropriate to the level of detail required by the individual involved.

There is a relationship between types and subtypes that corresponds to the relationship between classes and subclasses.

For example:

```
Type
    week_days = {mon,tues,wed, thur,fri,sat,sun};
    work_days = Week-days{mon..fri};
```

In this example, "work_days" is a subtype of "week_days."

Two questions: When is a class a subclass? Obviously when it has a superclass. Are there any classes that do not have superclasses? Oddly enough, the answer seems to be "no." For every class there must be a clear definition of the class. It must be possible to decide, for any given object, whether it is a member of the class or not. However by a law of logic, known as the axiom schema of separation, it is not possible to claim that a property universally applies without also specifying to what it applies. In other words, we must always specify what we are talking about. But what of the class that has no superclasses? It seems as though it must contain everything, so its definition must apply to everything; its definition is a property that is universally applicable. This is precisely what is disallowed by the axiom schema of separation.

Look at the consequences; in this case, what we need is an ultimate superclass—"US," the class that contains all subclasses. What we need then is a class such that

$$(\text{for all } x)\ (x \text{ is one of US})$$

Looking at "US" itself, is "US" an "US"? If it is, then there is a problem, for everything in "US" is a subclass, but "US" itself is not a subclass. If "US" is not one of "US" then there is still a problem because that means there is another class (all the things in "US" plus "US" itself) of which "US" is a subclass, so "US" is a subclass anyway.

The subclass–superclass convention should be treated as just that— a convention. For all practical purposes, every subclass can be treated as having a superclass of some sort—if nothing else, the class of all things, or in the context of a database, the class of all thing descriptions; databases, after all, only contain descriptions, although of course a description may be a thing in its own right.

It is advisable to remember though that when we start talking about everything in an unrestricted fashion, we are likely to get onto very slippery ground. This is the lesson to be derived from the problems associated with attempting to define "US."

Attributes

Classes are characterized by attributes. Attributes are essentially mappings from one class to another. An attribute value may be derived by accessing the entity in the class that is the range of the attribute; this entity is the value of the attribute. The entity may in turn be characterized by a set of attributes, which will be mappings to classes of some sort. Ultimately, such a chain of attribute references must be resolved (outside of the system anyway) by an outputtable *type*—that is, something that can be printed or displayed on a screen.

DATA VALUED (DVA) AND ENTITY VALUED (EVA)

An attribute that ranges over a type is a data-valued attribute (DVA). An attribute that ranges over a class is an entity-valued attribute (EVA).

The significance to the distinction between data valued (DVA) and entity valued (EVA) attributes is derived more from the use of the attributes in the context of query languages than from the significance of the attributes in the schema. Accurate classification is of concern in the schema; outputtable data is of concern in formulating queries.

CARDINALITY

Attributes are owned by a domain class; this is the class the attribute describes. Attributes map to a range class; this class provides the value, which characterizes the entity in the class described by the attributes.

Attributes, as mappings, may be characterized in various ways. The usual distinction is between multivalued (or MV) and single-valued (or SV) mappings. An attribute always has an inverse. The inverse of an attribute mapping S to P, is the same mapping considered from the other direction (i.e., a mapping from P to S). This provides the following usually recognized types of relationships:

Relationship Type	Cardinality	Cardinality of Inverse
1 : 1	SV	SV
1 : M	SV	MV
M : 1	MV	SV
M : M	MV	MV

NULLS

Attributes may be required, or they may have a null value. If an attribute is required—that is, it may never have a null value—then it is a total mapping from the domain or owning class to the range class.

Perspective Class

In dealing with a database that consists of a collection of classes, there will always be a class of interest, or the *perspective class*. The assumption is that in looking at the database, we are interested in something, some particular collection of things—be it people or cars or musical instruments. The class of things that we are interested in is assumed to dictate the way that the rest of the database will be viewed. Assuming that we are looking at musical instruments, other things in the database will be viewed relative to, or as attributes of, a musical instrument. Essentially, this means that whether something is an attribute value or an entity depends on how you are looking at things.

From the perspective of some particular entity in the database, potentially every other possible database entity is an attribute value of some kind. If there is a relationship to it, it is an attribute value. It is very unlikely, at least where classes are involved, that there will be any entirely isolated objects in a database (if there are, it is a most peculiar database).

Immediate, Inherited, and Extended

Given the classes and the two possible types of relationships between classes (subclass–superclass or attribute mapping), there are three different ways in which an attribute may be referenced.

1. As an immediate attribute of the class at issue: If "name" is an attribute of "person," for example, and the "names" of known "persons" are to be retrieved, "name" may be referenced as an immediate attribute of the class of interest, or the perspective class.

2. As an inherited attribute: If "student" is a subclass of "person," and the "names" of "students" are to be retrieved, "name" may be referenced as an inherited attribute. No special qualification is required, as "student" is embedded inside "person" (all "students" are known to be "persons"), and all "persons" have "names"; therefore, all "students" may also be assumed to have "names."

3. As an extended attribute: If "student" has a relationship "advisor" to an "instructor" (also a subclass of "person") the attribute "name" of "advisor" is an extended attribute of "student"; that is, it is an attribute, the value of which can only be derived from one or more relationship traversals.

Venn Diagrams

Venn diagrams were named after the nineteenth century mathematician and logician, John Venn. As is shown in this section, there is a direct equivalence between the components of a Venn diagram and the elements of formal logic. There is a similar equivalence between the SDM diagrams and Venn diagrams, and beyond this, there is an equivalence between the concepts of the SDM and the SDM diagrams. It follows that there is an equivalence between the concepts of the SDM and logic. This is important in a variety of ways. It is particularly important here in establishing a deeper understanding of the concepts of the SDM.

In a Venn diagram, a class is represented by a region labeled with the term that designates (or names) the class. For example, the class "dinosaurs," may be depicted as

Dinosaurs

The diagram is of a class, not a proposition. It represents the class "dinosaurs," but it does not assert anything about it. To represent the fact that the class "living dinosaurs" has no members, all the interior of the region is shaded.

Living Dinosaurs

This is actually the negation of a proposition, and it is equivalent to a denial of the proposition

(there exists x) (x is a dinosaur and x is alive)

Or, there exists an x such that x is a dinosaur and x is alive.

To represent the notion that there is at least one living dinosaur, an "x" (or some other lowercase italic letter) is placed in the appropriate region, giving

Living Dinosaurs

It should be noted that a diagram that represents a class also represents, by implication, all those things that are not a member of the class (i.e., the area outside of the region).

Propositions in logic come in standard forms. There are four standard form categorical propositions:

1. All S are P
2. No S are P
3. Some S are P
4. Some S are not P.

These propositions may be represented by using different regions of a diagram consisting of two overlapping circles:

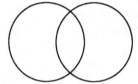

By asserting the existence of objects in some portion of the diagram or the nonexistence of objects in some portion of the diagram, the four standard form categorical propositions may be represented. For instance, in the proposition "All dinosaurs are extinct animals"

Dinosaurs 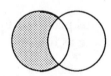 Extinct Animals

the shading indicates that there are no dinosaurs that are not extinct animals. Actually, the Venn diagram alters the expression of the proposition, but the expression is equivalent. The proposition "Some dinosaurs were amphibians" (having established that all dinosaurs are extinct the use of the past tense seems appropriate!) may be represented:

Dinosaurs 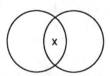 Amphibians

It should be noted that each region of the diagram indicates a class. In a diagram consisting of two overlapping circles, there are four regions. In the preceding example, dinosaurs, amphibians, amphibious dinosaurs, and all things that are neither dinosaurs nor amphibians.

Syllogistic reasoning may be represented using Venn diagrams. A syllogism is an argument form consisting of a major premise, a minor premise, and a conclusion. For example,

>All dinosaurs are extinct animals
>
>All sauropods are dinosaurs

Therefore,   all sauropods are extinct animals.

In the example, there are three classes of objects involved: "extinct animals," "dinosaurs," and "sauropods." These may be represented by three overlapping circles:

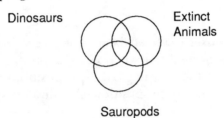

The assertions provided by the major and minor premise give the diagram shading as follows:

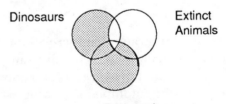

The conclusion may be seen from the diagram: All possible sauropods are extinct. There is an interesting and profound point to be made here. The so called "conclusion" derived from the previous diagram was actually there all the time. The convention of writing down syllogisms as a series of steps tends to give the impression that something new has been discovered, but with formal logic, this is never the case. In fact, it must not be the case. Any language for manipulating a formal system, such as a syllogism, should never derive something that was not implied by the system in the first place; if it does, the language is invalid.

Deciding the validity of a language used to describe or manipulate a database is by no means easy. In database terms, what is required is a language that will not allow conclusions to be drawn from information in the database that in some sense contradicts other information present in the database or that simply was not there in the first place. Note the assumption that the database itself is consistent, not just the information derived from it. Unfortunately, no system devised to date is both

1. Powerful enough to provide a full and useful description of a real-life application, and

2. Equivalent to some system of logic that can be formally proven to be correct.

What's more, there are very good reasons for believing that there never will be such a system! The reason for saying this is quite simple. Kurt Gödel's incompleteness theorem says something like this: If a system is powerful enough to perform arithmetic, then there are statements that are valid within the system that cannot be proven within the system. Formal logic can never provide a complete guarantee that a system is consistent and correct, but it is the best we have, so far as formal systems are concerned. An understanding of formal logic is essential to an understanding of the ideas behind systems such as the relational, functional, and semantic data models. But like anything else, logic is not a cure-all; we must, in the end, depend on our native wit to spot situations where the system has clearly gone berserk and someone needs to pull out the plug.

SDM Diagrams

SDM diagrams have to depict the following:

*   The subclass–superclass relationship—this may be taken as the same as the Venn diagram's inclusion relationship

*   Attributes, both DVA and EVA—the diagram has to indicate the name of the attribute, the class that owns the attribute, and the classes that inherit the attribute; the attribute must be an extended attribute to any class that has a relationship, direct or indirect, to the class that owns the attribute

- The cardinality of the attribute
- Classes of entities
- Queries—that is, subsets of a class of entities
- Individuals—that is, instances of a class.

A great deal is achieved in Venn diagrams simply by the ability to indicate where objects overlap. Overlapping may conveniently be depicted simply by ordering things from left to right. For example, in the following, A and B are overlapped by D:

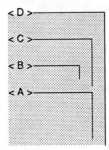

And B is overlapped by both C and D. This provides for all of the subclass–superclass relationships implied by the SDM. Note that it may not always be possible to depict an entire hierarchy without a particular class appearing more than once.

SDM diagrams will be provided by these conventions:

1. A class is indicated by a vertical line with a cross piece at the top. The name of the class is written between angle brackets (<, >) within the crosspiece. For example, here is the class "Dinosaurs":

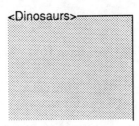

2. The attributes of the class are indicated by horizontal lines attached to the vertical line for the class. The line terminates with the name of the class to which the attribute maps. The line is labeled with the name of the attribute. The line terminates in a single arrow if the

attribute is SV, in a double arrow if the attribute is MV. The following is the class "dinosaurs," with attributes "name," "first era," "last era," and "locations":

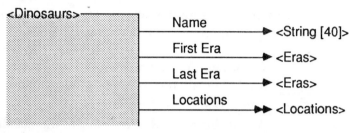

Where appropriate, the range class of an attribute may be included in the diagram. For example,

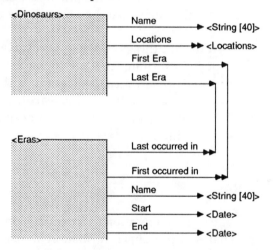

3. Subclasses are indicated by placing the line for the subclass to the left of the line for its superclass. The class "carnivorous dinosaur," subclass of "dinosaurs," with attribute, "prey," which ranges over "animals."

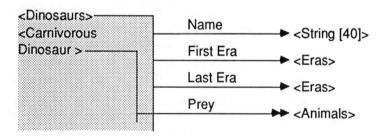

The implication of the diagram is that a "dinosaur" that happens to be "carnivorous" will have the attribute "prey," indicating what it eats, as well as the attributes "name" and "first era" and "last era."

There are a number of subsidiary conventions governing the layout and presentation of the diagrams:

- Classes may be *exploded* as often as necessary to obtain the desired level of detail; the convention does not assume that all classes are always represented.

- An attribute only has to indicate the class to which the attribute maps; the class does not have to be present on the diagram.

- If there is a single unnamed relation between two classes, the relation may take the name of the range class.

Note that things in angle brackets stand for something else. The analogy with things that are in angle brackets in railroad diagrams is intended. In a railroad diagram, a thing in angle brackets can be expanded to something else, usually another railroad diagram. In an SDM diagram, a thing in angle brackets can usually be expanded to a set of entities.

Query Diagrams

A *query* is an operation that extracts some information from a database. That is, it presents information about entities within the database, or instances of classes contained by the database. The diagrams so far have been used to describe classes—that is collections of entities—rather than some particular entity or particular collection of entities. A query diagram then represents a particular entity, or an instance of a class, rather than the class itself.

It is generally the case that the result of a query may represent one or more entities. The result in any event is regarded as a set of objects; the set may be null (a set with no members), a singleton set (a set with one member), or arbitrarily large within the limits of the class to which the query is addressed. Although it is necessary to represent the information about a single entity in order to represent a query result, it is also necessary to represent information about a collection of entities in order to represent the query as a whole. Regarding a single entity as a class with a population of one provides a technique for dealing with single entities; the model already provides a technique for dealing with multiple entities, which is the class itself. A class is a collection of entities; similarly, a query result consists (in part) of a collection of entities, and so may be regarded as a class.

In an SDM, a query has three parts:

1. A perspective class, or class of interest
2. A list of attributes, the values of which are to be returned
3. A selection expression, indicating which entities from the perspective class are to be included in the query result.

From a data modeling point of view, the query is doing essentially two things:

1. Establishing a new class—a subclass of the perspective class, with entities included in the class, where they satisfy the selection expression; if no selection expression is present, a new class is not established, but in either event, the query assumes a defined collection of entities (i.e., a class)
2. Establishing a view of the database—the list of attributes provided by the query specifies which parts of the database are visible while processing the query; in CODASYL terms, this is a *subschema*, which has similar characteristics to the database as a whole; it contains classes and subclasses, any related attributes, and may have queries performed upon it.

With a few minor extensions then, it is possible to see the SDM diagrams as representations of a query or a query result, as well as representations of a class.

• Queries are represented by subclasses with the restriction on the permissible values of the attributes of the subclass indicated with the range class; if it is more convenient, a condition may be stated along with, or as, the name of the subclass generated by the query. For example, carnivores that prey on protoceratops may be diagrammed as follows:

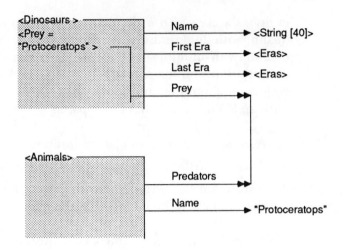

Two things are not shown by the diagram: (1) "dinosaurs" are a subclass of "animals," and (2) the range class of "predators" is actually "animals"

- An individual entity will be shown by supplying values for the attributes of the entity where the range class is normally shown. For example, the *Tyrannosaurus rex* may be diagrammed in this way:

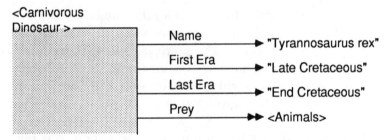

The derivation of the values displayed for "first era" and "last era" are explained in the discussion of label attributes, but for the moment, the diagrams simply assume that an attribute can be designated as a label attribute. Where the value of an entity-valued attribute (EVA) has to be displayed, the value of the label attribute of the range class is used.

Attributes represent mappings from one class to another. Circumstances can arise where it is desirable to be able to disassociate one use of an attribute from another use of the same attribute.

For example, if the "name" and "name of location of dinosaurs" is to be returned only where the dinosaur has been found in the region called "Northern Europe," there is an ambiguity in how the query is to be processed. Diagrammatically, what we have is the following:

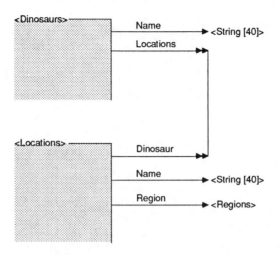

It may be that some particular dinosaur has been found in Leighton Buzzard and Redcar (which are in Northern Europe) and Gweru (which is in Africa). The trouble arises in Gweru. Gweru is not in Northern Europe, so it seems on the face of it that the information returned by the query should not reflect the Gweru location. In this case, this is reasonable enough. But it might be the case that what is wanted is all locations for any dinosaur that happens to have been found in Northern Europe, not just the northern European locations for these dinosaurs.

If this is what is needed from the query, then the query has to be broken down into its separate components. The first component involves the isolation of some portion of the database. This portion will constitute a subset of the data in the database as a whole. The second component involves the retrieval of the requested information, as found in the resulting subset of the database.

We begin with the isolation of the component of interest.

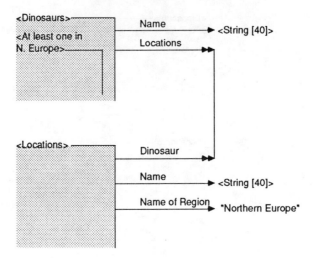

To find out those dinosaurs where at least one specimen has been found in Northern Europe is simply a matter of going through the instances of the class implied by the query, one example being the following:

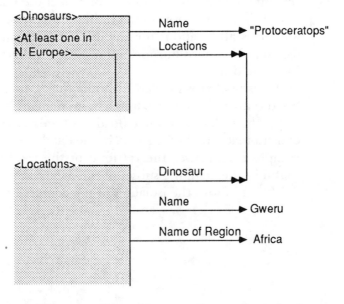

It is possible to perform this type of query in a single step. If this is done, the concepts of *variables* and *binding* have to be introduced, but these are more appropriately considered as a part of the implementation of the system.

Programming languages have a concept known as type coercion. *Type coercion* is a process whereby a value of one type can be used in an operation with a value of another, incompatible type. For example, it is not ordinarily permissible to add a person's age to his weight. It may be that in some circumstances this is a desirable thing to do, for example in computing some sort of health risk factor. In heavily typed programming languages, such as Pascal, special operators are provided, which allow things like ages and weights to be used together. In terms of SDM diagrams, the situation may be depicted in the following way:

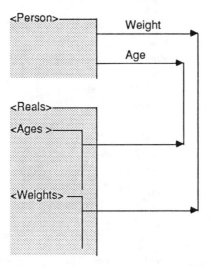

Weights and ages are clearly not the same things unless they are looked at as real numbers. This is what type coercion allows; it permits something at one level of the hierarchy to be viewed as though it were being seen from some other level in the hierarchy. In this case, we are looking at ages and weights as real numbers. It may be the case though that a real number is to be seen as an age, or an age as a weight, and so on. If, for example, there is a Boolean attribute, "overweight," of weights, it would be possible to see whether overweight, or age, looked at as a weight, is true (at what age is the overweight weight, expressed in kilos, the same as the age?). Not very sensible perhaps, but the point is that it is possible to coerce types anywhere across the hierarchy. A coercion operator is supported by the model: It is the ASA ("as a") operator.

Getting back to the query result: For a given entity (considered as a subclass with a population of one), all the relations the entity inherits from its superclasses may be taken as instances of the inherited relations, or more usefully as a limited and special case of the inherited relation. Consider, for instance, the relationship "found-in," between "dinosaur" and "location." The implication is that the relationship between "dinosaur" and "location" ASA "site" is not the same as the relationship between "dinosaur" and "location" ASA "quarry," or between "dinosaur" and "location" ASA <a quarry name>. Here, we have "dinosaur" and "location":

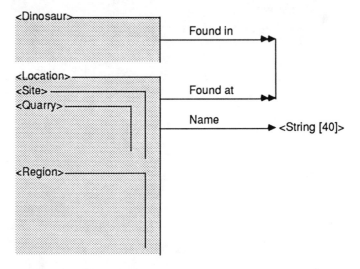

Assuming that some dinosaurs were known to have been found only in quarries, or that we are only interested in dinosaurs that were found in quarries, the meaning of the "found-in" relationship shifts. In another case, some particular quarry is of interest. We may have, for example, the following:

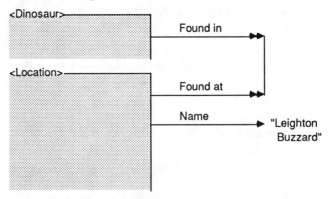

There is a clear shift of meaning in going from the first general case, where the relationship "found-in" is to a "location" that may be any one of a number of different types of things, to the second case, where the relationship is to a specific quarry. It is this shift of meaning whereby a generalized relationship becomes a particular relationship—that is, taken to be characteristic of the process of retrieving data from the database. There is a difference in degree, but not in kind, between the data in a query result and the data in the database itself. This is clearly as it should be.

Where a relationship apparently has more than one range class, it is necessary either to break the relationship into two different relationships or to provide some superclass, with the two range classes as subclasses, over which the relationship may range. Taking again the relationship "found-in" between "location" and "dinosaur," "location" contains "region" and "site." "Dinosaurs" may be found in "regions" and/or "sites." The connotations to the "found-in" relationship will be slightly different, depending on whether the "location" is a "region" or a "site." It could be modeled as two different relationships. A similar argument may be applied to the classes "Man-made" and "Natural," within "site," and so on down to the bottom of the hierarchy. For example, the "found-in" relationship could be depicted as follows:

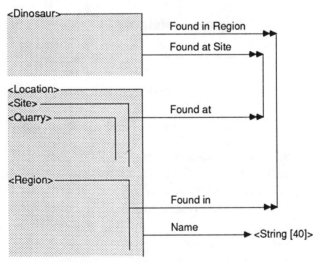

If the bottom of the hierarchy is a singleton class (in other words, the result of a query or a single entity), taking all of the instances of all of the inherited attributes to be attributes unique to the perspective entity is quite reasonable. The type and the context of the relationship still have to be borne in mind, but depicting the relationship as unique to, or qualified by, the entity in question provides a technique for representing a query result that is consistent with the technique used to represent the database as a whole.

At least so far as the diagrams are concerned, there does not have to be any substantial distinction between the representation of the description of a collection of things and the description of a particular thing. This is a highly desirable objective, given that the data in the query result (a) must be a subset of the data in the database and (b) must be seen as such if it is to remain meaningful.

THIRD DESCRIPTION: SDM SYNTAX

In this section, the syntax of a language that may be used to describe a semantic database is provided. It is directly equivalent to both the diagrams and the concepts.

The syntax is presented using railroad diagrams. For an explanation of railroad diagrams, see the description of PSL in Chapter 3, ServiceDB.

<Data Description Language Statement>

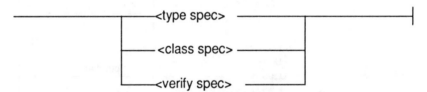

A *schema* consists of a series of DDL statements (that is, the type, class, and verify specifications in the preceding diagram). No particular order is implied, and in some cases (e.g., EVAs to a subclass), an item may have to be referenced before it is declared. Provision is also made for the declaration of types. Types are not distinguished from classes as a result of data modeling considerations but rather because of implementation considerations. As things that are independent from classes, they can be ignored for the time being.

\<Type Spec\>

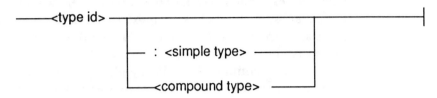

A type spec may be compound or simple.

Compound Type

A compound type may appear as the body of a class, wherein the class has attributes; a compound type within a class is essentially an embedded class, and as such, it should be treated with caution. A compound type provides the attributes of a class.

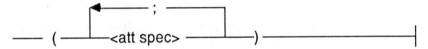

\<Att [Attribute] Spec\>

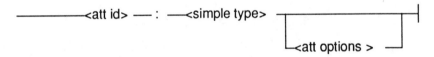

Entities are characterized by attributes and acquire attributes by participating in a class. An attribute may be said to be applicable to an entity if an entity participates in the class for which the attribute is declared. Attributes retain their usual meaning of a mapping from one class to another; for example,

```
CLASS Person
    (
    Name            :  Names
    . . . .
    ) ;
```

indicates that there is an association between the class "person" and the type "names," which may have been defined elsewhere to be a subset of the system-supported class "strings" (i.e., character strings; note that the class "strings" differs from the attribute type STRING, discussed herein later.

Attribute identifiers (<att id>) need not be unique either across the database or within a hierarchy. The assumption is made here that attributes have to be unique within the scope of the compound type within which the attribute is declared. This has implications for the data manipulation language (DML); that is, the language has to be able to allow for the fact that both extended and inherited attributes may not be unique. This does not represent a serious problem, however, as it simply means that the relevant attributes have to be qualified by owner name in order to make the attribute visible.

Attributes and Relationships

In the preceding example, the attribute "name" associates an entity in the class "person" with an entity in a subset of the system-supported class "string." A similar approach is taken toward relationships in general. For example,

```
SUBCLASS Minor OF Person
    (
    Guardian         :  Person;
    ) ;
```

The same way that "name" maps "person" to "names," "guardian" maps "minor" to "person." This provides a totally uniform approach to the declaration of attributes, regardless of whether the attribute represents a type (or relationship to a system-supported class) or represents a relationship in the usually accepted sense of the term.

Class Spec

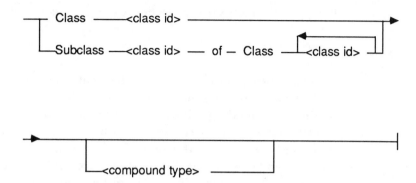

In a class hierarchy, there must be a single root class. A class cannot directly or indirectly be a subclass of itself, but a class does not have to have attributes.

Simple Type

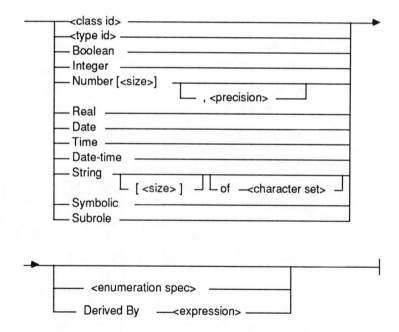

If <class id> is used as a type, an EVA (entity-valued attribute) is declared.

The <type id> indicates that the attribute type is a user-defined type. It is possible, for example, to declare a type, as follows:

```
Type Names            : String[40] ("A".."Z"," ");
```

This may subsequently be used in declaring any number of attributes. The use of a user-defined type serves both as a shorthand and as a method of including additional semantics into the database. Where two attributes are of the same type, it will usually be sensible to compare them and use them in the same expressions; if they are of different types, this may not be sensible at all. For example, what sort of sensible interpretation might be applied to adding a weight to a date? If they are both declared as being of type "integer," the anomaly may not be very obvious.

The following attribute types are commonly used in databases:

- BOOLEAN
- REAL
- INTEGER
- NUMBER
- DATE–TIME
- STRING
- SYMBOLIC
- SUBROLE

The BOOLEAN attribute type has a range of TRUE and FALSE. The normal logical operations (AND, OR, NOT) apply. REAL is a floating-point number and is practically useless for most commercial applications, as the precision cannot be guaranteed. INTEGER represents the positive and negative whole numbers. NUMBER must have a size associated with it, representing the number of digits to the left of the decimal point. The degree of precision, if specified, indicates the number of digits to the right of the decimal point. In operations on NUMBERS, fractional parts are truncated where necessary.

DATE and TIME are special types supported by the system, which allow for the manipulation of temporal information. Particularly important is the interpretation and compatibility of attributes of these types. A uniform method of representation is required, and a variety of specialized functions are needed for handling the DATE and TIME attribute types.

The attribute type STRING allows for the handling of ordered collections of characters of some specified set. The default set is the EBCDIC character set, but a variety of other character sets are possible, such as uppercase characters only. A further possibility is a requirement to be able to deal with character sets that contain more than 256 characters (which is the number in the EBCDIC set). For example, the Japanese Kanji character set contains about 60,000 possible characters.

The SYMBOLIC attribute type allows an attribute to be established that has an arbitrary set of database identifiers as its value. For example, if it is possible for a part in a parts database to be "current," "pending," "suspended," or "deleted," a symbolic attribute could be declared as follows:

```
Part-Status  :  SYMBOLIC
                (Current, Pending, Suspended, Deleted);
```

Expressions such as the following could be used (GTR refers to "greater than"):

```
Part-Status  =  Deleted or Part-Status GTR Suspended
```

SUBROLES are a related idea, except that in the case of the SUBROLE, the enumerations for the SUBROLE are implied by the subclasses of the class that contains the SUBROLE attribute. Using the part-status example again, the following would be needed to make "part-status" into a SUBROLE attribute:

```
Class Parts (
     Part-Name        :  String {40};
     Part-Status      :  SUBROLE;
);
Subclass Current of Parts;
Subclass Pending of Parts;
Subclass Suspended of Parts;
Subclass Deleted of Parts;
```

This differs from the SYMBOLIC version of the attribute; in the absence of an enumeration, no order is implied, so use of the GTR operator would not be valid with the SUBROLE attribute "part-status."

One of the major uses of the SUBROLE attribute type is in declaring the characteristics of the generalization hierarchy. A SUBROLE, as with other attribute types, may be specified as required, MV or SV and so on. In the preceding example, "part-status" could be required, in which case a part must always be a current, a pending, a suspended, or a deleted part.

Enumeration Spec

The <enumeration spec> enumerates the set of values that are allowed by the attribute type. The <expression> must be of an appropriate type. The collection of expressions contained within the curly braces have various constraints depending on the types involved. The SYMBOLIC type requires valid database identifiers. All ordered types may use the expression <value1>..<value2>, where <value2> is greater than <value1>, designating the set of all values from <value1> to <value 2>, inclusive.

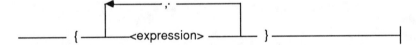

Derived Attributes

Where an attribute value can be derived by a computation on some other attributes, the attribute may be specified as being a derived attribute. A derived attribute has a DERIVED BY clause following the attribute type and is read only (i.e., it may not be written to by the user).

```
CLASS PERSON
    (
    Parent              : BOOLEAN DERIVED BY <expression>;
    . . . .
    ) ;
```

Both with derived attributes and with expressions in verify clauses, there may be considerable problems for the data management system in maintaining the derived values. Given that the DERIVED BY <expression> may contain inherited and extended attributes, as well as immediate ones, every time any attribute in the expression changes its values, the expression may have to be reevaluated. This, though, is an implementation consideration and is not relevant to a description of the model or to the design of a particular database.

It is of immense importance that a derived item be recognized and described as such. If it is not, it is almost inevitable that it will eventually become inconsistent with the data from which it is supposed to be derived. Age is a good example here. Age must be a derived attribute, derived by the following:

```
current date  -  date of birth
```

If the value for age is stored in the database as a number, representing age in years, it would be necessary to update the value every year on the individual's birthday. If this is not done, the stored derived attribute will become inconsistent with the data from which it should be derived.

Att Options

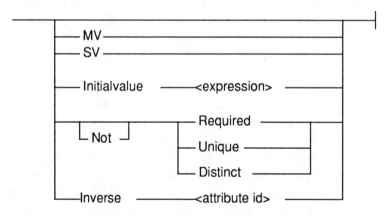

In addition to alternative attribute types, there are attribute options: REQUIRED, UNIQUE, DISTINCT, and INITIAL VALUE. REQUIRED and UNIQUE are redundant, as they could be specified by using a VERIFY operation ((COUNT) > 0 for REQUIRED, COUNT = 1 for UNIQUE). But both are useful and widely understood shorthands.

DISTINCT is applicable to an MV attribute, and it implies that there should be no duplicates for each of the attributes of any given entity, though it may be possible for different entities to share the same value. For example, "employee" may have an attribute "current-projects," referring to the projects to which the employee is currently assigned. It is reasonable for an employee to be assigned to more than one project, so the "current-project" attribute is MV. But it is not reasonable for a given employee to be assigned to the same project twice, so the "current-projects" attribute is DISTINCT.

If no other value is supplied, INITIALVALUE is the value that is used for the value of the attribute when the entity is first created.

MV (MULTIVALUED) AND SV (SINGLE-VALUED) ATTRIBUTE OPTIONS

By default, an attribute is taken to designate a 1:1 mapping between two classes. An M:1 mapping is indicated by specifying the attribute as MULTIVALUED, or MV.

MV compound attributes are not allowed to contain MV attributes. The reasons for this are related both to limitations in the DML and to the fact that an MV compound represents a set of dependent entities. It is convenient to be able to declare these as a part of the entity they are dependent upon, but this is not very good from a data modeling point of view. MV compounds particularly should always be segregated and declared as disjoint classes; if there is some compelling requirements (ease of use for example), they may subsequently be made into an MV compound, but there are very few cases where this is justifiable.

In practice, some upper limit on COUNT of MVs is likely to be applied. So far as the database design goes, MV limits are likely to be such that they can be ignored during the logical design phase.

Note that a class is just a MV'd object.

There are no structural implications to a MV'd collection. The system will ensure that each member of the collection is unique within the collection, making the collection a set. The user sees the collection as a bag, a *bag* being a set in which duplicates are allowed. If for example, "person" has an attribute "previous-assignments," indicating which departments a person has previously been assigned to, it may be the case that a particular individual has been assigned to the same department twice. "Previous-assignment," in this case, will have duplicate entries.

Arrays, lists, queues, strings, and so on may be declared by suitable use of MV attributes. A seniority list for a corporation could be provided by:

```
CLASS Corporation
    (
    Employees          :   Employee, MV;
    .  .  .  .
    )
SUBCLASS Employee OF Person
    (
    Senior-to       :   Employee;
    ) ;
```

Taking this type of general approach to MV (particularly arrays) may seem somewhat clumsy. The approach is justified, though, by the following facts:

- It is an accurate and complete description of the structure involved.

- The size of the structures is not limited; normal array implementation techniques are usually not suitable for data to be stored in a database.

- The data has to be dealt with on retrieval and input in a way that is as consistent as possible across the entire model. Unless a wide range of different operations are to be provided, it is necessary to reduce complex structures, such as arrays and lists, to some simple common denominator.

Inverse

Where it is desirable to follow a relationship from either end, it is necessary to name both ends of the relationship.

Consider, for example, "manages" and "managed-by":

```
SUBCLASS Employee OF Person
    (
    .  .  .  .
    Managed-by       :   Manager;
    ) ;
SUBCLASS Manager of Employee
    (
    .  .  .
    Manages            :   Employee, MV;
    ) ;
```

Clearly, if A is managed by B, then it must be the case that B manages A. If this is not so, the database is inconsistent.

The constraint on the "manages"–"managed-by" relationship is specified by having one attribute as the INVERSE of the other.

```
SUBCLASS Employee OF Person
    (
    .  .  .  .
    Managed-by      :  Manager;
    )  ;

SUBCLASS Manager of Employee
    (
    .  .  .
    Manages           :  Employee, MV, INVERSE Managed-by;
```

The use of the INVERSE clause allows an index to be explicitly specified:

```
CLASS PERSON
    (
    Name            :  Names, inverse Named;
    )  ;

CLASS Names
    (
    named           :  Person;
    Text            :  Character, MV;
    )  ;
```

In practice, the declaration of inverses for DVAs is never necessary however, as the model always assumes the existence of the inverse, even if it has not been explicitly declared.

Verify Spec

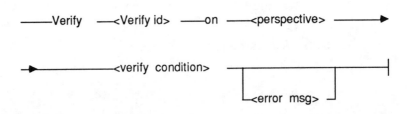

Verifies are applicable to **insert, modify**, and **delete** operations. Whenever the database changes, if necessary, the verify condition has to be checked to ensure that the information placed in the database is correct. If the verify condition fails, the change to the database is discarded and the error message is returned to the user.

Verifies are a type of constraint, as is the logical structure of the database. A REQUIRED attribute is a constraint: the attribute may not be null. A subclass is a constraint: an entity may not have the attributes of the subclass without being in the subclass.

Most of the structural constraints of the database are a part of the visible semantics of the system. This is desirable, as it makes the system easier to use and to understand. Verifies represent semantics that, while not exactly hidden, are not an immediately evident characteristic of the schema and so they should be avoided where possible.

FOURTH DESCRIPTION: THE METASCHEMA

A database is a mechanism for describing a collection of objects. For example, a parts database might describe the parts needed to make a sewing machine. The schema of the parts database will actually consist of a description of a sewing machine. From the schema, it might be possible to derive what parts a sewing machine contains, what relationships the parts have to each other, how big they are, and so on.

In the same way, it is possible to devise a database that can describe a database. Whereas an ordinary database contains data and has a schema, a database that describes databases contains schemas as data and its schema is a description of the data model used in implementing the system as a whole. The usual terms are *metadata* for the data that describes databases, and *metaschema* for the schema that describes the data model.

Data and Schema

The schema for a given database will be stored in the directory. In the case of a semantic database, the directory is itself a semantic database, containing classes and subclasses, these being described by various attributes. A variety of static characteristics of the system can be expected to be stored, as data, in the directory. Strictly speaking, any data in the directory is data about data and as such is *metadata.* In practice, whether a given piece of information ends up being stored as data or metadata depends, to some extent, on such accidental circumstances as the volatility of the data.

Consider, for example, a list of valid appliance types in an appliances database. If new appliance types are never added to the database, appliance type may be maintained as a list of valid types known to the system that has to maintain the database. In a semantic database, this implies that the appliance types are to be found in the schema—possibly in integrity constraints, possibly in the form of enumerated attributes of some sort.

But if appliance types are volatile, changing all the time, appliance type will probably be maintained as data in the database. But it is essentially the same information, used in much the same way.

The directory then has to be understood as an extension of the database as a whole. It is just as much a location for data as is the database itself. The difference is that the data in the directory is used to control the database, as well as being data so far as the outside world is concerned.

The Class Class and Its Contents

The directory contains a class for each of the different types of object in the data model. Accordingly, the directory contains a class called "classes." "Classes" contains various entities, including entities for all of the classes in the directory. "Classes" even contains an entity that stands for itself. The classes for the directory itself include the following:

Classes

Subclasses

Attributes

Derived Attributes

Types

Expressions

Any user-declared classes.

The class "attributes" contains entities for the various attributes necessary to describe the model. These include the following:

Name of classes

Name of attributes

Name of types

Subclass of Classes

Superclass of subclasses

Verifies of Classes

Range of attributes

Domain of attributes

Derivation of derived attributes

Any user-declared attributes.

Where an attribute has a known and enumerable set of values specified as a part of the system, these values may be specified as entities in the range class of the attribute. There are limits to the uses of this type of approach. In principle, it may be assumed that all relationships are explicitly represented in the directory; in practice, such complex objects as expressions or enumerations may be represented using other techniques, such as stored algorithms.

The Logical Entity Hierarchy

Largely as a matter of convenience, all of the classes in the directory are grouped into a single hierarchy under the class "directory entity." There are three main "legs" to the hierarchy immediately below "directory entity": "logical entity," "logical component entity," and "physical entity." The last two are discussed later on.

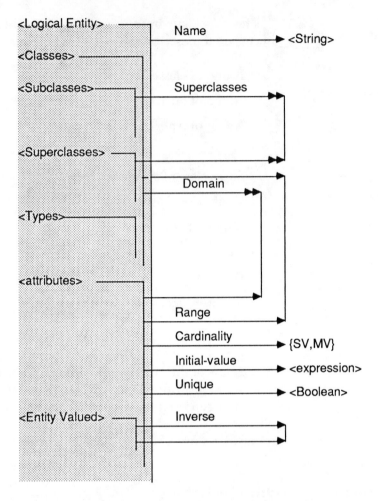

Note that the type of an EVA is a class, whereas the type of a DVA is a "type" (or system-supported class). The following SDM diagram illustrates the main classes and attributes in the type hierarchy.

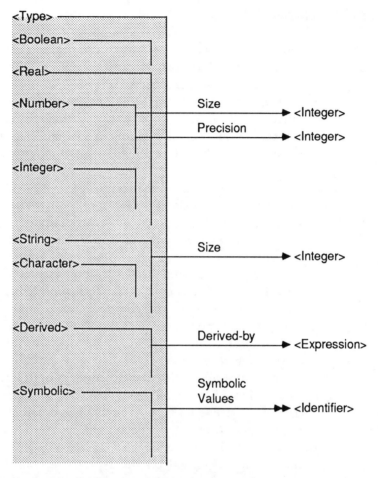

Attribute "type" is a subclass of class (as in the preceding diagram). BOOLEAN, SYMBOLIC, STRING, and REAL are mutually exclusive. Derived attributes of the BOOLEAN, STRING, REAL, or SYMBOLIC types are allowed.

The implications of insertions, deletions, and modifications of entities in the "logical entity" hierarchy are considered in the PaleoDB (paleontology database) discussion. The implications of altering the metaschema itself are also examined in the discussion of PaleoDB. For the moment, suffice it to say that adding a new class implies inserting an entity into the "classes" class; adding a new subclass to the "classes" class implies altering the model itself, which turns out to be a highly desirable thing to be able to do under a variety of circumstances.

Extensible Data Models

One rather unwarranted assumption that has been made so far is that the data model will provide an adequate mechanism for the description of all the types of objects likely to occur in the application domain. In a way, it can be argued that entities occurring in classes that have attributes are fundamental; anything that cannot be described using this paradigm is not susceptible to a formal, rational process and so is outside the realms of data management in any case. There is another side to this.

A type has been defined previously as both a collection or domain of values and an associated set of operations. While it is the case that it must be possible to conceive of any set of values as a class of entities that have attributes, clearly the operations represent another problem altogether.

The types supported directly by some implementation of the model may, for example, include date and time. It may be possible to add times, subtract times, and compare times. Addition, subtraction, and comparison here have a quite different meaning to that normally employed when dealing with simple numbers. Similar requirements may arise in any number of ways.

For example, consider the comparison, in terms of alphabetic position, of words using different character sets. There may be a requirement for e, ê, ẽ, è, and é all to be taken as the same character, although, at the machine level the representation of the character obviously must be different in each case. This can only be provided by allowing the operations permitted on the type to be explicitly declared in the metaschema. The database designer can then alter and extend the metaschema to allow for the particular requirements of the application.

At this point, the metaschema, and indeed the whole model, clearly becomes much more complicated. It would then be necessary to add two major features to the model to make these types of extension possible. First, as already mentioned, the operations permitted for a type would have to be explicitly declared as a part of the type definition. Second, the language used to define the operations (presumably the DML) would have to be extremely rich; in effect, it would have to be equivalent in expressiveness to a general purpose programming language. The DML that has been outlined so far does not fit this criterion.

One interesting development in this respect is the recent rise of object oriented databases, so-called OODBs. Many OODBs, such as the Orion system (Woelk, 1968), so far as the data modeling side of the system is concerned, are essentially indistinguishable from a database management system based on a semantic data model. Orion is somewhat exceptional in providing both the manipulative techniques typical of an object-oriented system, and a fully featured DML. There is no real dichotomy between semantic databases and OODB at least so far as the semantic databases are concerned, it is always possible to add object-oriented features to a semantic data model. The reverse, however, may not be the case. Where database type features have been added to existing object-oriented program environments, such as in Smalltalk or C++, the provision of a good, general purpose DML may not be so easy.

Comparing Metaschemas

Comparing metaschemas has a lot in common with comparing technologies; there tends to be an amplification effect, where apparently minor differences in some basic feature of the technology leads, in the final result, to vast differences of approach and vast differences in the final product produced.

For example, a technology based on steam engines, using coal as a power source, is likely to differ in a variety of ways from one based on draft animals and wind power. Vehicles on fixed tracks existed with both power sources, but they were used in quite different ways. Or comparing steam to the internal combustion engine, steam-driven trucks are perfectly feasible, but they take so long to warm up that a different approach has to be taken to the employment of people to handle them.

Most data management systems built on the relational model have a directory. The schema for the directory of a relational system describes the model in the same way as the directory did in the preceding discussion. But consider the contents of such a directory; it consists of three tables, somewhat as follows:

```
Relations (
    Name
    )

Attributes(
    Name
    Owner
    Type
    )

Type (
    Name
    )
```

There may be some implication that "owner" must be a relation and "type" must be a type, but this is not a part of the schema. Attributes in the relational model do not have cardinality, so there is no information present in the schema as to how many instances of an attribute a thing may have. For that matter, there is no real indication of what things there are in the database. Essentially, if you want to think of something as a thing, that is your business, and the database has nothing to say about it. In practice, relational metaschemas have information that indicates which attributes are required and which are unique. It may be possible to infer from this which attributes are entity identifiers, but again there are no guarantees. All this should sound quite familiar. These are simply the problems associated with record-based information models. The relational model is a record-based model, and as such, it inherits many of the problems associated with the record model.

The metaschema for a semantic database is itself a semantic database and manages to avoid many of the record-based model problems. It is far more expressive than the relational metaschema in that it contains far more information and its information is easier to access than in a relational metaschema. This becomes a difference in kind, not simply in degree.

The expressiveness of the model becomes evident in a variety of ways, but most especially in the variety and richness of information to be found in the metaschema. The metaschema, both as an expression of the model and as an object in its own right, has far more usable information in it than a relational schema can possibly have, while it remains a reflection of the relational model.

FIFTH DESCRIPTION: OPERATIONS ON THE SDM

A data model consists of two things: a way to manipulate data and a way to describe data. It should be fairly evident from the SDM diagrams that manipulating data and describing data are actually two sides of the same thing. Particularly where a database contains a description of itself, it is possible to describe data by manipulating data—that is, manipulating the metaschema. It is also possible to manipulate data by describing it; declaring a subclass is in many ways the same thing as performing a query.

This section describes a DML that has been specifically devised for accessing information in a semantic database. The DML is closely modeled on that used by the Unisys SIM system, which itself is a part of the Infoexec™ data management environment. SIM (the Semantic Information Manager) is a data management system based on the SDM and incorporates many of the concepts described in this book.

Much of the normal navigation (or aggregation) operations of other data models (such as the relational or hierarchical models) disappear in the semantic data model. In the model, simply knowing what you want is usually sufficient to also specify how to go about getting it. In the case of the attributes of a given entity, all the attributes (both immediate and inherited) applicable to the entity are implied by an access to the entity itself. In the case of attributes of related entities, simply using the name of the relationship as a qualifier is sufficient to indicate which attributes are being referred to and how they are to be accessed.

Relational-type **joins** may be used to navigate around the database; this, however, merely implies that there are relationships between entities that have not been declared (otherwise, what is the basis of the *join?*). This involves hiding information in the application program, which is precisely what the model is trying to avoid.

Inherited Attributes

As classes are arranged in hierarchies, it will always be the case that for a given entity, if it is viewed from some point in the hierarchy, it will be seen as having all of the attributes of the *perspective class* (i.e., the class through which the entity is being viewed), as well as all the attributes of all of the classes above it in the hierarchy.

™Infoexec is a trademark of the Unisys Corporation.

```
CLASS Person
    (
    Name                : Names;
    Age                 : Integer DERIVED BY
                          Elapsed-Years(
                            Todays-Date, Date-of-Birth);
    Date-of-Birth       : Date;
    ) ;


SUBCLASS Minor OF Person
    (
    Guardian            : Person;
    );
```

In the case of the class "minor," the class has not only the attribute "guardian" but also the attributes "name," "age," and "date-of-birth" inherited from "person." The implication of the placing of the attributes is that it is reasonable for a "person" to have an "age," but a "person" might not have a "guardian." If a "person" is also a "minor," it is reasonable for the "person" to have both an "age" and a "guardian" as attributes.

Extended Attributes

The class–subclass distinction represents a relationship between two classes (often referred to as the ISA ["is a"] relationship). It is convenient to allow inheritance of attributes across the ISA relationship, as the relationship has a special status, indicating a subset relationship between one class and another.

The very existence of any relationship, however, indicates there is some significance to be attached to the attributes at each end of the relationship, even if the significance may vary somewhat from case to case. This is recognized in the model in the concept of an extended attribute.

An extended attribute is simply an attribute of an entity to which some relationship exists. Using an "OF" notation to indicate qualification by the relationship, it is reasonable to refer to "age" OF "guardian," allowing relationship traversal to be represented as a natural extension of the idea of attribute reference. From the perspective of any particular entity, all the attributes of all the other entities in the database are, potentially, simply extended attributes. The significance of the attributes are provided by the type of the relationship, as well as the type of the attribute involved.

Entity Selection

It is possible to perform entity selection using conditions that include immediate, inherited, or extended attributes. The characteristics of an entity are provided by its immediate attributes, its inherited attributes, and the immediate and inherited attributes of any entities to which it has a relationship of some kind.

At least so far as one side of the Boolean condition used in selecting the entity is concerned, these attributes are the only ones that could possibly be used in selecting an entity. If the criterion used to select the entity does not use an immediate, inherited, or extended attribute of the entity, then it is no criterion at all.

The other side of the Boolean expression used in selecting entities is the values to which the entity's attributes are compared. These may just be constant values, such as a particular name or a particular age, or the values may be derived from other entities in the database.

For example, it may be that the entities to be selected are those that have an age that is less than the average age. Here, it is necessary to compute one side of the expression before it is possible to formulate the result of the query. Or it may be that the top 10% is to be returned, again requiring a pass through the database, determining some appropriate values before the execution of the query.

The possibilities are considerable, but for the most part, they may be ignored here. The implementer of the data management system software must provide for adequate optimization of the various types of queries likely to be encountered by the system—an immense task. The vast majority of these, however, are various combinations of uses of relationships and classes that have already been described. While it is desirable for the database designer to be aware of certain basic types of optimization strategies (especially when designing the physical database), these requirements are minimal and they are covered in Chapter 11, "SDM Implementation."

Functions

The types of functions required over a particular database vary from case to case. The following seem to be universally applicable:

COUNT may be applied to an MV collection of objects and will return the number of individuals in the collection. For example:

COUNT (Manages)

will return the number of individuals managed by the associated manager.

SUM also applies to MV attributes; in this case, the attribute is assumed to be numeric and SUM returns the total of all the individual values. For example the average age may be computed by:

SUM (Age of Employee) / COUNT (Employee)

MIN, applicable to MV attributes, returns the minimum value in the set.

MAX returns the maximum value in the set.

INVERSE allows a relationship to be traversed in the inverse direction even if the inverse is not or has not been explicitly declared. "Managed-by" is the same thing as "INVERSE (manages)."

TRANSITIVE may be used where it is sensible to repeatedly traverse a relationship. To find the average age of a particular individual's managers:

SUM (Age of TRANSITIVE (Managed-by))

COUNT (TRANSITIVE (Managed-by))

EXISTS will test for the existence of a relationship. Effectively, the EXISTS operator provides a test for a null value. It is equally applicable to EVAs and DVAs.

ISA has two parameters: (1) a selection expression, designating some entity, and (2) a class; it returns true if the selected entity participates in the class.

ASA is the type coercion operator. It allows the attributes of a subclass to be accessed. That is, where a class is being accessed and the class has subclasses, the attributes of the subclass may be accessed.

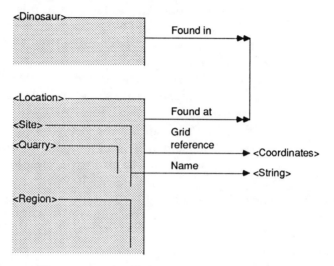

In the preceding example, if the names of the quarries in which dinosaurs have been found is to be retrieved, the relationship "found-in" OF "dinosaur" cannot really be used because it maps to the class "location," whereas the attribute "name" is an attribute of "site." "Location" does not have an attribute "name," either as an immediate or an inherited attribute. In such a situation, the ASA operator may be used, allowing the "name" attribute to be designated, using

Name OF found-in ASA Quarry OF Dinosaur

The ASA function can be made redundant by the simple convention of allowing the assumption that all relationships map both to the range class and to all of its subclasses, with the restriction that where an attribute of a subclass is being accessed, the subclass concerned has to be mentioned. The foregoing expression would then be

Name OF Quarry OF Found-in OF Dinosaur

DATE and TIME functions: A variety of functions are required for manipulating dates and times. A generic function in the form

Elapsed_<units>

is needed to allow dates and times to be converted into integers of a specified unit. The units being years, months, weeks, and days. For time, the units are hours, minutes, and seconds.

The operators likely to be present in a data model are determined by the types supported by the model. The time-related operators are a good illustration of this. Those outlined here are only a sample of the types of operators likely to be required in practice. It is highly desirable to be able to extend the operator set with the addition of specialized operators required as a result of the introduction of new types into the database.

One of the main advantages cited for object-oriented systems, as opposed to semantic data models, is that object-oriented systems provide a natural mechanism for the implementation of both new types and new operators. There is, however, no obvious reason why similar facilities should not be built into semantic data models.

Quantification

When dealing with an MV collection, it is desirable to be able to specify whether the entire collection is of interest, or a subset of it, or possibly none. The model has the concept of a quantifier to deal with this. The quantifiers are the following:

ALL indicating that all of the collection is being referred to. For example, the following could be used to determine whether all of the employees managed by a manager are over 21 years of age:

ALL Age OF Managed-by > 21

SOME requires that at least one of the set satisfies the associated condition. This is the default.

NO requires that none of the set satisfies the associated condition.

The ALL quantifier is the same as the universal quantifier (for all x) used in logic, the SOME quantifier is the same as the existential quantifier (there exists x).

Update

The process of modifying a semantic database must be understood in terms of the modification of sets of objects. This contrasts with the record-based approach, in which objects are modified one at a time within a processing loop of some sort. For all update statements (with the possible exception of **insert**), a collection of entities is being dealt with which may have one, many, or no members.

The general form of the update statement then is

<update type> <perspective> <attribute assignments>
WHERE <condition>;

The <update types> are **modify, insert,** and **delete.** The <attribute assignments> do not apply to **delete.** The WHERE <condition> does not always apply to **insert.**

The <perspective> is the class that either contains the entities being modified or will contain the entities being inserted. All update operations have to be performed from a single perspective. **Retrieve** operations may have multiple perspectives if a **join** is done as a part of the **retrieve,** but as already mentioned, this is an aberration.

For both **modify** and **insert,** attribute values may be supplied for both immediate and inherited attributes. It is not normally the case that attribute values are supplied for extended attributes, although there are some exceptions.

MODIFY

If the class specified as the perspective for the **modify** statement has any superclasses, all of the attributes of all of the superclasses may be altered as a part of the **modify.** If more than one entity is selected by the WHERE condition, all of the entities selected will have the same **modify** applied to them. If any errors are detected while processing the **modify,** no modification will be performed. That is, any partial modifications will be discarded by the system.

INSERT

Insert is assumed to take two forms:

1. Into a hierarchy where the entity did not previously exist in the

hierarchy—the entity is being added to the database for the first time; the entity will be inserted into the class involved, and into all of the superclasses of the class.

2. Into some lower level of the hierarchy, with the entity already existing on some higher level—for example, when an employee becomes a manager, it is necessary to insert that "employee" into the "manager" class.

With the second type of **insert**, any number of entities may be affected. With the first type of **insert**, only one entity may be involved, and the WHERE clause may not be present.

The following example inserts a location that did not previously exist:

INSERT Location (Name := "Leighton Buzzard");

or   **insert** can be used to insert an entity where the entity already exists, in this case making Leighton Buzzard a quarry:

INSERT Quarry FROM Location WHERE Name =
"Leighton Buzzard";

DELETE

Delete is asymmetric to **insert**. Whereas it is necessary to insert at the lowest applicable level in the hierarchy, it is necessary to **delete** at the highest applicable level. If, for example, the intention is to delete an entity altogether, the delete should be performed from the topmost level of the hierarchy. If an employee ceases to be a manager, the employee would be deleted from the "manager" class but would still participate in the "employee" class. If the employee leaves the company, the entity would be deleted from the "employee" class.

Delete operations then propagate downward through the hierarchy, while **insert** operations propagate upward.

Delete and **insert** then should really be thought of as role modification. The implication is that everything is assumed to be an entity—that is, a participant in the class entity. When something is deleted, it is being deleted from some subclass of the class entity and, in a sense, never ceases to exist. Similarly, if something is inserted, it is always inserted from some previously existing role.

Assignment

It is fairly simple to apply values to SV attributes for which either the type is a system-supported class (REAL, for example) or the attribute type is based on a system-supported class. Concepts derived from programming languages such as Pascal fit readily into the modification of these types of attributes. The standard assignment statement, in the form,

<attribute> := <expression>

is adequate in all cases, given that the system can evaluate the expression. The ":=" sign may be read as "takes the value."

Values for attributes with a type that is a user-declared class—that is EVAs—must be supplied in the form of a selection expression or a selected entity. Again, given that the expression is of a suitable type, the interpretation of the assignment statement represents no particular problem, although it is worth bearing in mind that the equivalent operation in a record-based system would be the establishment of a relationship between two or more records.

When supplying values for an MV attribute, it must be possible to indicate which values are to be replaced, or that the values are simply to be added to, or deleted from, the set of values. This requires some extensions to the assignment statement in the form of EXCLUDE and INCLUDE key words. An important point here is that all MV objects (basically classes or MV attributes) are considered to be unordered collections of entities. It is not then sensible to replace the first one, the second one, or the last one, because there is no first, second, or last.

The use of INCLUDE and EXCLUDE are illustrated in the following examples; the examples are based on the dinosaur-location schema used in the previous section.

```
Protoceratops has been found in Mongolia

Modify Dinosaur(
Found-in := INCLUDE Location WITH (Name = "Mongolia"))
WHERE Name = "Protoceratops";
```

To indicate that the ankylosaurus found in Leighton Buzzard turned out to be a scolosaurus, the following change would be made.

```
Modify Quarry (
     Found-at := EXCLUDE Dinosaur
                    WITH (Name = "Ankylosaurus"),
     Found-at := INCLUDE Dinosaur
                    WITH (Name = "Scolosaurus"))
     WHERE Name = "Leighton Buzzard"
```

Retrieve

The **retrieve** statement is used to specify the data that is to be retrieved from the database. By a convention of database theory, both updates and retrieves are lumped under the general heading "query," although normal English usage might lead one to assume that a query was purely concerned with obtaining information and so should be restricted to what is here referred to as a **retrieve**.

The general form of the retrieve is the following:

```
FROM <perspective> RETRIEVE <format>
     <target list> WHERE <condition>
```

The <perspective>, as usual, is a class. The <format> may be either structured or tabular (discussed here later). The <target list> is a list of expressions, the values of which are to be returned by the query. The WHERE <condition> indicates which entities are to be selected. The <condition> must be a Boolean expression, and it will be evaluated for each entity in the perspective class; if the expression is true, the entity will be included in the query result.

Local selection expressions are allowed. These may occur in the target list acting as a second level of restriction on the values to be returned. For example, the following query will return the names of all "dinosaurs" for which the "last-period" in which the dinosaur occurred was the Jurassic, but it will only return the name of the location of the dinosaur if the location happens to be in Asia; a null value will be returned otherwise. In other words, the "dinosaurs" name will be returned even if none of its locations are Asiatic ones.

```
FROM Dinosaur RETRIEVE
     Name,
     Name OF Location WITH(Continent = "Asia")
     WHERE Name OF Last-Period of Dinosaur =
     "Jurassic";
```

Another place in which local selection expressions occur is inside functions.

```
FROM Dinosaur RETRIEVE
     Name,
     AVERAGE(COUNT(Found-in WITH(Continent = "Asia")))
     Where Found-in ISA Quarry
```

For example, the preceding query will retrieve the names of all dinosaurs found in quarries. The average count of dinosaurs per quarry will be returned where the quarry happens to be in Asia. The COUNT of "found-in" is reasonable because it is possible for something to be related to something else more than once. The assumption is that if a dinosaur is found in a quarry multiple times, it will have multiple "found-in" relationships to that quarry.

Dealing with Query Results

Query results have to be returned in such a way that they reflect the structure of the data from which the query result was derived. This can be a difficult problem when a large number of attribute traversals are involved, if the attributes and entity dependencies used in the traversal are to be preserved.

A semantic database query processor must be able to return data that is an accurate reflection of the data in the database. The query processor must be able to extract data from the database and present it to the user in such a way that nothing implied by the original data is lost. At the same time, everything implied by the query result must be a fair reflection of some information in the original data.

Obviously, a great deal depends on the format of the extracted data. If the data is to be extracted and imported into another semantic database, preservation of the information in the original database is a matter of ensuring that the schema of the target database is equivalent to the schema of the source database. In the general case, establishing the equivalence of two schemas is a decidedly nontrivial problem. Given a few assumptions though, the problem can be rendered trivial.

If the format of the extracted data is to be an SDM diagram, again the problem is trivial, as there are exact parallels between all of the components of a class and the components of an SDM diagram. An SDM diagram is not a class, but it is a representation of a class; formulating and expressing query results, queries, or schemas using SDM diagrams is therefore relatively simple.

The difficulty arises when the format of the extracted data is a file of records. The chapter dealing with the problems with the record-based information model has already described, in some detail, the difficulties that arise when attempting to use records to represent entities. Many of these problems tend to come to the fore when the format of the data to be extracted by a query is one or more records.

The problem is that the set of records to be formulated by the query processor must be an accurate representation of the relationships, entities, classes, and attributes found in the original database. Returning to the dinosaur-location example, we are given a database with the following instance:

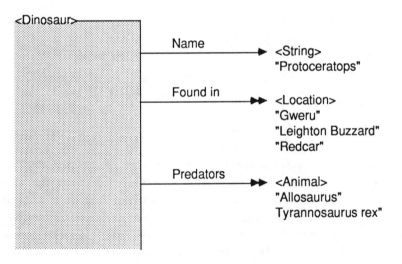

How is this information to be represented as a set of records? There are two possible formats: tabular and structured. The structured format is the easier of the two. For structured output, the query result is broken into a series of levels, each of which contains only SV items.

Indentation, or some equivalent mechanism, is used to indicate the dependencies among the different records in the query result. For the query

```
FROM Dinosaur RETRIEVE STRUCTURE
     Name,
     Name OF Found-in,
     Name OF Predators
```

the structured output for protoceratops would be the following:

```
01     Name - Protoceratops
     02   Name of Found in - Gweru
     02   Name of Found in - Leighton Buzzard
     02   Name of Found in - Redcar
     02   Name of Found in - <no more data>
     02   Name of Predators - Allosaurus
     02   Name of Predators - Tyrannosaurus rex
     02   Name of Predators - <no more data>
```

Assuming that protoceratops was the last dinosaur in the query result, the end of the query would be indicated by

```
01     Name - <no more data>
```

The <no more data> may be considered a special query result that may be returned for any attribute access. The process of looking at the structured query result as a whole may be thought of as a series of operations on the parts of the query. **Retrieve** operations begin with "01 Name," followed by retrievals of "02 Name OF Found-in," followed by retrievals of "02 Name OF Predators." Each series of retrievals terminates with the <no more data> result and then goes on to the next retrieval at the current or next level.

Tabular output, particularly from a programming point of view, tends to be rather more difficult to interpret. Using the dinosaur situation a tabular **retrieve** query might look like this:

```
FROM Dinosaur RETRIEVE TABULAR
     Name,
     Name OF Found-in,
     Name OF Predators
```

What has to be represented is that a particular dinosaur has been found in various places and may have been eaten by various other animals. But there is no association between where a dinosaur has been found and which animals it has been eaten by, so the following tabular representation is misleading:

Name	Name of Found in	Name of Predator
Protoceratops	Gweru Leighton Buzzard Redcar	Tyrannosaurus rex Allosaurus

In terms of dependencies, there is no dependency between predator and location. It is not the case that protoceratops in Leighton Buzzard was preyed on by allosaurus, or that protoceratops in Redcar lives without fear of being eaten by anything. An allosaurus will eat a protoceratops wherever it is found, and the table in this respect is quite misleading. To avoid misinterpretation, the table must actually be represented as follows:

Name	Name of Found in	Name of Predator
Protoceratops Protoceratops Protoceratops Protoceratops Protoceratops	Gweru Leighton Buzzard Redcar	Tyrannosaurus rex Allosaurus

All of the SV attributes have to be repeated for each row of the table to which they apply. Each of the MV attributes has to be presented on its own, without any other MV attribute values, in order to avoid a spurious appearance of dependency. The only dependency presented by the table is between the SV attributes and those dependent on them. That is true in this case, but consider the following query:

```
FROM Dinosaur RETRIEVE TABULAR
    Name,
    Name OF Found-in,
    Name OF Predators
    Name OF Found-in OF Predators
```

There is now a fourth column to the table, which is indirectly dependent on the original dinosaur name. Here, there must be repetitions of the name of the original dinosaur and, within these, repetitions of the name of predators, along with all of the locations in which they are found. It is very easy, even with a small amount of data, for these types of tables to become very large and very difficult to understand.

This is especially so if the original query is not formulated in a very sensible fashion. For example, if the primary name is omitted (as in the following example),

```
FROM Dinosaur RETRIEVE TABULAR
     Name OF Found-in,
     Name OF Predators
     Name OF Found-in OF Predators
```

the query result will be quite incomprehensible. Without the dinosaur name, it will be impossible to tell who is associated with what—particularly, which predators are associated with which dinosaur locations. There will be no definite breakpoint between the information for one dinosaur and the result. Largely as an attempt to address this problem, if a query contains an MV attribute, and the MV attribute is null for some entity accessed, a null row will be returned in the query result for the entity. Given this assumption, it would be possible (but certainly not easy!) to determine the dependencies in the absence of the name, as in the preceding query.

Error Handling

There are a number of different methods of establishing constraints on the data in a semantic database, the principle methods being the structural constraints implied by the declaration of classes, subclasses, and attributes and their characteristics, as well as the explicit constraints defined by the VERIFY statement of the DDL.

So far as **retrieve** operations are concerned, most of these are not an issue. The retrieval operations are constrained by the structure of the database, but only in the sense that what the user sees, and therefore what the user chooses to select from, is dictated by the structure of the database, as defined by the schema of the database.

Update operations are a quite different story: Ideally, a semantic database should enforce all the known constraints that can be enforced automatically. It should not be the case that some constraints are only enforced by a process that is used to access the database but is external to the database. This has a number of consequences.

Notably, in this context, it means that it is possible for a user to access the database using general-purpose query tools (an implementation of SDM diagrams, for example) and be reasonably certain of not applying invalid updates to the database. It is difficult to overemphasize the importance of this capability. It means that anyone who understands the schema and the query processor can freely update the database without having to code a special-purpose program to do the job. This is simply not possible on other systems that do not capture the semantics of the underlying application to the same degree.

One capability essential to the viability of such a system is adequate error handling. Good error handling and sensible error results assume a very important place in a semantic database because of the fact that a substantial portion of the semantics of the data will be known to, and enforced by, the database.

As diverse numbers and types of errors can be returned from any given update statement, it is desirable that a reasonably flexible data structure be used to represent the error results. The obvious solution is the use of a class that is automatically populated by the system to reflect the results of the last operation performed by the user. The class would appear somewhat as follows:

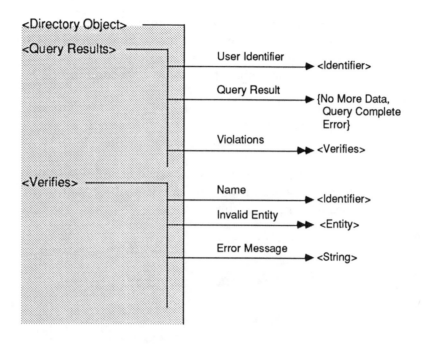

This arrangement assumes that the classes are private to the user concerned, which is a departure from the assumptions that have been made about the database presented thus far. It has always been the case with the previously considered databases that the database is intended to be shared by any number of users and that the contents of the database persist over time. The "query results" class is duplicated for each user of the database; its contents need not survive the user's session. Describing data structures external to the database, using the concepts of the model, is in itself useful. There is no particular reason why a semantic database should not be implemented in such a way that the data structures could actually be established, accessed, and maintained as well. In practice, most systems tend to accomplish the effect of the "query results" class by supplying rather inflexible and incomplete information regarding the result of a query. The information is supplied using the record structures typical of procedural languages such as COBOL and ALGOL. This is potentially a serious flaw in a semantic database management system.

So far as the constraints themselves are concerned, they are expressed using the operations defined for the model. That is, the various navigational features of the model, plus the functions and expressions supported by the model. The constraints are a part of the database description and appear as labeled assertions about the state of the database. The constraint has to be labeled in order to allow it to be distinguished from other constraints. It has both a condition and a message or series of messages associated with it. For example,

```
VERIFY Age-restriction        =
    Age OF Employee > 16
          "all employees must be over 16 years of age";
```

Some surprising results can arise when modifications to a semantic database start triggering and violating constraints. The following situation illustrates the point:

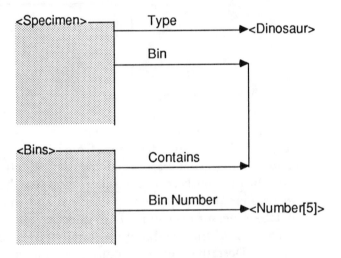

"Bin" OF "specimen" is required; "contains" OF "bins" is not. A specimen must be allocated to a bin, but a bin may be empty. Assume that the database contains the following:

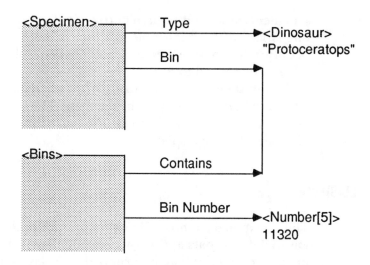

Then the following **modify** is applied to the database:

```
MODIFY Bins (
    Contains := Specimen WITH
        (Name OF Type = "Ankylosaurus")
    WHERE Bin-Number = 11320
```

This produces a required-attribute-missing error for the attribute, "bin" OF "specimen." "Bin" is the inverse of "contains," and so it is being assigned a value by the **modify** statement. One may ask, how then is it possible to get a required-attribute-missing error? The answer lies in the fact that the system is responsible for fixing up the inverse attributes. "Bin" OF "specimen" is an SV attribute when a value is assigned to it; this is interpreted to mean that the current value (if any) must be discarded. When "contains" is assigned a value, if the "bin" already contains something, the inference is that it is being taken out of the bin and replaced by something else. Its "bin" attribute becomes null—hence, the required-attribute-missing error. The error is not for the specimen being put into the bin; it is for the specimen that is already in the bin.

These types of consequential errors are likely to arise in any number of different circumstances. Another example occurs when both ends of a relationship are stated to be required; as is shown in a later chapter, there are mechanisms that render update of a relationship possible where both ends of the relationship are required. But with the update statements described so far, if both ends of a relationship are required, one is left in the impossible position of not being able to insert A because it has to be related to B, and not being able to insert B because it has to be related to A.

Verifies then are an essential part of the database, and they play a large part in the usability of the database. They can make the database safe for naive users, but they can also make the database impossible to maintain in some respects.

CONCLUSION

The semantic data model, in common with other models, provides a way to describe data and a way to manipulate it. The data is described in terms of entities that are grouped into classes, and the classes may have subclasses. The entities in a class are characterized both by the immediate attributes of the class and by inherited attributes and extended attributes.

The operations supported by the model mainly consist of isolating subsets of the entities in a class. From the resulting subset, any desired information may be extracted using the three attribute types. Navigation within a database is mainly just a matter of knowing what things are called.

On Inaccuracies

I'll give you four-oh green grow the rushes oh. What is your four oh?

Four for the Earth's wide Seasons. Three   for   the   r i vals

Two, two the lily white boys   Clothéd all   in   green oh

One is one and all a – lone and e-ver more shall be so

Meph is singing; Cmmn enters.

Cmmn. Hello there! When singing "The Dilly Song," you got "four-oh" wrong, you know. Four is for the gospel makers.

Meph. And three, I suppose, is for the Trinity?

Cmmn. No, for the three magi, I believe.

Meph. And the two lily white figures clothed in green? Where do these fit into your iconography? One at least we can agree on, as all things must surely have a beginning.

Cmmn. The interpretation of two is usually "Christ" and "John, the Baptist," though, I confess, why they should be clothed in green escapes me. Nonetheless, four is for the gospel makers, I am certain of it.

Meph. Well, you have confessed to some doubts, even if you are adamant about the makers of the gospel. Let's look at some of the other lines. What about seven? "Seven for the seven stars in the sky." Riddle me this, then?

Cmmn. Traditionally, this is taken either as the seven planets—or, perhaps, as Ursula, the Great Bear.

Meph. Ah, Ursula, the She-Bear, Mother of the Animals. Indeed a well-known member of the congregation. I think that you must admit that there is a little discrepancy between the words of the song and the way you would like it interpreted.

Cmmn. Then you explain the last three lines to me.

Meph. What about "nine for the nine bright shiners"? There is nothing the matter with that.

Cmmn. No. The last lines are, "Twelve for the twelve apostles, eleven for the eleven who went to heaven, ten for the ten commandments."

Meph. These have just been added on, not properly a part of the song at all. Surely you must accept that the song predates the dominion of the Christian church. How else is one to explain the references that you admit it contains? The world we must assume to be one with itself. If something supposes itself to be an account of the world, it too must be consistent with itself. The song is a record of the uses of the song over the ages; it is easy enough to see what has been added on by simply looking into the song for the oldest of the lines and reconstituting the rest of the song from there. Here we have inconsistencies. You must at least grant me some uncertainty as to the status of these interpolated lines you have quoted.

Cmmn.   Perhaps.

Meph.   Good. It is not such a big step then to go seeking some alternative that eliminates the inconsistency. Eliminate your last three lines, put back the earth and the seasons, and you have a sensible dilly song.

Cmmn.   I am not in the least sure of the propriety of what you say.

Meph.   Well if you feel uncomfortable with the seasons, let's try another topic. I recently came across this most remarkable paper. Leibniz has been trying to teach me some physics, to which end I was reading a paper in the *Journal of Physics*. This study examined the stability of the earth in its orbit, with a view to establishing what the effect would be if a celestial body were to pass near to the earth. A most remarkable thing was discovered—namely that, due to the irregularity of the earth's shape, it would take a mere 1/300th of the earth's rotational energy to make the earth turn completely upside down. The effects, of course, would be global and catastrophic. The Seven Stars in the sky would disappear and be replaced by stars characteristic of the other hemisphere. The sun would cease to rise in the west, and it would rise in the east instead. Some would see the sun set and then rise again over the same horizon! Are you all right? You look a little pale.

Cmmn.   Enough! This is not to be talked of as though it were an established fact; it is a mere hypothesis.

Meph.   But it so happens that this computation concerning the stability of the earth's orbit is the key to a whole cosmology. It is like the earth's wide seasons to the dilly song. It has been established beyond reasonable doubt that catastrophes have taken place, and not just in the age of the dinosaurs. For example, the earth's magnetic field has reversed polarity at least twice in recorded history. In recorded history, there have been widespread and catastrophic earthquakes, floods, and perturbations of the heavens. Wasn't it Joshua for whom the Sun stood still? It seems to me you must sacrifice the accuracy of the Bible to rescue the stability of the earth.

Cmmn.   I think I prefer your ideas on the dilly song.

Meph.   Yes, the dilly song looks innocent enough. But I think perhaps it has depths that could drown the unwary.

Cmmn.   I'm afraid I find nothing of any profit in this discussion at all.

Meph.   That is a little unfair. I fail to see how it is not possible to learn a little from an exposure of our ideas, or an exposure to the ideas of others.

Cmmn.   The exposure has to be to ideas—something that qualifies as a statement worthy of discussion. What you have to say about the stability of the earth, or about the likely original content of the dilly song, simply does not qualify.

Meph.   Why not? Come, you must be specific or be called unfair. Talking about the stability of the earth, are you saying the statements are inaccurate?

Cmmn.   The ideas are outlandish. As such, at the very least, I would want to be sure of both the measurements and the mathematics involved before I would consent to a further consideration of them.

Meph.   Good, so given accurate data and theories that matched the data, you might be persuaded?

Cmmn.   I am sorry, but I cannot say that under any circumstances I would be prepared to accept a theory asserting that the entire earth had been stood on its head. I think that if seriously challenged I should simply search for some data that would refute the theory.

Meph.   So you would judge the sufficiency of the degree of accuracy by the refutation of the theory. The data is insufficiently accurate if the theory has not been refuted. Accuracy, then, is to be measured by our current standards of what is outlandish. I find this a rather comical conclusion.

Cmmn. But what else do we have as a guide other than what is sane and sensible?

Meph. So anything new is merely a part of the lunatic fringe. Pity the poor innovators, hey? Well, let's try another topic then.

Cmmn. Must we?

Meph. You are familiar with the theory of evolution?

Cmmn. Yes, I have recently read Huxley's summary of the *Origin of the Species.* I confess myself unimpressed.

Meph. Good. Why?

Cmmn. Apart from the very dubious theological status that must be assigned to the theory, there is the question of its usefulness as a theory. It seems to me that the whole thing can be summarized by the statement, "in a competitive environment, over time, things will improve." This is hardly a subject worthy of study. It is neither provable nor disprovable. It does not even qualify as a program for research. What I would expect to see as a part of an account of evolution is some concrete evidence of the transformation of one species into another. This, as far as I can see, is totally lacking in the literature generated by the theory so far. Minor variations within a species are plentiful. Evolution is nowhere to be seen. On the contrary, all evidence points to the great stability of species within certain species-specific limits.

Meph. A commendable view. A theory must be *accurate* (that is, it must not conflict with the world), **and** it must actually *say something about the world.*

Cmmn. Quite so.

Meph. Does that not then recommend to you the theory of the unstable earth? It agrees with what is known, and it certainly says something about the world.

Cmmn. No. I'm sorry, but it is too large a pill for me to swallow. And I still do not feel comfortable with your dilly song. In fact, if necessary, I believe I would change the song myself if I found it not to my liking.

Meph. What about "seven for the seven tall candles," then? But I believe even there you will find yourself on unstable ground! Besides, changing a song to suit some personal preference is acceptable enough. A song (as a song and not as a record of the ideas of those who have sung the song over the years) is something that need only be shared with those who also want to share the sentiments of the singer. But a theory is something different. If we want to consider ourselves members of the community of rational thinkers, we cannot just treat a theory like the song and alter it to suit our prejudices. A theory is something that must be respected as an object that exists in its own right. We may not like the idea of the unstable earth, but either to deny it on the grounds that it is unthinkable or to attempt to defeat it by a pursuit of data suitable to the purpose will lead to humankind thinking in terms of Angels on pinheads. Scholasticism rampant again! Who knows—we might even begin the Inquisition again. Now, there's a thought!

8

Database Design

INTRODUCTION

Semantic data models (SDMs) were devised specifically to address the problem of database design. The model provides a clear, easily understood representation of the application being modeled. It is a representation that is easy to formalize and transform into a system description that can be interpreted and understood by a computer. So the database is designed, and, without having to go through further transformations, the design can be fed into a program, which then produces a working system. This chapter looks at how such a system should be used.

In particular, it looks at the relationship between the individuals participating in the design process and the *application domain* or, to borrow a term from logic, the *universe of discourse*. A clear and well-defined approach to database design is described. The approach is dependent on the use and understanding of an SDM, though not on the availability of an implementation of one.

Although this is the only chapter in the book purely devoted to database design, most of the book is really concerned, directly or indirectly, with database design. The remaining three applications, PaleoDB, CamDB, and SapperDB, contain material specifically relevant to logical database design. They each address a variety of different issues specific to particular database design problems. By contrast, this chapter deals with themes that are relevant to any database design effort.

The contents of the chapter are roughly as follows: "Designing the database" deals with the basic issues faced in designing a database. "The Problem of Induction" looks at how these issues relate to the ways we can understand and describe the world. It also looks at some of the fundamental limitations on how we can describe and understand the world. The implications of these limitations for what can be accomplished in the design process and how the design process is best carried out are described in "Approaches to Database Design." Finally, some further implications lead to some very concrete guidelines as to how alternative database designs can be assessed. This is dealt with in "Assessing a Design." The two concluding sections of the chapter take another look at the problem of induction and its solution, and how this fits with the business of assessing competing database designs.

The problem of induction is central to the argument; it justifies both the approach to formulating a database design and the approach to refining the design. This should come as no surprise. The theory of induction is central to the scientific method and essential to any rational account of the world around us. Any database design technique that does not confront the problem and incorporate an adequate solution to it cannot provide an adequate means of coming to grips with the real world—the world as it is.

DESIGNING THE DATABASE

A database is a model of some part of the world. It should represent the state of that part as clearly as possible. The representation should be to a degree of accuracy appropriate to the types of activities that are to be based on the data in the database. To be more precise, the degree of accuracy should be appropriate to the kinds of decisions that are to be based on the data in the database.

There are two important questions here:

1. What is to be the basis of the design of the model? This question is not concerned with the data model in the sense of the semantic, relational, or hierarchical models, but rather with the types of entities that are to be taken as making up the world to be modeled. For example, in a personnel database, there may be an interest in

employees and dependents, but not in parts and components. It is employees and dependents that are to be modeled; other things are excluded as being irrelevant. More than just this, it is necessary to find out what an employee is and how an employee behaves and can be described.

2.   How is the degree of accuracy of the data and the schema to be determined? Particularly, how is one database design to be compared with another in such a way that the relative degrees of accuracy can be assessed?

The first point poses the question "How do we know what we are talking about?" The second point assumes that we know what we are talking about and want to be able to compare different descriptions of the same thing: It asks the question "What is the best way to describe the thing?"

Question 1 has no definite answer. The world would be a terribly boring place if it did. What investigations there have been in this area are to be found in the study of knowledge itself, or *epistemology*. This is not the same thing as the study of logic. Epistemology embraces the study of logic, but it is broader than the study of logic. Precisely what it encompasses tends to vary from one philosophy to the next.

We do not now know, and we probably never will know how we come to understand things or just what is the basis for intuition, imagination, insight, Koestler's "Ah Ha!" or Archimedes' "Eureka!" Anyway, a formula that can generate every possible formula (presumably including itself) has a number of very fundamental logical problems. Understanding understanding is something that will almost certainly always elude us.

Therefore, Question 2 is what this chapter is really all about. It is actually a substitute for the eternal question, "how do I know whether or not I am being told the truth?" This question also has no definitive answer. We do not and cannot know whether someone is telling us the truth about the world. What Question 2 is aimed at is the alternative approach, which says, "If I am told X and I am also told Y, how do I choose between them?" To this question, there happens to be a quite definite answer.

First, we take a look at why we never know the truth about the real world, and after that, we take a look at how we can compare different and competing accounts of the real world. We begin with the frailty of proof and the problem of induction.

THE PROBLEM OF INDUCTION

Briefly, the problem of induction is the fact that our knowledge of the world around us takes the form of general statements, such as "all swans are white." The Greeks realized, and the case was most forcefully stated by the English philosopher Hume that such statements ultimately cannot be based on logic. If a statement is logically derivable from some other statement, the question then is "where did that statement come from?" Sooner or later, something external to the system of logic has to be appealed to; it is at this point that things break down and the problem of induction arises.

How are statements in logic to be derived from statements about the real world? Unless every possible thing in the real world has been examined, it is always possible that some circumstance that contradicts the statement may arise in the real world. It may or may not be the case that "all swans are white," but if you have not yet discovered Australia, how are you to know?

Worse yet, the whole point of this type of statement is to make predictions possible about things that have not yet been observed. Making useful statements about the world around us inherently involves saying something about things that we have not seen. Simply describing what we have observed says nothing. What counts are predictions about things that we have not seen, statements about events that we have not observed directly, for one of the following reasons:

- We cannot see them—they are on the other side of the moon or beyond the upper or lower limits of our eyesight, or otherwise beyond our sensory capabilities.

- They happened before we came on the scene—for example, the characteristics of the dinosaurs can only be inferred from what we see of their remains; nobody has ever seen a dinosaur.

- The event has not yet happened—the arrival of a comet, an eclipse of the sun, tomorrow's weather.

What all this amounts to is that useful statements are precisely those that have a doubtful status. The very effort to prove a statement or render it provable by limiting it to things that we can observe directly (whatever that means!) is self-defeating. The only way to render a statement even moderately certain, in this sense, is to make it useless.

The same idea applies to data processing systems. The only way to be absolutely certain that a program will never fail is to test every possible use of the program. This implies not just that every possible use of the program is tested but also that the outcome of the use is known in advance. This is needed so that if the program behaves incorrectly, the incorrect behavior will be spotted. But this means that the testing of the program will take almost as much effort as the actual use of the program. It would be easier, probably much easier, to just write out the user's reports by hand. Why use a computer when every line of output has to be specified in advance to such a degree of accuracy that an error can always be spotted? In the same way that proving a statement renders the statement uninteresting, establishing the correctness of a program may be more costly than not using the program at all.

It may be possible to specify some programs as formal systems and prove that the program is correct, but there comes a point where such a specification is no longer practical. The internal structure and the external relations of the program become so complex that a formal specification is out of the question. For such a system, it must be assumed that the system contains faults and that the system will evolve over time toward greater stability and greater usability.

This is recognized in common programming practice. It may appear that a system should work, but until

- It has had 3000 users using it simultaneously, and
- There is a disk or memory failure at precisely the undetected weak spot in the system,

how are the failures to be anticipated? The answer, as any programmer will tell you, is that they cannot be anticipated. This is the problem of induction. We do not actually know anything, the best we can do is make a guess at it. Furthermore, even if we do know the truth, it will not be the case that we know that we know the truth.

An operating system may be absolutely free of bugs, but proving it to be free of bugs is, to all intents and purposes, impossible. This is generally accepted to be true of large and complex programs such as operating systems, even though the conditions under which the operating system runs can be extremely well defined. It should not be surprising then that, when it comes to programs that have to model something as amorphous and difficult to define as a business organization, the programs must always be regarded as provisional and subject to change.

What then is the basis of our knowledge of the world around us? If truth is not a criterion, what is? It is Karl Popper's (Popper, 1968) great achievement to have formulated a sensible answer to the second question (he does not claim to have actually discovered the answer to the first one).

The basis of our knowledge is the idea of "best fit," based on the theory of truth developed by Alfred Tarski (see Popper, 1965). Two competing views can be assessed in terms of how closely they approximate what we see around us. The closer view wins.

Note that this does not assume that something is universally true, merely that it matches what we see, have seen, and expect to see. If we subsequently discover that the statement at issue does not match some circumstances that it was assumed to cover, then the statement must be taken as at least partially wrong.

The criterion for knowledge—that is, whether something is knowledge (as opposed to just verbiage)—is whether you can test it or not. If it is testable, and it fits, it is knowledge. The testability of a statement replaces the idea of proving a statement.

Because of the problem of induction, nothing can be proven in the sense of being established as true of the real world. But it is possible for something to be disproven. All that is needed is a single counterinstance. One contradiction is good enough, whereas no amount of confirmation will ever prove that a contradiction will not be encountered.

Our models of the world around us have to be formulated in such a way that they can be disproven. So long as they survive (i.e., are not disproven), despite being disprovable, they remain possibly true. It is also necessarily the case that if something is not disprovable, then it tells us nothing about the real world (it may of course be a useful statement about logic, but it will not say anything about the world outside of logic).

A statement need not be discarded even if it is disproven. It may be sufficient to modify it to accommodate the change in circumstances, thereby making it more accurate. Instead of "all swans are white" we may have "all non-Australian swans are white."

It is, however, important that a statement should not be altered in such a way as to make it immune to further tests. The statement should not become untestable. "All swans are white, except some" tells us nothing about the world at all. Here, the one thing implies the other; if a statement is immune to further testing (i.e., if it is not disprovable), it tells us nothing about the world. Similarly, a statement that tells us nothing about the world is not disprovable (unless it is a purely logical statement).

AN APPROACH TO DATABASE DESIGN

The practical implications of the problem of induction are best presented in two parts, reflecting the two problems facing the database designer. In this part, we address the question, "What will form the basis for the design?" The second question is addressed in the next part of this chapter.

The issue of identifying the entities of interest and their basic characteristics actually is not so difficult, given the right sort of environment. The simple, obvious, and only solution is to allow those who have to use the database to determine what it is to look like. The people who use the application must also be assumed to understand it. If this is not the case, several dire consequences will follow:

- Someone who does not use the application, and therefore probably does not understand the application, will have to design it.

- If the designer is not on hand to correct the design, as the application changes (and it will change) and as inaccuracies in the original design are discovered, the design will go uncorrected. Over time, the application will become a burden instead of a tool.

- Those who have to use the system, although they may understand the application, will be unlikely to understand someone else's model of the application. Either it must be explained to them, or they must continue in their ignorance.

- Those who have to use the system will regard it, quite rightly, as not having anything to do with them, and therefore as something to be subverted and circumvented, not used and improved.

When it comes to the business of the basic database design the answer is blindingly simple—let somebody else do it. The lesson to be learned from the problem of induction is that there is no one recipe or procedure that, when applied to a real-world problem, can be guaranteed to lead to a correct solution. Under no circumstances can we prove that some suggested solution is correct. So, and this is the main point of the approach, there is no formula that automatically allows us to derive suggestions because there is no procedure that allows us to establish that some given suggestion is correct.

All we can do is guess, and it may not be the case that my guess is as good as yours. If you happen to be working in the area, if you happen to have more experience than I have, and, most especially, if you happen to have daily and continual contact with the system, the chances are that, over time, your guess will be much better than mine. The closer the formulation of the design can be brought to the usage of the thing being designed, the better the design will be. Stated in these terms, the argument is almost trivial, but it is remarkable how often systems are produced that are regarded as inappropriate or ineffective by those who have to use them.

The approach, of course, assumes that it is possible to alter the application once it has been installed. Getting back to the problem of induction, the application will turn out to be invalid in some ways and will have to be changed in order to accommodate changes in circumstances or a new understanding of the requirements of the system. This will be a continuing process and is an integral part of the cost of the application. If it is not possible to change the application because it is too difficult or too expensive, the application, in time, will cease to be used, and the money will have been wasted anyway.

A database design that is not formulated, or at least criticized, in detail, by those who have to use it can be almost guaranteed to fail. Furthermore, a database that cannot be altered, once it has been built and come into use, will almost certainly become more and more useless as time goes by until it reaches a point where it is not used at all.

There is some comfort in the fact that in many installations, there is a tendency for design responsibility to be migrated out to the users. Systems analysts tend to be seen as being concerned with gathering requirements, rather than with specifying them. They have to rely on the users to describe the applications to be developed. So their main task is to act as a translator between the user's realm and the data processing realm. Such an arrangement is inevitable under some circumstances, but it should be clearly understood that it compromises the principal requirements for a good implementation of an application—that is, user involvement and flexibility.

What, then, is the role of the database administrator in all this? He or she should be confined to an advisory and watchdog role. The administrator should make sure that what goes into the database is sensible and practical, that the database is maintained in such a way that there is a continuity to the various parts of the database.

This alone is more than enough to keep most people busy. And in practice, most database administrators actually do very little by way of database design work. Most of the database design is done by people who are external to the database administration function. This is necessarily the case. One person is unlikely to be able to understand all of the functions and characteristics of even a small organization while knowing enough to be able to look after the database properly.

ASSESSING A DESIGN

There remains the issue of how to assess competing techniques for modeling some given application area, something a database specialist can reasonably expect to have to give advice and guidance on. Some fairly definite answers can be supplied. They involve, to begin with, a consideration of the status of the data in the database.

Database systems usually recognize a number of circumstances in which the values of an attribute may have an uncertain or indeterminate status. The term *null* tends to be indiscriminately used for all of the following attribute states:

1. *Inapplicable,* in which case the attribute is associated with some entity for which it may not assume any value (e.g., the attribute "wife" of an entity of type "female")

2. *Unknown,* implying that it is possible that the attribute has a value, but the value is not present in the database

3. *Uncertain,* suggesting that the attribute may have one of a (limited) number of different values; various arguments related to both possible and probable values may be applied to the attribute

4. *Invalid,* in which the attribute value contradicts some assertion about the database.

It is important to understand the implications of all four attribute states. A proper understanding of the possible attribute states allows the database to be assessed in terms of its match with the real world.

Particularly, the subject of attribute states leads to a criterion that may be used in comparing different and competing database designs. The following sections then look, in some detail, at the attribute states.

Inapplicable Attributes

Inapplicable attributes should not occur in a semantic database that has a complete and accurate schema. An entity that has a correct type should not have any attributes associated with it that are not applicable to it. If this occurs, it is merely an indication of an incomplete database design. A nonapplicable attribute simply means that there is some additional level in the hierarchy that has not been declared.

For example, the subclass "theropods" of the class "dinosaurs," is discovered to have in it some individuals that eat other dinosaurs. "Theropods" is therefore given an attribute "prey," indicating which dinosaurs were supposed to have been eaten by individual species within the class. It is subsequently decided that certain theropods did not eat other dinosaurs—that is, the "prey" attribute does not apply to them. For any of these theropods, the "prey" attribute is said to be null.

Obviously, what we are dealing with is two subclasses of the class "theropods"; "carnivores" and "herbivores." This is always the case with an inapplicable attribute. The fact that the attribute is null for some members of a class simply divides the class into those to whom the attribute applies, which will be a subclass of the class as a whole, and those to which the attribute does not apply. In the case of the "theropods," what is needed is a subclass "carnivorous theropods" which has the attribute "prey." The superclass "theropods" and the subclass "herbivorous theropods" does not have such an attribute.

Nulls in Query Results

Another place where the inapplicable attributes may be said to arise is in the case of query results: If the query result is regarded as a table derived from a set of related entities, probably of different types, then arguably there may be cases for which the query result may contain null values (i.e., some rows of the table returned by the query may have certain attributes with legitimate values; others may have the same attributes with no values).

Again, this is not the case. The database can be viewed as a collection of relations, one relation per class. If there are no attributes in the database that may be null, any **join** based on entity identifiers (which is what a relationship traversal is) cannot, by the definition of the relational **join** operator, return nulls. It may be possible to derive query results that contain nulls if an outer **join** is used. This may be regarded as an aberration so far as the SDM is concerned. The problem of nulls in a query result may be taken as a reflection of the inadequacy of the relational model in dealing with data in SDMs.

An SDM query processor may legitimately use the operations of the relational model to describe data access and retrieval. But considerably more has to be added to the SDM query processor. The relational model is not expected to take account of normalization in processing queries; this, however, is precisely the task that has to be undertaken by an SDM query processor if the meaning (semantics) of the data is to be preserved. An SDM query processor that had to rely entirely on the operations of the relational model to represent query results would be very clumsy indeed. In practice, the conventions of structured and tabular output have to be devised to allow query results (that, of course, are full of nulls) to be interpreted correctly.

The rest of the discussion assumes, unless otherwise stated, that databases do not have inapplicable values in them—that is, only unknown or invalid data may be present in a database.

Unknown and Uncertain Values

Unknown values are actually a special case of uncertain values. It will always be the case (in an SDM) that although the value of a given attribute may be unknown, the type of the attribute will be known. Assuming that the type is not in question, and the applicability of the attribute is not in question, the database management system can take the value of the attribute as being within the range of values designated by the type. This, so far as the SDM is concerned, covers the case of possible values.

It is perfectly reasonable in the case of the query:

```
RETRIEVE eye-color, hair-color
    WHERE name = "Bridget"
```

for the system to reply:

```
  eye-color = green,
 hair-color = ONE OF
{brown,blonde,black,red,white,grey}
```

The schema of a semantic database may be taken as designating a set of possible states applicable to a given entity. If the entities in the database are defined to a sufficient degree of accuracy, it may be possible for the database management system's query processor to provide useful information even in the case of the value of an attribute being unknown.

A reasonable approach to dealing with uncertain values in a query result would be to allow a special qualifier to deal with them. Query processors commonly recognize qualifiers such as ALL, SOME, FIRST, and so on. Uncertain values could be dealt with using the qualifier POSSIBLE, allowing queries such as the following:

```
RETRIEVE name
    WHERE POSSIBLE hair-color = blonde
```

The system replies,

```
→ name = "Bridget"
```

This is not actually very useful, given that a similar effect could be achieved by extending the interpretation of existing operators, but the principle is important.

If inapplicable attributes are not allowed in the database, any absent values should merely be taken as unknown. If inapplicable attributes are allowed, a distinction must be drawn between inapplicable and unknown if use is to be made either of the schema or of statistically derived values in returning the result of a query.

Particularly, if nulls are not allowed, it may be possible for semantic databases to allow the insertion of entities for which some required attributes are *not* specified. If an attribute has no value, it should just be interpreted to mean that the value is not known at the present time. Actually, in the absence of nulls, all items are required.

If the absence of a value does just imply that the value is not known, the query processor, in returning information about an entity, can take account of the absence of data in the preceding ways, allowing, for example,

```
RETRIEVE name OF paternal-grandmother
    WHERE name = "Bridget"
```

The system responds

```
→ name OF paternal-grandmother = <unknown>
```

Inferred Values

It is reasonable to take a further step and maintain information of a statistical nature concerning the values of certain attributes. Particularly, the database may keep information regarding the correlation between the values of different attributes and the distribution of the values of various attributes (a number of optimization schemes, for example, require the maintenance of these types of statistics).

Given some fairly simple statistical analysis of the data placed in the database, the system could be queried with the following:

```
RETRIEVE height
    WHERE name = "Thomas"
```

If height is unknown and "Thomas" is a male Caucasian, 3 $\frac{1}{2}$ years old, the system might respond with the following:

```
→ probably about 3 ft. 6 in.
```

This type of analysis of the data may be especially useful in the case of updates, in which all values have to be regarded, until validated, as having an uncertain status. Ordinarily, types and various other explicit constraints are expected to be used in data validation.

Statistical data may also be used to add a further level of checking by allowing an analysis of update data in terms of the probability of the data. If the data in the database is known to conform to a normal distribution, exception reporting could be provided on any attribute values supplied with a probability below some specified value.

This type of approach to data validation is already a feature of many application systems. For example, it is common practice to check such things as electricity bills against a pattern of values, invoking exception reporting where the values stray from some specified bounds. Inevitably, when types are specified for a range of values that obey a normal distribution, the upper, and possibly the lower, bounds of the type will represent extremely improbable values and warrant some special attention if the data in the database is to be taken as meaningful and reliable.

Invalid Data

If a database contains a value that contradicts some assertion about the database (whether it should be there at all is addressed here subsequently), the value of the associated attribute has to be regarded as being of an indeterminate status. There are three distinct kinds of situations where an attribute value may contradict a database assertion:

1. As a result of an *empirical conflict*—the value is known or believed by some external agency to be correct, but it conflicts with some assertion in the database

2. As a result of some *change in the assertions*

3. As a result of the *logic of the assertion itself* (e.g., Bertrand Russell's barber, who shaves all those who do not shave themselves [who shaves the barber?]).

In the process of designing a database, all three problems will have to be confronted; and all three may be solved within the scope of Popper's solution to the problem of induction. The idea of "best fit" allows for a sensible interpretation of invalid data. It must be taken as representing a potential conflict between the model and the real world that can only be resolved by a reassessment of both the data and the model.

A BASIS FOR INDUCTION

As we have already seen, Popper proposes the alternative, so far as science is concerned, of substituting falsifiability for proof, justifying the scientific status of some theories, not in terms of proof, but in terms of the fact that the theory is potentially falsifiable by some apparently possible observation.

Popper takes the normal course of theory development to be one of the following:

1. Proposal of a hypothesis
2. Statement of the hypothesis in a falsifiable form
3. Refutation by some statement of greater information content—on the assumption that it accounts for the old theory while superseding it.

There are a number of interesting characteristics to this process. For example, designating the information content of a statement "a" as CT(a), in terms of the calculus of probability, the conjunction of two statements "a" and "b" (e.g., dice A and B both showing a six) is less probable than either statement taken on its own (e.g., dice A showing a six). The content of two statements taken together, Ct(a,b) is greater than either statement taken individually, leading to the following inequalities (P(a) indicates the probability of a; LEQ signifies "less than or equal to "; GEQ signifies "greater than or equal to"):

$$Ct(a) \text{ LEQ } Ct(a,b) \text{ GEQ } Ct(b)$$

and

$$P(a) \text{ GEQ } P(a,b) \text{ LEQ } P(b)$$

Or, more simply, the more information in a statement, the less probable it is. This, taken with the idea of falsifiability, leads to a clear statement of the goal of science:

1. Falsifiable theories
2. Of increasing content
3. And decreasing probability.

The first prerequisite for any progress is a criterion that allows progress to be recognized. This is precisely what Popper supplies. The same three criteria are clearly applicable in the areas of database design and usage.

The idea that increasing information implies decreasing probability is sometimes regarded as being paradoxical. This is only true, though, if a traditional approach to induction is assumed. Traditionally induction, as formulated by Bacon, requires that we look for increasing probability by attempting to verify statements as widely as possible. The idea is that if a sufficient number of observations are made confirming the theory to be tested, the theory will eventually become so probable that for all practical purposes, it can be taken as being true. It has always been recognized that this approach, though attractive, is of a very doubtful validity. Hume established a clear set of arguments undermining it in the 1700s. The final major blow came when Einstein's theory of relativity demolished Newtonian physics, which had always been cited by the Baconians as a shining example of the results of traditional inductive methods.

DATABASES AND INDUCTION

A database is a model or hypothesis concerning the characteristics of the world it is intended to model. In Popper's terms, it is a theory that will have a certain information content and that may be more or less probable. As such, the following must be expected;

- No design is likely to be correct; certainly, no design will be demonstrably correct.

- It is only possible to increase the information content of the database at the price of increasing the improbability, both of the schema and of the data.

- Through a series of changes, the design of the database should be expected to evolve, providing an increasingly accurate, though never completely accurate representation of the world being modeled.

Semantic data models seem to be well suited to this view of database management systems because they emphasize the following:

- A clear and complete statement of the schema

- Which allows for the possibility of evolving the schema as the understanding of the data evolves

- While maintaining the meaning of the data across the different schemas.

A variety of different features in SDMs facilitate this.

A semantic database may be viewed as a collection of related entities. The entities are arranged in hierarchies with increasingly specialized types as the lower levels of the hierarchy are reached. At a certain level of abstraction, everything in the database may be viewed as an entity, or, more accurately, as a representation of an entity, regardless of the actual type of the entity (or, what amounts to the same thing, the classes in which it participates). This allows the database to represent both relationships and entities that are not clearly defined or completely understood.

If the type of an entity is uncertain, an entity representation can always be inserted into the database as an entity (i.e., in the class "entity"). If a relationship is not properly understood it can always be represented as a relationship of indeterminate type between, if necessary, two entities.

This capability allows the database to deal with exceptions and schema violations in a consistent and reasonable manner. This allows information to be preserved and evaluated even if the information happens to violate some integrity constraints in the schema.

A semantic database should be able to deal with special cases and exceptions, allowing data to be preserved for subsequent evaluation, which would lead to one of the following:

- Modification of the schema

- Rejection of the data

- Preservation of the exception.

For example, let us assume that there exists a relationship between person A and person B in a database that already has the following classes:

```
Class Person
   father
   mother
   sibling

Subclass male
   wife

Subclass female
   husband INVERSE wife
```

It is quite reasonable to add the relationship "relation" to the class "person," allowing the fact that A and B are related to be represented even though the type of the relationship is unknown. This closely parallels the idea of increasing information content, allowing relationships and attributes to be moved down the hierarchy, reflecting more detailed information, and incidentally increasing the probability of finding some counterinstance, while decreasing the probability of the schema, a necessary corollary of increasing information content.

Null values may be interpreted in this context as reflecting a lack of "fit" between the database and the world being modeled. Allowing nulls in the database decreases the number and extent of the inferences that may be drawn, both from the schema and the data. This is a straightforward reflection of decreasing information content with increasing probability. In the extreme case, if any attributes may be null, any entity will fit.

The designer of the database must then balance the needs and requirements likely to be placed on the database by its users against the cost of meeting those needs. It must always be borne in mind that the more information there is in the database, the more difficult it will be to achieve a correct and accurate design. However, the more information there is in the database, the more can be expected from it.

Information can only be had at a price. The cost will be measured in the time it takes to implement the system, the amount of effort that has to be devoted to maintaining it, and the ease with which it can be understood.

9

Paleontology Database (PaleoDB)

INTRODUCTION

The previous chapters have described the concepts and structures of the semantic data model (SDM) and the operations that may be used to define and manipulate a semantic database. They also provided an introduction to the subject of designing databases using an SDM. The level of detail provided by the chapter on database design is sufficient to deal with the design of fairly simple databases. It is also sufficient to provide the intellectual tools required to understand a substantial portion of the databases that are likely to be encountered in the commercial world. Therefore, if you do not have an interest in database design, you may choose to leave this chapter on the PaleoDB until a second reading of the book.

The problems dealt with in this chapter are quite easy to describe using the SDM, but they are, generally speaking, not quite so easy to solve. The problem descriptions are provided using a number of different database examples, notably, portions of the ServiceDB system, a paleontology database (PaleoDB), and examples based on data dictionaries and computer-aided design (CAD). The paleontology application serves as the focus of this chapter, as it particularly represents some almost insuperable difficulties for a semantic database. But almost all of the databases, even the ServiceDB system, experience these problems in one form or another.

There is some consolation in the thought that in many data models, it is difficult even to describe these problems, while finding solutions verges on the impossible. The problems, briefly, are as follows:

- *Classes as data*—we have already seen, in the form of the directory, an example of a class in which the entities in the class do not describe real-world objects. The objects described are objects that themselves describe other objects, so the directory has (a) classes that contain attributes (or, more accurately, descriptions of attributes), (b) classes that contain types, and (c) classes that contain classes. This sort of thing tends to make one go mentally cross-eyed trying to visualize a strange self-referential world where things often turn out to be much more than what they seem. Unfortunately, this sort of thing is not by any means confined to database directories but frequently crops up, in all sorts of disguises, in ordinary commercial databases. How are classes of classes to be understood and dealt with?

- *Multiple-entity entities*—some entities are clearly made up of other entities. They are compound entities. This is not the same as the aggregation concept whereby an entity is characterized by other entities: A person being characterized by a name or an address is not the same thing as a car being made up of a chassis and an engine. If Joe Soap gets run down by a steam roller, his name and address do not cease to be valid. But if a car gets turned into scrap metal, its engine goes along with it. An engine is a part of a car; "Joe Soap" is not a part of Joe Soap, it is just his name. What precisely is this "part of" relationship?

- *Versions and temporal data*—how can a database be established in such a way that it is possible to represent the state of an application at different moments in time?

- *Relationships that have attributes*—a given type of part may be stored at many different locations, and a given location may store many different types of parts. Where should the count of the number of parts at a location be stored? It cannot be stored with each part; parts could be at many different locations. It cannot be stored with each location; locations may be associated with many different parts. An "intersection" class has to be invented as a place holder for the "location-part" count. How can such a thing be incorporated into the model in such a way that it makes sense?

The SDM does not provide ready-made solutions to the aforementioned problems. These problems will be encountered by the database designer as common features of commercial databases. Please note that it is highly desirable to be able to recognize them, not to solve them. Half the trouble with these issues is that they lead to the introduction of kludges that are not properly understood. These, in turn, lead to the addition of yet more kludges. Kludge mounts upon kludge until the whole database and everything associated with it turns into a tangled morass that can only be dealt with by consigning it to the scrap heap.

CLASSES AS DATA

The idea of different levels of description has already been encountered in a number of different forms, one notable example being the directory. The directory is not very suitable as a basis for an explanation of levels of description, as it carries too many complexities of its own. We begin, then, with a simple example, a fragment of the schema for ServiceDB.

The schema is presented using DDL rather than the SDM diagrams because it is desirable here to emphasize the difference between *schema* and *data*, whereas SDM diagrams are designed specifically to avoid making a distinction between a schema and data. The ServiceDB DDL follows:

```
Type maintenance-agreement
              :Symbolic {None, Prime-time, Anytime} ;

Class Person (
    Name        : String, Unique, Required;
    );

Subclass Customer of Person (
    Address     : String;
    Owns        : Appliance, MV;
    Maintenance-Contract
                : maintenance-agreement, Required;
    ) ;

Class Appliance (
    Name        : String, Unique, Required;
    ) ;
```

Some examples of data that might be found in the ServiceDB, using a layout that emphasizes the difference between schema and data:

```
Name        Address                     Name of
                                        Appliance

Pscl        111001 Back Door            thermithometer
            The Maze

Desc        01000000111 Front Door      zakanaka
            The Maze

Gola        00001                       rootitutti
            Another Maze
```

The table is a representation of the following query:

```
From Customer Retrieve Name, Address,
  Name of Appliance;
```

The names and addresses are attributes of some of the customers serviced by the appliance servicing system. The attribute value "Pscl" is different from the name "address," but both are information about the database. "Pscl stands for something outside of the database; it designates some individual to be found at "111001" in "The Maze." "Address," however stands for a whole collection of things. It is defined, from an extensional point of view, by all of the addresses stored in the system. These in turn stand for other things—in this case, locations in mazes. So while data items, such as the name "Pscl" (usually), stand for things in the real world, schema items, such as address (usually), stand for collections of data items. It is a fundamental aspect of the model that schema items are themselves data.

The concept of different levels of description may be applied to the data that makes up the database. There is the distinction between data and schema, a schema being considered to be at a higher level than data, although a schema is still inclusive of data. In this case, "name," for example, is *schema*, "Pscl" is *data*.

The idea of different levels is analogous to the similar concept of levels as found in logic. Logic distinguishes various levels of statements: Level 0 corresponds to individual signs; predicates that contain only assertions about individual signs represent first-order statements, or Level 1; predicates that contain assertions about first-order predicates are second-order predicates, or Level 2, and so on.

Any number of levels are allowed. A given statement may be made up of components drawn from any number of levels. The level of a given statement is taken to be one greater than its highest-level component statement.

In these examples, the statements are on the left, and the logical forms are on the right:

- Statement x

- The preceding statement x ISA y
  is a Level 0 statement

- Any statement that refers to $(x$ ISA $y)$ ISA z
  another statement such as the
  preceding statement is a Level 1
  statement.

Of course, the last statement was a Level 2 statement because it refers to a Level 1 statement, and this statement is a Level 3 statement because it refers to itself. Or perhaps it is a Level 4 statement because it refers to itself and it is a Level 3 statement. But if it is a Level 4 statement, then it must be a Level 5 statement. . . . At which point we arbitrarily stop. Self-reference can lead to hopeless logical tangles, and it is sometimes best swept under the carpet.

A schema is usually concerned with asserting that some collection of individuals share some property or other (a name or an address for example).

The following DDL statement

```
Class Person (
     Name              : String, Unique, Required;
     );
```

is equivalent to the following:

> (for all x (Person(x) →
> Name (x) NEQ null &
> (for all y (Person (y) →
> Name (y) NEQ Name (x)))

Or "for all x, x is a person implies that x has a name and for all y, y is a person implies that y's name is not equal to x's name." Note that this is not a second-order statement. There is nothing in the definition of the class "Person" that specifies that a variable, such as x, stands for a proposition rather than an individual sign. In this case, individual signs are the entities in the database.

Second-order logic then is a much wider case than first-order logic because in second-order logic, it is possible to have conditions about conditions. In database terms, this is the type of logic that is implied by the description of the data model itself.

For example, given the subclass–superclass relationship, if every member of one class is also a member of a second class, then the first is a subclass of the second. This may be rendered as follows:

> (for all A) (for all B) (there does not exist x)

> (A(x) & Not B(x) → Subclass(A,B))

The predicate calculus form turns the statement around a little to "for every A and every B, if there is no x such that x is an A and x is not a B, then A is a subclass of B." It also implies that a class with no members, the null class, is a subclass of every class.

Life would be disarmingly simple if this sort of thing were confined to the definition of data models, allowing people concerned with the definitions of databases to stick to the relatively secure realms of the first-order logic. Things would even be quite simple if second-order statements were only encountered when dealing with the schema.

But consider the following case. A library has a rule that if there are no more copies of an edition of a book kept by the library, the information about the book should be deleted from the database. What does this look like in predicate calculus terms?

$$(for\ all\ y)\ (there\ does\ not\ exist\ x)\ (y(x) \rightarrow delete(y))$$

Or, for every book, y, if there is no copy, x, such that x is a y, delete y.

The "y" should be in capitals—Y is clearly a proposition, not an individual sign. Particularly in situations such as this, where things become dependent on other things, second-order logic is likely to be encountered in the data, as opposed to the schema. The consequences as we see are not to be taken lightly.

Where Level 2 data is to be altered, by definition, the fundamental characteristics of all relevant Level 1 data will be changed as well. The Level 2 data determines the general shape and form of the Level 1 data, and accordingly can frequently only be changed at the expense of drastic and wide-ranging changes at Level 1. In the library example, if a book is deleted, all of the volumes that are copies of the book ought to disappear as well. To take a more extreme example; what would be the implications of saying that no attributes in an SDM database may be null. This would involve a fundamental reinterpretation of the data model and therefore of all the data in every database that is an instance of the data model.

The Level 0–Level 1 distinction is relative. In particular, it is frequently quite difficult to determine clearly where the Level 1 data starts. Something that might appear to be Level 0 data may turn out, on closer inspection, to be Level 1.

It is quite common to find commercial databases in which data that would ordinarily be taken as Level 0 data (i.e., just data) is in fact Level 1 data (i.e., it is really a description of some class or collection of objects).

There are at least two examples of this in the ServiceDB database. First, the "Customer" attribute, "Maintenance-contract," has as its type, "Maintenance-agreement." From a data modeling point of view, what exactly are the symbolic values of "Maintenance-agreement"? Consider the following version of ServiceDB:

```
Subclass Customer of Person (
     Address       : String:
     Owns          : Appliance, MV;
     Maintenance-Contract
                   : Contract, Required;
);
Class Contract (
     Maintenance-agreement
                   : Subrole {None, Prime-Time, Any-
Time}
                   Required;
);
```

So it turns out that "none' is a class! a subclass of contract, to be precise.

A further modification of ServiceDB provides another example of a multilevel schema. The following illustrates how ServiceDB might be altered to keep track of individual appliances:

```
Subclass Customer of Person (
     Address       : String
     Owns          : Appliances, MV;
     Maintenance-Contract
                   : maintenance-agreement, Required;
);

Class Appliances (
     Serial-number
                   : Number (12), Required;
     Appliance-type
                   : Appliance, Required;
);

Class Appliance (
     Name          : String, Unique, Required;
);
```

Life has suddenly become much more complicated. In fact, the entities in the class "appliances" are instances of the entities in the class "appliance." That is, there is the same relationship between the class "appliance" and the class "appliances" as there is between the class "class" and the class "appliance." This can be represented as follows (the numbers in parentheses represent the level of the associated objects):

$$\text{(2)Class} \xleftarrow{\quad\text{ISA}\quad} \text{(1)Appliance} \xleftarrow{\quad\text{ISA}\quad} \text{(0)Appliances}$$

"Appliance" is an instance of an entity in the class "class," and an appliance in "appliances" is an instance of an entity in the class "Appliance." Logically speaking, "appliance" occupies the same level as is normally occupied by the schema of a database. This is terrible! A sizable proportion of the software that makes up a database management system is devoted to this complex task of correctly maintaining the "instance-of" or ISA relationship between a class and its entities. But in this new version of ServiceDB, ordinary programs can create and destroy classes as a by-product of creating and deleting apparently ordinary entities.

The problem is that a three-level schema has to be represented in a two-level system. In many cases, the consequences are not serious, but there are likely to be difficulties with insertion and deletion. Users may not appreciate that there is an ISA relationship between an entity in "appliance" and entities in "appliances"; difficulties are bound to follow.

A Profusion of Levels

So far as multilevel systems are concerned, paleontology represents an extreme case. Paleontology has some very complex and highly structured classification techniques. This is especially so with respect to the classification of life forms. Life forms are classified in two ways: (1) using a system that indicates various types of classification, and (2) specifying classes and subclasses of life forms, based on the types of classification. The types of classification are as follows:

Kingdom

Phylum

Class

Order

Family

Genus

Species

Where appropriate, the prefixes super, sub, and infra may be applied. For example for a certain type of animal, a subfamily may be specified that is somewhat more general than a genus but less general than a family.

The following is an example of the use of the kingdom–phylum hierarchy, in this case, as applied to the species *Homo sapiens*:

Kingdom	Animalia
Phylum	Chordata
Class	Mammalia
Order	Primates
Family	Hominidae
Genus	*Homo*
Species	*Homo sapiens*

As an example of the use of the prefix conventions, a classification, Hominoidae has been identified as a superfamily of Hominidae.

The kingdom–phylum classification of individuals into species and genus could be dealt with in a number of ways. One approach that suggests itself is to take the obvious ISA relationship between *Homo sapiens* and species, *Homo* and genus, and so on, and have one database class for each classification type, giving a list of database classes that contain a database class for species, genus, and so on. In this way, *Homo sapiens* would be stored in the database as an instance of a species.

You may remember that the test for the validity of a hierarchy is to look at the hierarchy from the point of view of some supposed instance of a class in the hierarchy. Looking at the situation from the point of view of some individual of the species *Homo sapiens,* the suggested arrangement of the database classes is clearly not correct. According to the definition of the SDM, an individual is supposed to (1) have all the attributes of his immediate database class, and (2) inherit all the attributes of the superclasses of his database class.

Joe Soap clearly ISA *Homo sapiens; Homo sapiens* ISA species; therefore, Joe Soap ISA species. This is obviously wrong. The applicable ISA relationship, so far as Joe Soap is concerned, is the relationship *Homo sapiens* ISA *Homo.* Therefore, Joe Soap ISA *Homo,* ISA Primates, ISA Mammalia, and so on.

There are obviously two types of ISA relationship involved. The relationship between *Homo sapiens* and *Homo,* indicating that an instance of the database class *"homo sapiens"* is also an instance of the database class *"Homo,"* whereas the ISA relationship between *Homo sapiens* and species indicates that *Homo sapiens* ASA class ISA species, but some instance of the database class is not.

It follows that the correct method of modeling this is to provide a database class hierarchy with Animalia as the root database class. Animalia has Chordata (etc.) as subclasses, and so on down to *Homo,* with the various species of the genus *Homo* as its subclasses.

What the kingdom, phylum, class hierarchy defines, then, is a hierarchy for defining generalization hierarchies. The *Homo sapiens, Homo,* Hominidae hierarchy is an instance of the kingdom, phylum, class hierarchy. Therefore, what we have here is not merely a database class that can be used to define other database classes, but a whole structure that can be used to define other structures. In theory, there is no obvious reason why this process should stop here; perhaps structures that define structures of structures are possible.

In practice, the kingdom, phylum, class hierarchy is probably about as complex an object as is likely to be encountered in a commercial database. Apart from any other considerations, anything more complex than this would simply not be understood. Note that kingdom, phylum, class, and so on could still be modeled as separate database classes with some sort of relationship between them and the database classes such as *Homo* and *Homo sapiens.* But this is still unsatisfactory, as it does not indicate that something that is a database subclass to a kingdom must be a phylum and something that is a database subclass to a class must be an order, and so forth. This is clearly a case of lost semantics.

Subroles: A Partial Solution

Subroles do provide a partial solution. A subrole describes a relationship between a class and its subclasses. "Person" may, for example, have a subrole "profession," which indicates that "person" may be either a "researcher" or a "lecturer." "Person" will have a corresponding subclass for every possible value of its subrole "profession."

Clearly, kingdom, phylum, class, and so on may be considered to be subroles. For example the database class *"Homo"* (which is actually a genus), will have subrole "species," the values of the subrole "species" being all of the species of the genus *"Homo."* Even here though, there is still nothing to enforce the rule that something that is a subclass to a kingdom must be a phylum.

MULTIPLE ENTITY ENTITIES

CAD databases have to deal with situations where the objects that are routinely manipulated in the database are not simple atomic objects, but actually collections of objects. Collections are of two distinct types: (1) collections that are classes (i.e., object types), (2) collections that are related sets of entities (such as a VLSI [very large scale integration] chip), which have to be established by declaring relationships among the classes that participate in the structure.

In both cases, the model has to supply the ability to manipulate three things: (1) both Level 0 and Level 1 objects, (2) both entities and descriptions of entity types, and (3) both relationships and descriptions of relationship types. The real problem that has to be solved by the model is how to reconcile the alteration of the description of a class or relationship with the existence of instances of the class or relationship.

Dictionaries are a similar case. A sizable proportion of the data in a data dictionary is likely to be in the form of structures of one type or another. For example, a database may be depicted as follows:

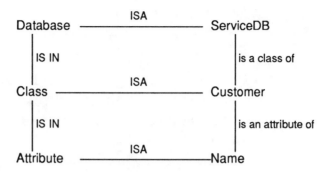

This means that there are structural semantics in these types of databases. The interpretation of the relationships within the structure is heavily dependent on the fact that the relationships are being used to define a structure.

This becomes particularly evident in the types of operations that might reasonably be performed on the structure. We have already seen how in a generalization hierarchy, which itself is just a type of structure, **delete** operations propagate downward in the structure. If something is deleted at the midpoint of the structure, everything below it disappears, but everything above it is unaffected. The same applies here; if a class in a database is deleted, the attributes contained by the class must disappear as well; the database itself and other classes remain unaltered.

Data dictionaries and CAD databases have to deal with structures and with multilevel data. They can be used to illustrate a number of other problems.

VERSIONS AND TEMPORAL DATA

According to one approach, a CAD database has to be able to represent the following:

- *Realizations and interfaces*–the *interface* is the general form of the object; the *realization* is the technique used to implement the form

- *Configurations of entities*—the CAD database has to be able to represent, construct, and manipulate configurations of entities

- *Multiversion entities*—it has to be able to deal with multiversion entities; the versions themselves may represent the following:

* Alternative strategies

* Revisions of previous entities

* Different views (as interface or as realization)

- *Means of entity selection*–the CAD database must provide entity selection, with rules for providing some default version of the entity

- *Means for using previously defined entities*—it must allow for usage in various contexts

- *A history of the different versions of an entity*—it must also explain the reason for alterations to the entity.

Adequate version handling is crucial to the success of a CAD database. Multiple versions are characteristic of both CAD databases and data dictionaries and are a useful introduction to the subject of temporal data.

Version handling tends to be very complex. Much of the complexity may also be attributed to confusion regarding levels. This is not to say that confusions about levels can be avoided in the interfaces to the system or in its implementation. But it is desirable to avoid confusions about levels in the formal specification of the system.

Versions may be handled as different manifestations of the same thing. Consider a dictionary that supports multiple versions and allows entities to be copied as new versions. If, for example, one has different versions of a program P, that produces random numbers, being P_1, P_2, ... P_n. All of the programs P_1 through P_n are essentially members of a class—that is, the class of random-number-producing programs of type P. Declaring the program in the first place is essentially declaring a class. The process of copying P_n as P_{n+1} is in fact just inserting an entity into the class P, and not a copy at all.

The situation may be represented diagrammatically as follows:

$$\underset{\text{(3)Class}}{} \xleftarrow{\text{ISA}} \underset{\text{(2)Program}}{} \xleftarrow{\text{ISA}} \underset{\substack{\text{(1)P(random}\\ \text{number}\\ \text{program)}}}{} \xleftarrow{\text{ISA}} \underset{\text{(0)}P_n}{}$$

What is involved is a three-level logic being represented in a two-level system. In both CAD databases and data dictionary systems, the definition of Level 1 tends to be very problematic. This is what interface and realization are all about.

In a CAD context, the interface must always be the same, and it may be taken as representing the class description; changing the interface creates a new class. The realization may vary within the limits of the interface, and it represents the instances of the class. Drawing on concepts from the field of modular programming, what is involved is the *visibility* of the various characteristics of the object being modeled. Those characteristics that are only visible internally represent data that may vary from one implementation to the next, whereas those characteristics that are visible to external objects have to be fixed for all the instances of the type.

The internal–external distinction is useful, as it underlines the fact that visibility is context dependent. Going back to the data dictionary. In some cases, it may be important as to which language a program is written in; in some cases, it may not be. If the language does not matter at all, the language may be changed without generating a new version. If the language does matter but does not change the interface, the language may be changed, but it may imply a new version. The language then is a part of the realization. If, however, a language change implies a change to the interface, a whole new class results (i.e., a different type of program).

There are then three possible types of changes:

1. Changes that do not make any difference (nonchanges—there is no sense in which a new entity is created or an old version superseded)

2. Changes that result in a new version (i.e., represent a new entity, but still an entity of the same type)

3. Changes that result in a whole new type of entity (i.e., they imply the creation of a new class).

Currently available database management systems only support changes of Types 1 and 2 via a DML. Changes of Type 3 are expected to be performed using the DDL. This is based on the assumption that a clear distinction can be drawn between the data to which types 1 and 2 changes apply and the data to which Type 3 changes apply. All of the databases examined so far have precisely this problem; they all have to be able to apply Type 3 changes to data, which is itself described by data to which Type 3 changes may also be applied. They contain data that is simultaneously data and descriptions of data, and the DDL–DML distinction collapses.

The previously cited data dictionary example bears a reexamination in the light of the view that different versions of an object are different instances of a class of objects. The previous diagram could be expanded to the following:

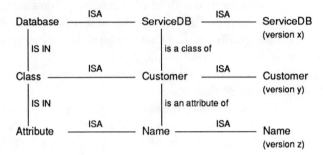

This is (at least) a three-level schema with

- The database–class–attribute schema describing the database structure
- The ServiceDB–Customer–Name schema describing an instance of the structure
- Version x–Version y–Version z being an instance of the ServiceDB structure.

It may be the case that "customer" (version y) has a relationship to "appliance" (version w). The system has to be able to deal with the fact that there is a description of this relationship between "customer" and "appliance." If this description of the relationship is to be modified, all of the instances of the relationship must be modified as well. This implication is essentially carried by the ISA relationships. Another way of saying all this is that if the schema is modified, all of the instances of the schema will have to be modified as well.

RELATIONSHIP ATTRIBUTES

Another concept, somewhat obliquely related to the topics dealt with so far, is the concept of *relationship attributes*; it also frequently, though not always, results from a confusion of levels. An example from a data dictionary illustrates this. If an item appears twice in the same report, then the item may have relationship attributes, the attributes specifying where the item is located in the report. This is a *relationship attribute* because it cannot be kept with the item; the item may appear in many different reports or even many times in the same report. And the report location cannot be kept with the report because a given report will normally contain bits of information from many different items, each at a different location. What is actually happening is that the item represents a class of objects, each usage of the item being an instance of the item. This then gives (at least) a three-level hierarchy:

```
          instance of        instance of          Instance of
(3)Class  ◄────────(2)Item  ◄──── (1)Item A  ◄────────(0)Usage of item A
```

"Item" is an instance of "class"; that is, "item" ISA "class." "Class" then, in this case, is a Level 3 object.

In this presentation, the relationship attribute goes away. There is no problem as to where to put the relationship attribute, "report location." It is merely an attribute of the Level 0 entity, "usage of item A."

Returning to the version of ServiceDB that keeps track of individual appliances, a relationship attribute arises between "customer" and "appliance," indicating the number of appliances owned by a given customer. This is also a confusion of levels, clearly evident in this case, given the previous discussion of the data dictionary example. Properly speaking, the relationship is among "appliance" (as a class of appliance types), a specific instance of the appliance, and the owner of the instance of the appliance. The number of entities participating in the relationship gives the number of appliances of the given type owned by the given customer. The relationship between "appliance" and "appliances" is, of course, an ISA relationship.

It is almost always the case with relationship attributes that a structure is implied. A special type of attribute inheritance applies within the structure. The Level n–1 entities inherit the characteristics of the Level n entities. For example the size of a "usage of item A," is given by the Level 1 "item A." The Level 0 entities "pick up" all of the characteristics of the Level 1 entities. The same is true between Levels 1 and 2, 2 and 3, and so on.

Relationship attributes, too, usually imply a confusion of levels. The relationship attributes, rather than applying to a relationship between object A and object B, apply to entities related to "class A," which are instances of "class B."

A LIMITATION IN SDM

There remains the question of how to capture all of the information in the kingdom–phylum hierarchy. The hierarchy actually describes a structure. It describes permissible configurations within a set of related entities of different types, which are expected to behave as a group, as a collection of entities, even as an entity made up of multiple entities. Thus, permissible configurations of collections of entities, not just permissible states of a single entity, are involved.

The kingdom, phylum, class hierarchy is very similar to the database structure. The kingdom, phylum, class hierarchy provides relationships among subroles. This implies that anything that has a family as a subclass must itself be an order, anything that is a genus must itself only have species as subclasses. In a similar way, in a data dictionary, what is specified is that anything that is a database must have classes as components; anything that is a class must have attributes as components; anything that accesses a class, by implication, may access all of its component attributes.

Taking the kingdom–phylum hierarchy as a structure, the situation may be depicted somewhat as follows:

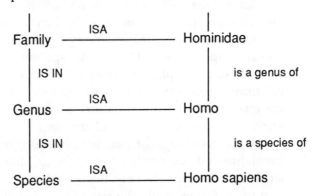

Although this is very similar to the database structure, the similarity should be treated with some caution. The significant difference is that the relationship species between *Homo* and *Homo sapiens* is a subrole, whereas the relationship "item" between "customer" and "name" obviously is not. "Name" is not a "customer," though *Homo sapiens* is a *Homo* (i.e., a subclass of the database class *"Homo."* This is because instances of the "is a species of" relationship between *Homo sapiens* and *Homo* imply membership in a class or, more correctly, a generalization hierarchy; whereas instances of the "is an item of" relationship between "name" and "customer" indicate participation in a structure—that structure, however, is not a generalization hierarchy.

Generalization hierarchies are a special case of a structure, and it is somewhat unusual to find a multilevel database containing, as data, a full-blown secondary generalization hierarchy, such as the life-forms classification. Structures such as the database, class, attribute structure are very common.

Another minor issue that arises here is the description of a subrole as a multityped relationship. Subroles are often referred to as multi-typed relationships on the grounds that the subrole represents a relationship that spans a number of different subclasses. The type of the subrole varies, depending on the value of the subrole, hence the name "multityped relationship"; the relationship may assume many different types.

The subrole is commonly described as providing a method of naming the relationship between the various components of a class hierarchy. This is incorrect; it really represents a mapping from one logical level to another. The relationship only appears to be "multi-typed" because it is being looked at from the wrong point of view. In the following example,

```
Class Person (
    Name            : String;
    Role            : Subrole {Employee, Customer} , MV;
    );
```

the directory for the database will have a class "class," which will contain, among other things, entities for the three classes represented here—namely, "person" and its two subclasses, "employee" and "customer." These may be represented as follows:

<Person>

<Customer>   <Employee>

Consider an individual, Joe Soap, in the "person" class, who is an "employee." As a result of being both a person and an employee, he is related by his role attribute both to "employee" and to "person." The role attribute is simply a name for the ISA relationship. This may be shown as follows:

<Person>

<Customer>   <Employee>

ISA
       ISA

Joe Soap

The relationship maps the given entity to one of a number of different classes; the collection of classes the entity is related to are themselves all of the same type (they are all members of the class "class"). The relationship then is a decent, well-behaved, single-typed relationship, although participating in the relationship has unusual consequences; it implies not just that the participating entity acquires some extended attributes, but also that it thereby becomes an entity of a particular type.

To summarize thus far: Wherever there are dependencies (as opposed to simple relationships) between different Level 0 data, it is very likely to be the case that the data is not Level 0 at all. It may be Level 1, as with the entities in the "appliance" class; it may even be Level 2, as with the classifications of life forms. Where Level 1 or Level 2 data is being dealt with, the normal rules of data manipulation do not apply. Where the entity representing a class disappears, all of the entities that the class contains must disappear as well. Where the entities of a class are themselves classes, the insertion and deletion of entities has side effects beyond those normally associated with the insertion and deletion of Level 0 entities. A milder form of the same type of phenomenon may be encountered in the case of structures in which the relationships that make up the structure are not ISA relationships.

LANGUAGE FORMS IA AND IB

Before discussing Language Forms IA and IB, we describe their origin. Carnap (1954) proposed the concept of an object as the aggregation of all the spatio–temporal instances of the object. Carnap described "Thing Languages," where "a thing occupies a region in a four-dimensional space–time continuum. A given thing at a given instant of time is, so to speak, a cross-section of the whole space–time region occupied by the thing. It is called a thing slice (or a thing moment)."

(Carnap, 1954, p. 158). Carnap then proceeded to distinguish different language forms on the basis of the different types employed in the languages, the basic distinctions being the following:

- What do expressions of the individual type designate (i.e., things or thing moments)
- To what type do the designations of the things belong? (i.e., are things Level 0 objects and just represent themselves, or are they Level 1 objects, representing the class of all their thing moments?)

From these distinctions, a number of different language forms are identified, notably Forms I, II, and III, and coordinate languages. A consideration of Language Form I is adequate for the current discussion. In Language Form I, individuals are taken to be space–time regions—particular things. There are three subdivisions of the form:

IA. According to this subdivision, only four-dimensional space–time regions are taken to be the individuals. "Things" are taken to be individuals, but "thing slices" are not. Carnap noted that this "choice is the simplest so long as sentences of the language are not expected to contain references to different time moments. (Such is the case, e.g., if assertions are to be made only about permanent properties of things, or if things are to be described only at a fixed instant of time, or during a given interval of time within which changes are to be ignored.)"

IB. In this subdivision, individuals are taken to be space–time regions of a definite but finite extent. "Things" and "thing slices" count as individuals, but not as space–time points. Carnap said that this form is "most convenient when we are content to speak of small but definite space–time regions instead of space–time points, yet wish—here departing from IA—to distinguish between various instants of time."

IC. Within this subdivision, all space–time regions, including space–time points, are taken as individuals. This language type undoubtedly has implications from a data modeling point of view, but it is not used in the current discussion.

Language Form IA is the language provided by current data management systems. The systems assume that descriptions of objects are static over time. For example, an account, having been declared, may always be considered apart from its previous and future states. When dealing with databases such as a data dictionary database, what is involved is clearly a type IB language. It should also be apparent from the cited examples that even in databases that have traditionally been regarded as type IA systems, any number of data modeling distortions (e.g., multityped relationships and relationship attributes) have been introduced. These have been introduced in order to deal with the fact that a type IA language is being used to deal with a type IB situation.

AVOIDING LEVEL CONFUSION

The distinction between Level n and Level $n+1$ data has long been recognized in the distinction between data and schema. Alterations to the schema cannot be undertaken lightly, as they imply that all of the "old" data has to be brought into a state in which it is consistent with the new schema. In the general case, it will not be possible for the system to allow such a change because the information necessary to transform the "old" data simply cannot be assumed to be available. It is largely as a result of these problems that the distinction has grown between data manipulation languages (DML) and data definition languages (DDL).

Database systems have accumulated whole collections of operations, grouped under the heading "reorganization," to allow some schema changes to take place. The handling of the schema change usually involves a series of ad hoc measures, the selection and implementation of which are dependent on specialist database administration personnel. This situation is not simply going to disappear: in fact, the types of applications covered in the current discussion are becoming more common. Therefore, any generalized solutions are well worth considering. Specifically of interest are situations in which it is possible to allow data at Level n to be freely modified, even when data at Level $n-1$ is present in the database.

One common feature of the databases that have been looked at is the idea of a structure. This usually takes the following form:

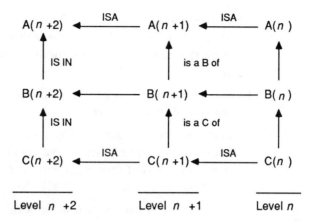

The A(n)'s are instances of the A($n+1$)'s; these in turn are instances of the A($n+2$)'s. The A ($n+2$) can be taken as defining the root of a structure. The Level $n+1$ objects can be taken as defining an instance of the pattern specified by the Level $n+2$ objects. The $n+1$ objects are themselves a schema and constitute an instance of the structure defined at Level $n+2$. The instances of the structure are at Level n.

The generalization hierarchy is an example of such a structure; returning to genus and species, we have the following:

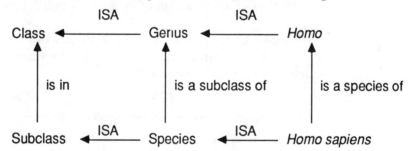

The generalization hierarchy is a good example of a structure; it provides a summary of the characteristics that distinguish a structure:

- The structure makes up a multicomponent entity.
- There are relationships among the components, which define the structure.
- The characteristics of the relationships define the characteristics of the structure as a whole. For example, if a relationship is universally required, the structure can only exist as a complete unit.

- The structure is a rooted tree. The root must always be present for the structure to be valid. An apparently optional root would merely indicate the presence of substructures that may exist in their own right.

- In accord with the preceding characteristic, structures may be composed of substructures.

- Operations on the top level (in the sense of the highest level present in the database system as a whole) cannot be controlled by the system because there is no structure pattern to use in controlling such operations.

- Modification to entities in middle levels of the structure may be allowed, provided that only internal attributes are affected ("internal" refers to context-dependent visibility, as mentioned previously).

- Deletion at Level n implies deletion of all entities at all levels lower than n (although entities shared among different structures present some thorny issues here).

- Creation at middle levels allows the possibility of creation at lower levels (and may, as in the case of the data dictionary, imply the creation of a default set of lower-level entities as well).

Although operations on the top level may not be controlled by the system, there is an interesting relationship between class and subclass, which may be presented as follows:

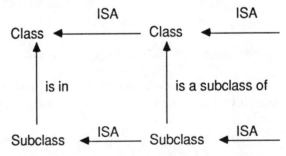

The class–subclass relationship is potentially self-referential, allowing the system at least to participate in analyzing itself and possibly even to participate in changing itself.

The existence of structures within most databases is difficult to avoid. As such, in considering the design of a particular database, it is essential to be aware of their existence. A two-level structure involving ISA relationships (i.e., a generalization hierarchy) can be dealt with by directly using the concepts of the SDM. Where there are more than two levels, or where the structural relationships are not ISA relationships, it will be the responsibility of those using and programming the database to ensure that the consistency of the data is properly maintained.

It is also possible to provide a partial solution to the problem of how to describe a structure in a semantic database, by using the concept of a dependent entity. The idea is that an entity's existence can be declared to depend on another entity (i.e., to be "existence dependent"); if the one entity disappears, then the other must as well. In the other direction, if the relevant attribute is required, the one entity must already exist before it is possible for the other entity to exist.

Taking the generalization hierarchy as an example of a structure, the "subclass-of" relationship is a dependent relationship. If the superclass is deleted, all the subclasses must disappear as well; if the subclass is inserted, all the superclasses must already have been inserted.

Some level of explicit representation of a structure may be achieved then through a simple attribute qualifier. Here, the word DEPENDENT is used and is taken to imply that if the associated attribute becomes null, the entity on the other end of the relationship should be deleted. Returning to ServiceDB, the relationship between "appliance" and "appliances" may be altered, as follows:

```
Class Appliance (
     Name           : String, Unique, Required;
     instances      : Appliances, MV, Dependent;
     );

Class Appliances (
     Serial-number
                    : Number (12), Required;
     Appliance-type
                    : Appliance, Required;
);
```

The implication of the DEPENDENT specification is that if the appliance "zakanaka" ever ceased to be supported, went out of production, and was no longer of any interest to the company, deletion of "zakanaka" from the class "appliance," would result as a side effect in the deletion of all "zakanaka" instances from the class "appliances."

Precisely the same considerations apply to relationship attributes, versions, and situations in which databases have multiple logical levels of data. Not all of the semantics of these situations can be captured using the DEPENDENT qualifier, but simply recognizing and stating the existence dependency will help enormously in designing and managing the database.

A DESIGN EXERCISE

The classification of life forms has already been considered. This section considers another area where paleontology has some fairly elaborate classification systems: the classification of time. It may be useful to consider how a database might be designed to incorporate information about the following:

- Classifications of life forms

- Individual species *(Tyrannosaurus rex)*

- Individual members of species (Specimen 1X.183, a member of the species *T. rex*)

- Locations where species, genera, etc., and individuals have been found

- Times in which species, genera, etc., and individuals have been found.

The design should be formulated on the assumption that all of the data is to go into a single database. The consequences of both adding individuals to classes (i.e., inserting) and deleting them from classes should be outlined and examples formulated using SDM diagrams. Note that because the diagrams make no real distinction between schema and data, it is possible to formulate both the kingdom–phylum hierarchy and the Animalia–Chordata type hierarchies in a single, consistent fashion. It should be remembered that the implications of such a formulation are beyond the capabilities of any existing commercial implementations of the SDM.

Just to limit the scope of the exercise somewhat, focus on providing diagrams that would allow for the formulation of the following queries ("retrieve*" means "retrieve everything"; the question usually is, "What would you get back?"):

From phylum, retrieve name, name of first-epoch

From Mammalia, retrieve name, where order of ancestor ISA primate

From *Homo sapiens*, retrieve* (*retrieve* means to retrieve all immediate and inherited attributes)

From species, retrieve*

From Primates, retrieve name, name of first-epoch, name of location of specimen,

where descendant of primate ISA *Homo*

From Primate, retrieve name, count(descendants)

From specimen, retrieve name of species, name of location

Something that should be evident from the design is that any attribute that is a partial mapping from one class to another defines a subclass in the range class. Any database is going to be positively thick with classes. The manipulation of any data should always be done with an eye to the metalevel consequences of the manipulation.

 # 10

On Orthodoxy

Isaac is sitting in the lobby reading something. Dasd walks by.

Cmmn.   Just look at this. What has the world come to? It can only be the work of a twisted soul. A spirit at war with itself.

Dasd.   Hi, Newton. What are you muttering about?

Cmmn.   Here. Read this:

> *Hylas.*   I am glad to find there is nothing in the accounts I heard of you.
>
> *Philonous.*   Pray what were those?
>
> *Hyla.*   You were represented in last night's conversation, as one who maintained the most extravagant opinion that ever entered into the mind of man, to wit, that there is no such thing as *material substance* in the world.
>
> *Phil.*   That there is no such thing as what Philosophers call *material substance*, I am seriously persuaded: but if I were made to see anything absurd or sceptical in this, I should then have the same reason to renounce this that I imagine I have now to reject the contrary opinion.

Hyl.   What! can anything be more fantastical, more repugnant to common sense, or a more manifest piece of scepticism, than to believe that there is no such thing as matter.

(G. Berkeley, *Three Dialogues between Hylas and Philonous*, 1713)

Cmmn.   And again. This is even worse.

Dasd.   What now?

Cmmn.   Here, look.

The plain consequence is (and it is a general maxim worthy of our attention), "That no testimony is sufficient to establish a miracle, unless the testimony be of such kind, that its falsehood should be more miraculous, than the fact, which it endeavours to establish; and even in that case there is a mutual destruction of arguments, and the superior only gives us an assurance suitable to that degree of force which remains after deducting the inferior." When anyone tells me that he saw a dead man restored to life, I immediately consider with myself, whether it be more probable, that this person should either deceive or be deceived, or that the fact which he relates, should really have happened. I weigh the one miracle against the other; and according to the superiority, which I discover, I pronounce my decision, and always reject the greater miracle. If the falsehood of his testimony would be more miraculous, than the event which he relates; then, and not until then, can he pretend to command my belief or opinion.

(Hume, *An Enquiry Concerning Human Understanding*, 1748, Ch.10)

Dasd.   Well, what are you so upset about?

Pscl and Meph enter.

Pscl.   Hey, Mephisto, here's a likely pair. Madame, Sir Isaac, Good day.

Meph.   Good day, all. Sir Isaac, you look as though you lost a guinea and found a penny.

Dasd.   Lost some innocence and found some experience perhaps. Have a good moan?

Cmmn.   Consider the implications of this passage.

Pscl.   Which is that?

Cmmn.   Here—have a look . . . the one by Hume. . . . His argument is this: If a man tells me something concerning some event I have not myself seen, then either I may believe what he tells me, or I may consider that he is mistaken. What I must do is balance the probability of the event described against the probability of the man being mistaken. Hume would then have us believe that if the event is one that I have not seen myself, and therefore may judge to be improbable, I should take it that it is more probable that the man is mistaken. I should take the man's account to be false.

Meph.   Sounds reasonable.

Cmmn.   But is it? Consider where it leads. Another way of stating the same position is in terms of authority versus the judgment of the individual. Essentially, the question is, do I believe what some individual tells me, even if it flies in the face of authority and established tradition? It seems to me that Hume's reply would be "No." By this argument, I am never allowed to progress beyond the restrictions of my immediate physical environment or beyond the intellectual restrictions of the prejudices and misconceptions of my fellow men.

Dasd.   Never mind your own prejudices.

Cmmn.   Precisely. For that matter, how often do our eyes deceive us? Should we, according to Hume, deny not only what others see but also what we see ourselves? It is a view that is simply not compatible with a full and meaningful existence in the world in which we live. Hume's denial of miracles is a blasphemous denial of the world around us—a denial of God—a view that can end only in cynicism and despair.

Meph.   Is it so bad though? Surely it is no more than a reflection of the need for orthodoxy. Merely one of life's little necessary evils . . .

Ivle.   Hello there. Did somebody call?

Dasd.   No, Ivan, you must have been hearing things.

Meph.   Orthodoxy—we are all subject to it in the end. We all contribute to it in the end. Even you, Sir Isaac. Let me tell you a story. There was once this man immersed in an attempt to come to an understanding of the world. He got hit on the head by an apple; this dislodged a thought in his mind that lead to a realm of understanding unimagined before. The secrets of the universe seemed to open up before the eyes of his contemporaries. The ideas that the Apple dislodged took on a life and an existence of their own and came to be the accepted and given truth to the people of the time. Does this sound familiar? But then, many years later, another Apple dropped; here, I happen to have an account of some of its consequences. Ah but wait, you may read it, but you must make a pact with me first. You must tell me honestly what you feel when you read it.

Cmmn.   Very well.

Meph.   Here it is.

Memorandum

There are two kinds of geometry—a geometry in the strict sense—the Euclidean; and an astral geometry.

Triangles in the latter have the property that the sum of their three angles is not equal to two right angles.

This being assumed we can prove rigorously:

a) That the sum of the three angles of a triangle is less than two right angles;

b) That the sum becomes ever less the greater the area of the triangle;

c) That the altitude of an isosceles right-angled triangle continually grows, as the sides increase, but it can never become greater than a certain length, which I call the Constant.

The Euclidean geometry hold only on the assumption that the Constant is infinite. Only in this case is it true that the three angles of every triangle are equal to two right angles: and this can easily be proved as soon as we admit that the Constant is infinite. (Schweikart in C. F. Gauss, *Werke*, Bd. VIII, pp. 180–181)

Meph. Well, tell me what did you feel?

Cmmn. As you say, we all contribute to Orthodoxy in the end. I find the ideas repulsive.

Dasd. Never mind, Newt. We all start with the best of intentions, even if we don't move things as far as we'd like, it's always worth having a try. Look at COBOL now. There's an orthodoxy if ever there was one. It started out as a great idea, liberating the world from the tyranny of assemblers. Making programs as easy to read as English, the universe renewed. Of course it was nothing like that. The people who designed COBOL knew that right from the word "GO." COBOL isn't the answer to even a small portion of the problems of making a machine usable, but it's a start. The terrible thing about it is that people have turned it into an orthodoxy. From being a liberation, it has become a trap. But you can't blame the people who designed it for that. It's the idiots that carry on using it when there are other better ways of doing things available. Worse yet are the people who deliberately suppress other better ways of doing things simply because they don't want to see the orthodoxy superseded.

Cmmn. Yes, we must all struggle to find our own balance and avoid bigotry where we can.

Ivle. I don't know, some of my best friends were bigots.

Meph. Orthodoxy still has its place, I feel. People need a sense of security; they like not to have to think too much.

Cmmn. Thought and decision are a part of the human condition.

Pscl. As is uncertainty, you know. In fact, it seems to me that we can measure the amount that something tells us simply by regard to how unlikely it is. If someone makes a statement about the world around us, such as "the sun will rise tomorrow," this seems reasonably certain, and as such, it doesn't really tell us very much. If someone makes the statement "there will be a total eclipse of the sun tomorrow," then we take notice. This is highly unlikely, and as such, it tells us a great deal; it puts far more knowledge at our disposal. If the same man should subsequently tell us that by the same principles, he has deduced that there will be a total eclipse of the moon tomorrow, we would be much inclined to believe him. He will have added a great deal to our knowledge of the world around us, unlike the man who tells us that the sun will rise tomorrow. The measure of the amount of knowledge involved is directly related to the improbability of the statements involved. What it amounts to is that increases in information content are only possible as a result of decreases in probability.

Cmmn.   So! It is by acts of faith that we come to know the world.

Meph.   Excuse me, I have an appointment with a couple of cherubs. Coming Ivan?

# 11

SDM (Semantic Data Model) Implementation

INTRODUCTION

This chapter describes some aspects of the implementation and use of a semantic database. The description is not meant to be so detailed that it could be used as a basis for actually building a semantic database management system. Rather, the description is meant to provide a basis for understanding the behavior and some of the features and limitations of such a system.

One of the main justifications for the use of an SDM is the fact that it allows the physical layers of the system to be separated from the logical ones. As such, this section can be omitted by those database users simply concerned with how to extract data from, or put data into, a semantic database. However, those concerned with the design or maintenance of a semantic database, or with designing high-performance, high-volume transaction systems, should be familiar with the issues covered here.

The discussion of the implementation of the model is in two parts: (1) a discussion of some of the basic internal features of the implementation of a semantic database, (2) a discussion of the implementation of a data processing environment using a semantic database.

Although it is reasonable to lump both of these under the "implementation" heading, they are actually two quite separate issues.

A fairly complete description has been provided of the characteristics and usage of an SDM. The model provides a good basis both for arriving at an understanding of an application area and for communicating this understanding to others. Up to this chapter, it has been important to avoid implementation issues, as these invariably cloud the understanding both of the model itself and of some particular use of the model.

At this point, it is desirable to introduce the idea of the database mapping hierarchy. There are multiple levels within the hierarchy. Each level is built on and uses those below it. At the bottom of the hierarchy are the primitives of the system—that is, the ultimate atomic operations—in terms of which all of the rest of the system can be described. The level above this aggregates the atomic operations into more complex operations, and so on up to the topmost level of the hierarchy.

The hierarchy is described in terms of access methods, objects accessed, and the data structures needed to support and control the objects and the accesses.

It is important to realize that in some sense, the atomic operations are not any less abstract than those at the top of the hierarchy. The following database mapping hierarchy does not reflect degrees of abstraction; it is concerned with implementation strategies:

Database Mapping Hierarchy

	Access Methods	Objects Accessed	Data Structures
1.	Saying what you want, rather then how to go about getting it	entities	logical schema description
2.	Programs doing Finds, Stores, Deletes, and so on. The programmer as navigator	records, sets, views, indexes, files	logical and physical schema description
3.	Manipulating variables internal to the data management software. Making sure that programs do not mess things up	physical records, access paths, cursors	free space tables, key tables, translation tables
4.	Lower-level data management variables, looking after the buffers	segments, pages	page tables, absolute disk addresses
5.	Operating system file management	files, blocks	system directories

The main advantage to be had from the use of the SDM is that it allows us, when concerned with the logical design of a database, to focus our attention purely on Level 1 of the mapping hierarchy. The problem with other models is that they collapse two or more levels together. For example, the relational model collapses Levels 1 and 2; the network and hierarchical models collapse Levels 1, 2, and 3.

An attempt to understand the relationship between the class "dinosaur," the species "*Tyrannosaurus rex*," and some individual of the species as found in some location is quite difficult enough. Attempting to understand this while visualizing how it may be stored in terms of disk addresses, record identifiers, field and record types, and other lower-level considerations is almost impossible. Precisely the same considerations apply to understanding CAD/CAM databases, data dictionaries, or even the appliance servicing system ServiceDB. It is vital to deal with the system one level at a time.

Once the description of Level 1 has been formulated and agreed upon, it is then possible to go on to the other layers of the system. The SDM then becomes an adequate basis for a complete and formal description of a data processing system. It can be used to describe the topmost layer of the system and then may be used as a means of controlling and coordinating the development of the other layers of the system. The model may be used both as a means to control the implementation of a system and as a basis for describing the data to be stored by the system. Even in the absence of a working semantic model that may be expected to handle many of the lower layers of the system automatically, a considerable benefit is to be derived from a familiarity with, and usage of, the concepts of the model.

It is well worth reiterating that all applications have semantics. The data must be meaningful if they are to be useful. It must be possible somewhere, and in some way, to be able to get what you want by simply stating what you want. In most systems, this statement of what you want may have to be made to a data processing clerk, or even to a systems analyst. But the fact remains that the topmost level of the system is always there. The difference between someone who has a working SDM and someone who does not is that the person who has the working model can usually rely on being able to satisfy an unusual request with a great deal less trouble. The person does not need quite so many people in the data processing department.

FUNDAMENTAL INTERNAL ISSUES

The problems posed by the implementation of a semantic model of data revolve around the representation of the following:

- Entities, mainly involving how an entity is to be identified
- Relationships
- Hierarchies, a special case of a 1:M relationship, where the presence of the relationship is always required on one end

- Attributes, especially complex types not supported by the underlying system, such as enumerated or symbolic types

- Query results and data to be applied to the database; some ideas from the theory of normalization are of interest here.

Note especially that it is not necessary for the data management system to provide all, or even most of the features of the model to make the model useful in the design and maintenance of an application built on the system. And all of these issues may have to be faced by any application regardless of the data model being used.

The model provides an explicit description of the characteristics of the data. For example, because "manager" ISA "employee," it is not reasonable to delete a (former) manager as "employee" if he is not also deleted as "manager" as well. These types of structural considerations are very difficult to detect, let alone describe accurately, without a good model of data. The point is though, that these considerations are still there. Whether it is recognized or not, the relationship between "manager" and "employee," if not properly maintained, will result in corruption of the database, ultimately rendering the database useless.

These types of relationships in nonsemantic databases end up being enforced by the programs that access the database. This may work, but in the absence of very carefully formulated system descriptions, whether or not it does work will probably be practically impossible to tell. The program can only be maintained if based on an adequate description of the underlying application; in this function particularly, an SDM may be invaluable, providing a basis on which a system may be maintained and understood.

A description of the strategies that might be used in implementing a semantic database is justified because of the following:

- Given an understanding of how to implement a semantic database, it is possible to use the model as a basis for designing and maintaining an application built on a nonsemantic data management system.

- The available implementations of the SDM may be used with existing systems. That is, the model may be used to provide a high-level view of an existing application built on a nonsemantic data management system. Using an SDM in this way implies a good understanding of which elements at the lower, physical levels, correspond to the structures present at the higher, logical, semantic level. How, for example, would one recognize a generalization hierarchy in a relational database?

- For the foreseeable future, there will be a need to understand the lower levels of the system. The hardware is limited in its capacities; the software and the hardware can be expected to fail periodically. The age of the kludge is not yet gone.

REPRESENTING ENTITIES

An entity is represented by an entity identifier. The entity identifier (sometimes referred to as a "surrogate") has some important properties and uses related to the issues discussed in Chapter 4, in the section "Problems with Record-Based Information Models":

- Given an entity identifier, it should be possible to locate an entity. That is, given an entity identifier, it should be possible to (efficiently) access the attributes of the entity.

- The entity identifier should either be read-only (i.e., not modifiable) so far as the user of the system is concerned or should not be visible at all. Because the identifier will occur wherever there is a reference to the entity (i.e., it may be scattered all over the database), the entity identifier cannot be changed.

Given these uses of the entity identifier, the following is clear:

- There must be some sort of index or other adequate access method associated with the identifier.

- The identifier must be reasonably small and compact, both to ensure a suitable basis for an index and to allow reasonably efficient use of the identifier as a foreign key.

- There is nothing preventing an entity from having several different identifiers, so long as there is no possibility of confusion among them.

- If the identifier is to be generated by the system, it must be possible to provide a new identifier in a reasonably efficient and secure manner. The implications of reusing identifiers are complex and extensive. If identifiers *are not* reused, an adequate "space" (such as the time to some level of precision) has to be found that is large enough and will not result in two entities being allocated the same identifier (there must be no possibility that the identifier will be allocated to two different entities).

- If it is possible to get duplicates during the process of allocating identifiers, the system must be able to detect this and keep trying until a unique identifier is obtained.

- If the identifier is to be provided by the user, the item must be required and there must be a 100%, cast-iron guarantee that the item will never change.

- If and *only* if an entity does *not* have *any* relationships to other entities, no entity identifier is required.

It is a function of the **insert** operation to ensure that all required attributes are supplied, including the surrogate. The **insert** operation must be able to generate the surrogate wherever appropriate.

There are two possible systematic approaches to establishing entity identifiers:

1. It is possible to have one surrogate per entity. Wherever a record exists that represents information about the entity, or wherever there is a relationship to the entity, the same value will be used in identifying the entity. This approach is not as self-evident as it seems. With an existing nonsemantic database, it is often not at all easy to decide which records belong to which entities. Different manifestations of the same entity may be labeled in quite different ways, depending on such factors as when the label becomes available (e.g., Social Security Number may not be known when an immigrant first arrives), user convenience (e.g., one department uses internal identifiers, others use some external standard identifier), and so on.

2. Have one surrogate per class per entity. Where an entity participates in more than one class, it will have one surrogate associated with it for each of the classes in which it participates. The easiest approach here is to have an additional field in the first type of surrogate, indicating the class type.

But things may not be as tidy as all that. When dealing with an existing nonsemantic database, it is necessary to examine the database for the existence of foreign keys. Anything that has been used as a foreign key is then a surrogate. This is a reasonable rule of thumb but not very practical in some cases. The problem is the number of different approaches that may be encountered in practice, which, of course, is at least a part of the justification for using an SDM in the first place. Some of the different approaches to implementing relationships, and their interpretation, are discussed in a later section of this chapter.

When dealing with an existing database, it is necessary to accommodate whatever schemes have been used in the evolution of the system over time. In practice, these often can only be fully understood by examining the programs that access and maintain the database. It is astonishing how complicated even so simple a thing as a 1:M (one-to-many) relationship may become. It is very easy for a large database to become quite unmanageable if careful control over such things as the implementation of relationships and entity identifiers is not exercised.

When designing a new schema, it is highly desirable to adopt a systematic approach to the implementation of entity identifiers *unless* the database (1) is unlikely to change, (2) is extremely simple, *and* (3) will not require an extensive programming effort.

Note: It is possible that a full implementation of entity identifiers will actually improve the efficiency of the database, especially where the database contains a reasonably large number of relationships. This is because the processes of entity maintenance can be confined to specially optimized code and data structures, which will have to be written anyway, even when taking an ad hoc approach. But with the ad hoc approach, the code is scattered around whatever other routines have to be supplied in order to access and maintain the data. This may be optimal for some short-term situations, but over time, it can be guaranteed either to deteriorate as the system changes or to cause the maintenance costs to be prohibitive.

The Class Entities

Surrogates may be understood from a data modeling point of view—that is, from the point of view of the SDM. When implemented with one surrogate per entity, what is being provided is a representation of the class of all the entities explicitly stored in the database.

An alternative view of this is the fact that all generalization hierarchies terminate in one root class: the class of entities. Returning to the subclass–superclass relationship, the class X is said to be a subclass of the class Y if every member of the class X is also a member of the class Y (it should also be the case that not every Y is an X, or Y and X are just the same). For the class "entities," everything that participates in a class is an entity, and every entity, by definition, is an entity; therefore, every class is a subclass of the class "entities."

What then are the attributes of the class "entities"?

Obviously, surrogate must be one attribute, but there are a number of other possibilities that serve to underline the algorithms necessary to handle the creation and deletion of entities. The following attributes are likely to be stored in a single record representing the entity:

- Surrogate (must be a value suitable for use as a record identifier—its characteristics have already been outlined)

- Creation time stamp (marking the time at which the entity was created)

- Reference count (the number of required relationships that range over this entity)

- Subclass information (map indicating which classes the entity participates in).

A more complete account of the interpretation of a surrogate may be provided by representing the class "entities" as a class, rather than just indicating what might be provided in a minimal record layout to support it. The following diagram illustrates the class "entities":

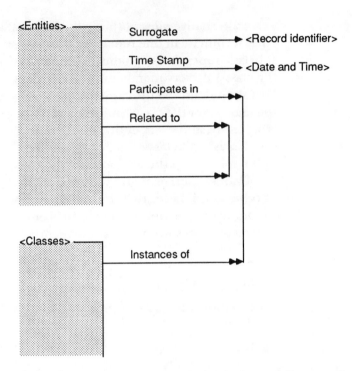

In data modeling terms, the class "entities" actually contains a representative of everything in the entire database. Each thing in the database may be "related-to" other things in the database (via entity-valued attributes—EVAs). Each thing in the database will "participate-in" one or more classes—that is, it will be an "instance-of" the class.

The "related-to" and the "participates-in" relationships lie at the heart of any database, not just a semantic database. They are essential to the integrity and maintenance of the database, but almost invariably they are not explicitly represented. Nor is it necessarily desirable that they should be. Two key points to recognize are that (1) entities are instances of classes, and (2) they have relationships to other entities. And most of the data in the database is concerned with just these facts.

The ability to manipulate entities based on being able to label them is fundamental to the SDM. It leads to an architecture that allows great flexibility for the model in terms of the types of data it can manipulate and the types of data management systems it can handle.

There are two obvious consequences here. First, an SDM lends itself to use with nonstandard types of data. For example, provided that a graphic image can be labeled, it is possible to establish relationships to it. Therefore, it is possible for it to have attributes, and it may participate in a hierarchy. If suitable operations are provided for the manipulation of the image, given that the image can be labeled, it may even be possible to **insert, delete,** and **modify** images using precisely the same syntax as is used for the manipulation of ordinary accounting information. It is not necessary for the database to be able to actually store the image itself; all it needs is a reliable label and the rest follows.

A second consequence of the flexibility of semantic databases is their ability to provide a way of looking at other database systems. In a data management environment where a number of different database management systems are in use, the SDM allows the environment to be unified. All databases can be viewed as semantic databases. A single well-defined approach is provided for the manipulation of data regardless of how it was originally established. Thus, an environment that contains relational, hierarchical, and network-based database management systems can be enormously simplified.

The reason why a semantic database may be successful in a heterogeneous environment is best understood in terms of the ANSI/SPARC three-layered architecture:

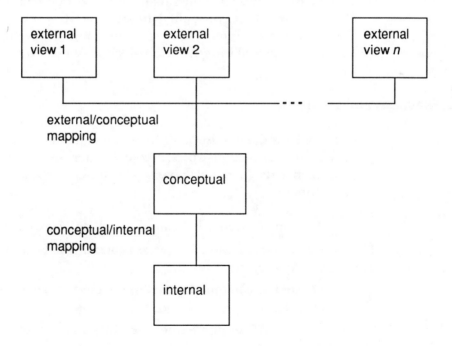

The SDM provides the conceptual layer of the system. The internal layer is provided by whatever data management facilities are available in the environment in which the system as a whole is implemented. The external layer is provided by the application or by whatever tailored user environments exist on the system. The SDM is rich enough and general enough to act as a superset of other data models. If the system is implemented appropriately, and if an appropriate internal– conceptual interface is provided, a semantic database can be built on top of any data management system that offers a reasonable implementation of relationships.

The advantages of this are enormous. It means that it is possible for a user of an SDM both to move to a better and more sophisticated database management system and to preserve existing systems within the new environment. This, of course, assumes that a working, appropriately implemented SDM is available. In any event, an appreciation of the potential advantages of the model may help in understanding some of the design decisions implied by the current description of the implementation of the model.

The external layer is the subject of the second half of this chapter. The features of the conceptual–internal interface is the subject of the first half of this chapter. The chapter on tuning and performance is also largely concerned with the internal layers of the system.

Functions and Entities

Throughout the discussion of the implementation of the system, it is assumed that functions will be provided, where necessary, to access and maintain data in the database. The functions will always use the following:

- An entity identifier indicating which entity is to be operated on
- One or more input parameters containing data to be used in entity selection or entity update
- One or more output parameters to be used in returning data about entities
- A result indicating whether the function was successful.

This type of approach (hiding the implementation details from the user) will be true either in the case of a full implementation of the model or in the case of a nonsemantic data management system. It is essential that the characteristics of entities be hidden from the users of the database. In this way, the complications of the representation of the entities inside the database may be hidden, and the usage and maintenance of the entities can be reliable.

REPRESENTING DATA-VALUED ATTRIBUTES (DVAS)

Representing attributes that resolve to types supported by the underlying system is not a problem. But in most other cases, the attribute will range over a class of more complex objects and will require an abstract type to allow access to it. This involves a function (as described in the previous section) that may be called to manipulate the attribute and that will be responsible for the details of attribute storage and maintenance.

This concept of an abstract type fits in very well with the entity orientation of the SDM. The types of data that may be manipulated and described by the model are only limited by prohibiting data for which it is not possible to define (1) a label, and (2) an abstract type. The label is essential to using the instances of the type as entities; the abstract type is essential to using the type as the range of an attribute.

For example, to adequately integrate the manipulation of graphic images into a semantic database, it would be necessary to be able to label them. Having labels, they can be stored as entities. To allow graphic images to be used as attribute values, it must be possible to manipulate them, compare them for equality, delete or insert them, and so on. Given the ability to manipulate an object (or more accurately the characteristics of an object), the graphic image can be used as an attribute value—that is, as the range for an EVA (entity-valued attribute). Remember that a type must be an "outputtable" object: the concept is deliberately not confined to a "printable" object. Any output device will do, line printers and graphics processing systems being considered equals in this respect.

Traditionally, DVAs (data-valued attributes) are considered to range over types rather than over classes. This, however, is an implementation consideration, as it relates both to the way in which the members of the class are represented and (in some cases) to the way in which the members of the class are to be accessed.

Classes that are represented by types (such as the classes of "integers," "reals," and "strings of length 2") are always classes the members of which are in some sense self-identifying. That is, some particular member of the class is a simple atomic object the minimal description of which says everything about it that we need to know. For example, the number 124 is an integer and represents a particular value. It is not ordinarily necessary for us to be told that it is equal to

$$1 \times 10^2 + 2 \times 10^1 + 4 \times 10^0$$

and that it is an integer, that it is divisible by 4, and so on.

Classes that can be represented by a simple atomic object are essential to the working of a database, because ultimately the data has to be stored in a form that, in this sense, "stands for itself," that needs no further description. These kinds of classes are usually distinguished by the term *type*.

TYPES

A type is a system-supported class. The following two assumptions underlie a type as defined within the model:

1. There is some formula that allows instances of the type to be recognized. This means that it is not necessary to store all possible instances of the type. Recall that there are two possible techniques for defining a class (i.e., by intension or extension—by describing the class or by listing its members, respectively). Types are classes that can be described to the system with sufficient accuracy that the system can always recognize something as either being or not being a member of the class. An explicit list of the members of the class is not required.

2. The representation of an instance of the type encapsulates all the relevant characteristics of the instance, given the type. Given that you are dealing with a number, the symbol "19" tells you everything you need to know about it. This is of course only true given that the number base may be assumed and that no units of measurement are involved. Issues such as these become relevant once semantics have been infused into the system.

Primitive Types

The primitive types that have to be recognized by the system must include the following:

- Character
- Real
- Boolean

Given a few other assumptions, real and Boolean types may be seen as subclasses of the type "character"—not a view to be recommended when talking about the implementation of the system! Reverting to the definition of a type though, a type should specify both a set of values and an associated set of operations, which take the set of values as their domain. The utility of distinguishing "character," "real," and "Boolean" is based on the fact that different operators apply to them.

Within these types ("character" and "real," at any rate), it is useful to make further subdivisions on the basis of the meaning of the sets of values. Here, we return to the Pascal language's idea of a user-defined type, and the associated concepts of type compatibility. It is possible to declare user-defined types, using "character," "real," and "Boolean" as a basis. Note that the Pascal-based idea of a record disappears, and it is replaced in the SDM by the class hierarchy.

Most systems of course recognize a number of types beyond just "Boolean," "character," and "real." One may also expect to see "string" and "integer," as well as any number of other more complex structured types such as "queues," "lists," and "arrays." Again, note that the different types are distinguishable largely on the basis of the operations that may be performed on them.

Subtypes

Types may be structured into hierarchies in a way similar to the structuring of classes into generalization hierarchies. Types may be declared as a base type such as the following:

```
TYPE Ages   = INTEGER;
```

Types can then be declared as related to a user-defined type (**note:** the

<integer>..<integer> notation denotes a subrange, as in PSL; "maxint" means "maximum integer value"), as follows:

```
TYPE Teenage      = Ages 13..19;
TYPE Adult  = Ages 20..Maxint;
TYPE Middle-age   = Adult 40..59;
TYPE Old-age      = Adult 60..Maxint;
```

In a similar way to the class hierarchy, the type hierarchy can be arranged into a directed graph; in the following case, the graph is a simple rooted tree:

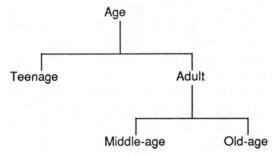

Constructed Types

A variety of other types are found in programming languages based on the aforementioned "character," "real," "Boolean" (and "record") types, such as the following:

- Complex numbers
- Lists
- Queues
- Arrays
- Sets
- Strings

All of these types can be constructed from the types mentioned already. The precise mechanisms used to construct the types are related to mechanisms associated with attributes. Accordingly, these types are considered along with their attributes.

For the moment it is sufficient to note that the types are usually characterized by a set of associated operations that allow variables to be manipulated in various ways. The potential for complexity here is practically limitless; in some cases, entire languages have been established for the manipulation of a particular type. For example, APL ("a programming language") was developed for handling matrices, SNOBOL for handling strings, and, of course, LISP ("list processor") for handling lists.

REPRESENTING RELATIONSHIPS

Wherever there is a relationship to an entity, there should be some assurance that the consistency of the relationship will be maintained. When an attempt is made to delete some entity from the database, one of a number of different things may happen:

- If the relationship has no other constraints on it, the system may then "fix" up the other end of the relationship as a part of the entity **delete** operation.

- The **delete** operation may be disallowed—if, for example, the relationship is required or will cause some other constraint to be violated.

- The **delete** operation may just be ignored, so far as any referencing entities are concerned. In this case, the system makes the assumption that it is possible to fix up the relationship if some subsequent traversal reveals that the referenced entity has been deleted. This is only possible if the relationship is not required.

There are a number of possible strategies so far as maintaining relationships is concerned:

- The existence of the relationship may not always be obvious to all of the parties involved, so the relationship may be maintained in such a way that it is reasonable to traverse the relationship in order to determine whether it exists or not. For example, if a foreign key is used, then a foreign key might be maintained on both ends of the relationship, allowing the existence of the relationship to be readily detected.

- A count of the number of references may be maintained. If the entity is deleted and the number of references is zero, no traversals are required. If this is the normal case, it may be possible to implement the relationship in such a way that the traversal is expensive (in terms of time and/or effort), on the assumption that it will not have to be done too often.

- The relationship may be maintained in such a way that there is only one thing that represents the relationship (typically a record). For the entity to be deleted, all such records may then be deleted (or modified) before the deletion of the entity itself.

Maintaining relationships is an extremely complex business and comprises a substantial portion of the code that has to be written in order to implement a (nonsemantic) database.

As illustrated, the types of maintenance necessary for a relationship very much depend on the type of the relationship itself. Various possibilities may be allowed or precluded by the type of the relationship, whether it is required, many-to-many (M:M), and so on. Therefore, it is important to be aware of the different ways in which relationships may be categorized, some of the more important ways being the following:

Cardinality
     1:1
     1:M
     M:M

Presence
     Required both ends
     Required one end
     Not required

Direction
     Traversable both ways
     Traversable one way

Random access
     To the objects on both ends
     To the objects on one end
     To the objects on neither end

Dependency
>   One entity cannot exist without the other
>   The entities are independent of each other

There are therefore at least $3 \times 3 \times 2 \times 3 \times 2$ (or 108) possible types of relationship; many of these imply quite distinct implementations. In many cases, for a given relationship type, there are a number of possibilities. In all cases, the implementation possible for a relationship can only be formulated in terms of a full description of the characteristics of the relationship. Particularly, just the cardinality of the relationship is not enough. In the following sections, implementation strategies for some of the 108 possible relationship types are described in some detail. These are only provided as a reasonable sample of the approaches that might be used.

In what follows, data structures and, where necessary, algorithms are provided for some of the more important combinations. The examples use sequential, direct, and random structures. These may be spanned by any number of random or index-sequential indexes. Direct and random structures declare an *access*, which is a syntactical device used to indicate the keys to be used in accessing the structure (for a detailed description of the characteristics of these structure types, see the chapter on performance).

One-to-One (1:1) Relationships

BOTH ENDS REQUIRED; ACCESS FROM ONE END ONLY

For "person" and "address," every person must have an address, and an address can only be associated with a person; that is, there is no way to represent an address without a corresponding person.

```
Employee Sequential File OF
     Record
     Emp-Number      : 1..9999999;
     . . .
     Emp-Address     :
          Record
          Addr-Street: string [1..20];
          Addr-town  : string [1..20];
          Addr-Code  : string [1..20];
          End;
Employee-by-Number Random Index OF Employee
     Key is Emp-Number;
```

In the preceding example, the employee's address is embedded as a subrecord inside the record for the employee. "Access from one end only" implies that access will only be via the employee. That is, it will be possible only to retrieve the address when given an employee number, not the employee number for a given addresss.

The example may appear to be a trifle odd, as the address looks like an attribute, not a relationship. But that is precisely the point; an attribute *is* a relationship, or at least one half of a relationship. The other half of the relationship is the inverse attribute in the class to which the attribute points.

ONE END REQUIRED; RANDOM ACCESS FROM BOTH ENDS

In this example, for "employee" and "address," it is desired to know either the address at which a given employee lives or the employee living at an address.

```
Employee Sequential File OF
     Record
     Emp-Number      : 1..9999999;
     . . .
     Emp-Address     :
          Record
          Addr-Street: string [1..20];
          Addr-town :  string [1..20];
          Addr-Code :  string [1..20];
          End;

Employee-by-Number Random Index OF Employee
     Key is Emp-Number;

Emp-By-Address Index-Sequential Index OF Employee
     Key is Emp-Address;
```

The access via the address is provided by simply making "address" a key for an index. It is important to realize that an index represents a relationship in its own right. The relationship is between the key item values and the things in the file that the index spans. When going from a thing to its attributes, given a thing of type "person," it is possible to find out the person's "name." When going from an attribute to its things, given a thing of type "string," it is possible to find out what "person" has that "string" as "name." The point is that a name is a thing just as much as a person is, and it, too, has relationships.

It is worth noting that the "emp-by-address" arrangement is very inefficient. It wastes space because all of the address information is duplicated in the "emp-by-address" index, and address is far too large an item to be used as a key (unless of course there is no other choice!). It would be far better to use some portion of the address if possible. In the United Kingdom, for example, the postal code is unique to the street level and so on its own would provide a reasonably efficient technique for accessing the address. In the U.S., nine-digit zip codes do the same.

Another alternative would be to separate the address items into another file. The file would be a random file, with address as the access to the file. In this way, the records disk address (i.e., location on the magnetic media) could be computed from the postal address. Given a postal address, it would be possible to access the record efficiently. The file could then have a foreign key relationship back to the original "employee" file.

Random Access Required in Both Directions

In this example, for "department" and "manager," a manager can only manage one department, and a department can only be managed by one manager. It is also necessary to be able to go both from department to manager and from manager to department:

```
Employee Random File OF
    Record
    Emp-Number   : 1..9999999;
    Manager      : Boolean;
    Managed-Dept : 1..99999;
    . . .
    End;

Employee-by-Number Access OF Employee
    Key is Emp-Number;
```

```
Department Random File OF
    Record
    Dept-Number    : 1..99999;
    Managed-by     : 1..9999999;
    . . .
    End;

Department-By-Number Access OF Department
    Key is Dept-Number;
```

Here, the two-way relationship is provided by storing a relevant foreign key on both ends. In SDM terms, there are two relationships one being the inverse of the other.

ONE END REQUIRED; RANDOM ACCESS FROM NONREQUIRED END

In this example, for "person" and "name," every person must have a name (though every name does not have to have a person), and a name is a string of characters.

```
Employee Sequential File OF
    Record
    Emp-Name       : string [1..30];

    End;
Emp-By-Name Sequential Index OF Employee
    Key is Emp-Name;
```

A major difference from the previous two examples is that "employee" has no employee number. Unless "name" is used as the employee record identifier, it is not possible to have any relationships to employee.

Note that in both this and the previous three cases, the relationships are assumed to be 1:1. In the case of "department" and "manager," this seems reasonable. But in the other two examples, this means that no two employees live at the same address and that no two employees have the same name. Neither assumption seems very reasonable. The relationships between "person" and "address" and between "person" and "name" are both likely to be 1:M; there will be more than one person living at a given address and there will be more than one person with a given name. Another way of putting this is that "address" and "name" are nonunique attributes. The only item seen so far that is likely to be unique is the employee number, and it is often the case that an item such as the employee number has to be invented just to identify the entity. The existence of such items tends to muddy the waters when it comes to answering the question of what constitutes an entity. Entity identifiers should be specified after the entity has been determined. All too often, this is not the case.

When dealing with duplicate identifiers, such as employee names, recall that the word "duplicates" after the key allows duplicate entries in the index-sequential index.

A number of these examples may strain the imagination somewhat so far as the capabilities of the file management system are concerned. Nonetheless, there are systems capable of supporting all of the features mentioned here.

One-to-Many (1:M) Relationships

RANDOM ACCESS NOT REQUIRED ON THE MANY END

For "employee: and "dependents," it is assumed that a "dependent" is not also an "employee."

```
Employee Sequential File
    Record
    Emp-Number    : 1..9999999;
    . . .
    Dependents Sequential File
        Record
        Dep-Name  : string [1..30];
        . . .
        End;
    End;

Employee-by-Number Random Index OF Employee
    Key is Emp-Number;
```

In this example, one file is embedded inside another. Each record of the master file owns any number of records of the embedded file. Random access to the master file is possible, but to the embedded file, it is difficult if not impossible.

This is typical of hierarchical data management systems. It assumes not just that the embedded structure cannot be accessed randomly, but also that the embedded structure is unlikely to have any relationships to anything other than its master record; in practice, this assumption is frequently very unrealistic. Most hierarchical systems have to compromise in this respect and allow pointers of some sort to the embedded records; this inevitably leads to complications in the software, which is oriented toward the maintenance of a strict hierarchy in which access can only be via the root of the hierarchy.

The implications are particularly serious from the point of view of the need for consistency. Assuming that multiple simultaneous accesses to a file are allowed, the following might occur: One process may access an embedded record, accessing it directly and bypassing the root. At the same time, if some other process accesses the root and attempts to delete it, or to drastically modify it, the software will have to have any amount of special code built into it in order to sort out the resulting mess. An alternative to that is for the software to have to always assume that there may be accesses going on to any record in the hierarchy and search the entire hierarchy any time any reference to the hierarchy is made—in which case it is no longer a hierarchy!

Another version of this is the following:

```
Employee Sequential File
    Record
    Emp-Number     : 1..9999999;
    . . .
    Dependents     : array of
        Record
        Dep-Name : string [1..30];
        . . .
        End;
    End;

Employee-by-Number Random Index OF Employee
    Key is Emp-Number;
```

The array (or in COBOL terms, "occurring item") allows multiple items to be stored together with some master record. Logically speaking, it is very similar to an embedded file, although the implementation is quite different.

This, along with any other scheme that involves multiple occurrences of an item being associated with a single record, violates the relational model's first normal form. That this type of arrangement is disallowed by the model is curious, especially in the light of examples such as the following (this example uses the Pascal idea of a set wherein a range of distinct values may be assumed by an attribute, each value being just an identifier):

```
Employee Sequential File
    Record
    Emp-Number    : 1..9999999;
    . . .
    External-activities : Set OF
                    {Golf, Tennis, Squash, Handball};
    End;

Employee-by-Number Random Index OF Employee
    Key is Emp-Number;
```

The point is that it is possible for "external-activities" to include both "tennis" and "squash." The attribute is multivalued (MV). The relational model would require that "external-activities" be placed in a separate file that could be joined with the "employee" file, using a foreign key. This is not based on some puristic objection to violations of first normal form. It is mandated by the operations of the model. The relational model simply does not have operations that can deal with an MV object such as "external-activities." The SDM does recognize that "external-activities" fundamentally is a relationship, but with the SDM, this is just turned into an attribute, and all attributes can be manipulated in a uniform fashion.

The relational model is more properly confined to Level 2 of the mapping hierarchy; it is unreasonable to expect it to be applicable to the operations and data structures characteristic of Level 1.

RANDOM ACCESS REQUIRED ON THE MANY END

In this example, for "employee" and "department," an employee may work in only one department, but a department may have many employees.

```
Employee Random File OF
    Record
    Emp-Number    : 1..9999999;
    Dept-Number   : 1..99999;
    . . .
    End;

Employee-by-Number Access OF Employee
    Key is Emp-Number;

Department Random File OF
    Record
    Dept-Number   : 1..99999;
. . .
    End;

Department-by-Number Access OF Department
    Key is Dept-Number;
```

The preceding is the typical foreign key arrangement. The relationship is traversable in one direction only—that is, from "employee" to "department." Given an employee number, it is possible to look up the appropriate employee record, extract the department number, and then look up the department record. Given a reasonable data management system, this should involve no more than two I/Os.

By contrast, to find all of the employees that work for a given department would require that every record in the employee file be read. This may be acceptable for some types of batch applications but it would not be acceptable for an on-line system in which a large number of employees are involved.

RANDOM ACCESS REQUIRED IN BOTH DIRECTIONS

Here, as in the previous example, an employee may work in just one department; a department may have many employees working in it.

```
Employee Random File OF
    Record
    Emp-Number    : 1..9999999;
    Dept-Number   : 1..99999;
    . . .
    End;

Employee-by-Number Access OF Employee
    Key is Emp-Number;

Emp-By-Dept Index-Sequential Index OF Employee
    Key is Dept-Number, Duplicates;

Department Random File OF
    Record
    Dept-Number   : 1..99999;
    . . .
    End;

Department-by-Number Access OF Department
    Key is Dept-Number;
```

In this case, it must be possible to gain access in both directions: from "employee" to "department" and from "department" to "employee." This access is provided by the simple device of adding an extra index on the employee file, with duplicate entries allowed in the index.

The traversal from the employee file to the department file works as in the previous case of the simple foreign key. For the traversal from the department file to the employee file, given a department number, it is not necessary to access the department. The department number may just be used to access the employee file via the "emp-by-dept" index. Successive **find** operations on this will return all of the relevant entries in the employee file (hence the reason for it being index-sequential rather than random; it must be possible to efficiently "find next" on it).

Note that the word "duplicates" must follow the key for the index-sequential index in order to allow duplicates therein.

It is interesting to compare the operations necessary to maintain the "department managed by" relationship with the "department employs" relationship. To make an employee the manager of a department requires a modification to both the department and the employee record. But to assign an employee to a department just requires a modification to the employee record, assuming that the data management system automatically maintains the indexes. The number of I/Os (input–output operations) then is likely to be the same, but the programming effort involved is considerably greater. Also both relationships are traversable in both directions, but in the case of the relationship from department to employee, a traversal will involve an extra I/O to the index prior to the access to the employee record.

Many-to-Many (M:M) Relationships

ACCESS IN ONE DIRECTION ONLY

In this example, for "department" and "location," a department may use many locations, and a given location may be used by many departments (i.e., they have a many-to-many [M:M] relationship). However, it is assumed that it is never necessary to go from location to department.

```
Department Random File OF
    Record
    Dept-Number    :      1..99999;
    . . . .
    Dept-Location Partial Index-Sequential Index OF
        Locations;
    End;

Department-by-Number Access OF Department
    Key is Dept-Number;

Locations Sequential File OF
    Record
    . . . .
    End;
```

A previous example illustrated a case in which a file was embedded inside another file. This example shows an index embedded inside a file, in which the index spans some file other than the file in which it is embedded (although this need not be the case). Recall that with the embedded file, a given record in the master structure owns any number of *records* in the embedded *structure*. With the embedded index, a given record in the master structure owns any number of *references* in the embedded *index*. Duplicates are not allowed for a given master record, but they are allowed within the sets of references as owned by different masters.

This type of arrangement is typical of the network data model. In the network model, the database is presented as a series of cross-connected files, the connections being provided by embedded indexes. In the network model, these are referred to by the rather confusing term, "set."

In this implementation of the "department" record, a given master record may have references to any number of "locations," and a given "location" may have any number of references to it.

In this case, the cost of traversal from the nonoptimal end is prohibitive. A process to traverse from "location" to "department" would have to go through each department record, traversing each of the "location" relationships to see whether the relevant location was returned. The number of I/Os would be the number of records in the department file multiplied by the number of records in the locations file!

ACCESS REQUIRED AT BOTH ENDS

```
Department Random File OF
     Record
     Dept-Number     : 1..99999;
     . . .
     End;

Department-by-Number Access OF Department
     Key is Dept-Number;

Locations Random File OF
     Record
     Loc-Number    : 1..999;
     . . .
     End;

Location-by-Number Access OF Locations
     Key is Loc-Number;

Dept-Loc Sequential File OF
     Record
```

```
    Dept-Number     : 1..99999;
    Loc-Number      : 1..999;
    End;

Dept-to-Loc Index-Sequential Index OF Dept-Loc
    Key is (Dept-Number,Loc-Number);

Loc-to-Dept Index-Sequential Index OF Dept-Loc
    Key is (Loc-Number,Dept-Number);
```

This exemplifies the typical intersection file, a structure that is more or less unavoidable if an M:M relationship is to be provided. What it actually consists of is two 1:M relationships between "department" and "location."

Note that there is an assumption that it is possible to access the index without accessing the file itself, which is the reason for including both identifiers in both indexes. Given this assumption, it is only necessary to access the file when creating a relationship, not when traversing it. As a result, an access via this structure is no more expensive than an access via a directly spanning index, as in the previous example. The price is paid at the time of **insert** and **delete** operations, when a number of extra I/Os are required.

The M:M relationship can also be expressed in terms of the entity–relationship model:

Removing the bit in the middle

This leaves an M:M relationship. In a file-based system, however, it is not possible to represent a M:M relationship directly; it must always be represented as two 1:M relationships.

For example, consider the following alternative approach to the "department"–"location" relationship:

```
Department Random File OF
    Record
    Dept-Number   : 1..99999;
 .  .  .  .
    Dept-Location Partial Index-Sequential Index OF
        Locations;
    End;

Department-by-Number Access OF Department
    Key is Dept-Number;

Locations Sequential File OF
    Record
    .  .  .  .
    Location-Dept Partial Index-Sequential Index OF
        Department;
    End;
```

Again the M:M "department"–"location" relationship can be provided as a two-way relationship by providing two 1:M relationships. When viewed from the perspective of the code required to maintain the relationships, it is difficult to maintain the fiction that these are a single relationship. When inserting the relationship, accesses have to be performed to both ends, and updates may have to be performed to four different file structures.

Many-to-many relationships have a rather dubious formal status. A pure functional model, for example, does not support them, as the theory of functions only allows 1:1 and 1:M relationships.

A Generalized Approach

The greatest problem in the implementation of 1:M or M:M relationships tends to be the proliferation of files needed to represent the relationships. Effectively, if directly spanning indexes are used, as in the examples above, there will be at least one file per relationship, with three files per M:M relationship.

Even in a relatively small database, this is likely to be unacceptable; fortunately, the "one file per relationship" approach is quite unnecessary. The following set of files may be used to implement almost any 1:1, 1:M, or M:M relationship, and they may be used for any number of such relationships:

```
Relations Sequential File OF
    Record
    Relation-Number          : 1..9999;
    Identifier-1             : 1..Max-Integer;
    Identifier-2             : 1..Max-Integer;
    End;

Relations-By-1 Index-Sequential Index OF Relations
    Key is (
        Relation-Number,
        Identifier-1,
        Identifier-2
        );

Relations-By-2 Index-Sequential Index OF Relations
    Key is (
        Relation-Number,
        Identifier-2
        Identifier-1
        );
```

Each type of relationship must be allocated an identifying number, and the relationship traversal may be performed using the following routine:

```
Type
        Surrogate                = 1..Maxint;
        Relation-number          = 1..9999;
        Directions               = {1to2,2to1} ;

Var
        Direction                : Array {Relation-number}
                                   OF Directions

Surrogate Function Traversal (
    Relation-id : Relation-number;
    Id-1        : Surrogate;
    Id-2        : Surrogate      ) ;
Begin
```

```
    If Direction[relation-number] = 1to2 then
        Begin
        find Relations-by-1 at
            Relation-number = Relation-id and
            Identifier-1 = Id-1 and
            Identifier-2 GTR Id-2;
        If NotFound
            Traversal := Null
        Else
            Traversal := Identifier-2;
        End
Else
        Begin
        find Relations-by-2 at
            Relation-number = Relation-id and
            Identifier-2 = Id-1 and
            Identifier-1 GTR Id-2;
        End;
        If NotFound
            Traversal := Null
        Else
            Traversal := Identifier-1;
        End;
End;
```

The caller of the function supplies both the surrogate of the domain class entity in Id-1, and the last returned surrogate in Id-2, or, if this is the first call, Id-2 should be zero. The function returns either the surrogate for the range class entity as the function value or null if there are no more instances of the relationship.

"Directions" is an array that indicate the direction that has to be used in traversing each relationship type. For each relationship, it will be necessary to go either from Id-1 to Id-2 or from Id-2 to Id-1. Which is to be used for a particular case is arbitrary.

"Directions" is required on the assumption that it is not possible to have more than one index entry per file record. If the file key could be an array of items in a record, allowing, in this case, two items for each record, a single index might suffice for the generalized relationship mechanism.

The approach also has the interesting property that it is possible to add and delete relationships more or less at will. Provided that the "directions" array can be handled dynamically and a relationship number can be allocated in a sensible fashion, relationships can be allocated "on the fly" (i.e., by the user, while using the database), with very little cost to the system as a whole.

REPRESENTING HIERARCHIES

Hierarchies are a special case of a 1:M relationship, whereby one end of the relationship is always required, and the relationship may actually be a group of "related" relationships.

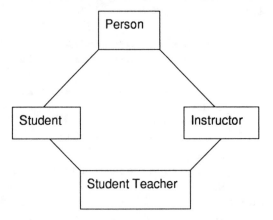

The preceding diagram depicts a class, "person," with subclasses "instructor" and "student," which in turn share a subclass, "student teacher." The relationship between "student" and "person" is not the same as the relationship between "instructor" and "person." It might be specified, however, that a "person" cannot be both a "student" and an "instructor," thereby establishing a connection between the two relationships (and making "student teachers" an impossibility!). This recalls the anomalies surrounding the subrole concept. It also serves to underline the usefulness of the concept; it is very convenient to be able to state constraints, such as the preceding one, in terms of subroles. The same could be accomplished using "verifies" and the ISA function, but the semantics would not be as obvious.

The subrole is also useful as a guide to the type of representations that may be used for the hierarchy containing the subrole. For example, it may permit the use of *variant records* (such as those in Pascal, which allow a particular record to be one of a number of variant types). It is usually the case that the variant may itself have variants. It is also usually the case that a given instance of a record may not participate in more than one variant at the same time. For example, if a record may be Type 1, 2, or 3, a given record may not be both Type 1 and Type 3.

Given a semantic database that has to be mapped to a file system supporting this type of representation, if each subclass in a hierarchy is to be mapped to a record variant, with the base class mapped to the base record, it must be the case that all of the subroles in the hierarchy are single valued (SV). It actually would be possible to concoct combinations of record items for each of the possible combinations of inherited class attributes, but the number of variant records would very rapidly get quite out of hand.

Where subroles are multivalued (MV), it is usually necessary to map hierarchies to multiple files with one file per SV subrole hierarchy segment. It also may be possible to map subroles to records that support arbitrary configurations of items, the records containing item directories indicating how the record is to be interpreted. These types of records, however, are unusual and not typical of the record concept as used in this book.

Therefore, from a practical point of view, there are only three approaches available for the implementation of a hierarchy. The viability of these approaches depends heavily on the types of structures supported by the underlying database.

1. A record may be used that contains the union of all the data-valued attributes (DVAs) present in the hierarchy; many items in such a record may be null. The record will have to contain an item capable of indicating which classes the associated entity participates in.

2. As mentioned, variant records may be used where (a) they are provided and (b) the hierarchy does not allow an entity to participate in more than one class at a given level. For example, the "student teacher" class would present difficulties in this respect. A variable format record might be used to allow for all possible combinations of subclasses, but in a large hierarchy this is likely to be impractical.

3. Separate records, one for each subclass in the hierarchy, may be provided. This may avoid wasted space, but it may be very expensive to maintain, given the large number of I/Os necessary to assemble all of the attributes for some subclass at the bottom of the hierarchy. This approach to the implementation of a hierarchy is commonly

used in nonsemantic databases. It is often the case that multityped entities, although they may not be recognized as such, are implemented using multiple records. This approach is therefore not a break with established practice.

OPERATIONS ON THE HIERARCHY

It is necessary for the function that performs class insertion to be able both to insert an existing entity into a subclass of which it is not currently a member and to insert an entity into a hierarchy in which it did not previously appear at all (e.g., inserting "person" into the "instructor" class, as well as a new person into the "person" class.

Deletion may operate either from the root of the hierarchy (in which case the entity is deleted from the database altogether) or from some intermediate level of the hierarchy (in which case only the subclasses below the perspective class are affected). In either case, a side effect of the **delete** operation should be the deletion of any dependent entities and the deletion of any relationships in which the entity formerly participated. For dependent entities, of course, the whole process is repeated.

Both the **delete** and **insert** operations have to have some means of "understanding" the way that the hierarchy is represented. Given the diverse mappings available and the fact that they could be mixed, the **delete** and **insert** routines could become very complicated.

In the case of **insert, delete,** and **modify,** any applicable constraints must be checked as a part of the operation. In the case of hierarchies, some elaborate algorithms are required to ensure that all required and MV constraints on all of the subroles throughout a hierarchy are not violated.

An ISA function must be provided for each of the classes supported; it will indicate whether a given entity participates in a given class. It may be necessary to support this function at a very low level, given that determination of class membership depends heavily on the mapping type. For variant records, class membership is given by record type; for separate records, class membership is given by a foreign key (or other relationship) traversal.

NORMALIZATION AND THE SDM

Normalization is a process usually associated with the relational model; however, there is no reason in principle why the normalization process should not be used with any data model. It is primarily a technique for detecting the presence of certain types of potential anomalies in a given database design.

Normalization is of a rather limited use in the design of a database built on an E–R-based model because normalization is based on an analysis of dependencies. The dependencies in turn are based on the identification and description of the entities in the database. Given reasonable techniques for identifying and describing entities, normalization becomes essentially redundant.

There are a number of problems that normalization is intended to avoid:

- *Redundancy*—that is, having the same information present in the database in several physically different locations. Particularly when deleting or changing information in the database, a number of problems may arise. It is necessary to ensure that all the representations of a thing either get deleted or undergo the same changes.

- *Potential inconsistency* (update anomalies—generally as a result of redundancy)—in the presence of redundant information, the problem likely to be encountered is that one version of the information can become different from other versions. If, for example, a person's age is stored several times, the database could, after a series of invalid updates, represent the person as having several different ages.

- *Insertion anomalies*—no way of storing entities without storing some associated entity—for example, a database cannot have a supplier who does not supply anything. If supplier information is kept with the information about whatever is supplied and nowhere else, and a supplier happens not to supply anything, there is no way of storing information about the supplier.

- *Deletion anomalies*—the opposite end of the preceding anomaly (i.e., entities are deleted if some associated entity is deleted)—for example, suppliers disappear when they cease to supply anything. As in the previous case, where a supplier ceases to supply anything, the supplier disappears altogether.

All of these anomalies are addressed by the SDM:

- *Redundancy* only arises where entities exist that have not been identified during the database design process. Correct design of the database avoids redundancy, and it can best be accomplished within the context of a clear and concise statement of the characteristics of the data, such as is provided by the SDM. Incidentally, if the entity has not been identified somewhere along the line, normalization will not spot the problem either. Remember that normalization relies on the identification of dependencies; dependencies can only be derived from an identification of entities (or some logically equivalent operation).

- *Potential inconsistency* (update anomalies) also only arise where the database design is incorrect (i.e., entities exist that have not been identified in the schema). The SDM not only assists in avoiding the problem but also helps when it comes to fixing it. An SDM gives a clear account of the implications of adding new entity types to a database, especially where data about the entities is already present in the database.

- *Insertion anomalies* are simply a question of accurate and complete entity description.

- *Deletion anomalies* also reduce the problem to accurate and complete entity description.

The SDM provides, as a by-product, the same type of physical-level integrity-constraint specification as is provided by normalization. Given reasonable physical-level mapping protocols, normalization should not be necessary. However, normalization may be useful in the context of an SDM if the data extracted from the database is dealt with using a model other than the SDM. If this is the case, it is highly desirable to preserve any dependencies implied in the original data. If the dependencies are not preserved, even though the data may be correct in the database, it will be incorrect as seen by the end user.

Here, normalization is being used as a basis for the design of the query processor, and it is only possible because of the clear statement, in the schema, of the entities stored in the database, and their relationships to each other.

PROGRAMMING A SEMANTIC DATABASE

In the absence of a full implementation of the SDM, the functions necessary to support the entities in a database must be provided by writing special-purpose programs. An outline of the type of structure necessary for these programs has already been provided. The programs provide a set of abstract types that can perform database operations necessary for storing and retrieving data. Such abstract types may be provided at the level of the database, where the entities and corresponding functions can be expected to be well defined. This is the usual and accepted province of the database designer, even if the need for some programming effort is not always recognized.

From the present description of the database design process, it should also be fairly obvious that it is not necessary, or even desirable, to stop using the SDM at this level. It is possible and reasonable to apply the concept of clearly and explicitly defined entities, with associated sets of operations, all the way out to the end user.

McLeod (Hammer and McLeod, 1978) sees the external level of the database (in the ANSI/SPARC) sense as a set of subclasses, tailored to the needs and perceptions of particular users. A given screen or report is a representation of a (sub)class, or collection of associated classes, and it is just as much a representation as is a string of magnetized spots on a disk drive. The two representations are subject to the same problems and are likely to benefit from similar solutions. It makes sense to use the SDM as widely as possible, if only from the point of view of controlling the data processing environment. Further, because a screen or report has to be recognized, and dealt with, as a representation of a set of classes, subclasses, and their associated attributes, to derive full benefit from the use of a SDM, it must be used not only by the database administration staff but also by those responsible for writing programs that run against the database.

The model offers considerable benefits in the area of database design. And it has even more to offer as a vehicle for communicating with those who generally have to use and maintain the data processing environment. This is, of course, a consideration that has been of paramount importance from the beginning, and it is precisely the problem that is not addressed by the record-based model.

THE METASCHEMA AND THE PHYSICAL DATABASE

As with the logical description of the database, it is necessary to store information in the database directory about the physical description of the database. This amounts to a description of the underlying database, using the terms of the SDM. This physical representation of the database must then be related to the logical representation, indicating how particular classes and attributes are implemented.

The precise nature of the classes and attributes used to describe the physical side of the database will be determined by the type of system used as the underlying database. It is not necessary that there should be only one type of underlying database. It is reasonable to have the type of the underlying database specifiable as a generation-time option. In this case, the system directory (i.e., the collection of classes used to describe the system as a whole) should contain a description of a semantic database, plus any number of other databases.

The classes presented here represent a mapping for the file system used as a part of the PSL, which has already been encountered, for example, in the description of the representation of relationships. It is assumed that only one implementation strategy per structure type must be provided.

Not all of the attributes necessary to represent the physical level are depicted. The schema for the physical level is likely to be much more complex than the schema for the logical level; this is quite acceptable, given that the physical level will not ordinarily be visible to the end user.

The main types of information that have to be provided by the physical level are generation information and query compilation information. Generation information allows the structure of the files in the underlying database to be determined. If necessary, it has to be possible to generate a schema for the underlying database. The information also has to encompass situations in which the database being generated already exists and the generation is actually a reorganization of the database.

Query compilation information must be provided to (a) allow a query to be expressed in terms of the logical-level objects (i.e., classes, subclasses, DVAs, and EVAs) and (b) translate the query into a series of statements about physical-level objects (i.e., files, items, and indexes). This task may be particularly difficult; it can be very complicated and must be done fairly efficiently. For an ad hoc query processor, it will directly affect the user's perception of the performance of the system. At the very least, it is going to have an impact on the compiler's performance.

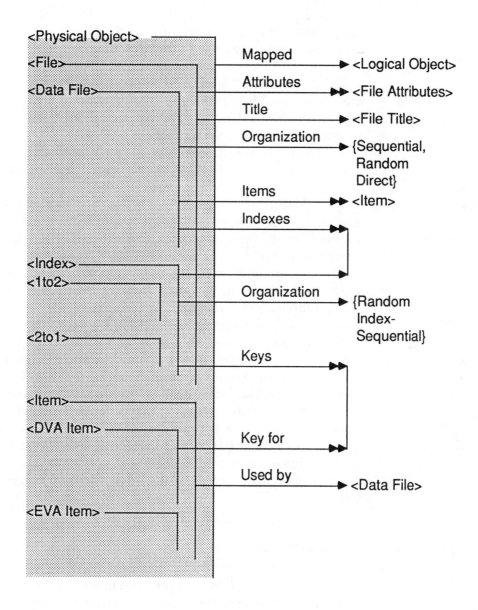

For any given implementation of a system there will be a structure (such as in the preceding illustration) indicating how the logical side of the system has been represented as a physical object. There are a number of possible extremes in this respect. At one extreme is a system such as Smalltalk-85, in which the system, right down to the interfaces to the hardware, is described using the structures and concepts of the logical model. This is a truly remarkable achievement and represents one of the logically "cleanest" data processing environments yet devised. It is arguable that the object orientation of the system detracts from the user-friendliness of the system, but as a conceptually pure environment, it is difficult to improve on it.

An extreme in the opposite direction is represented by the Apple Macintosh system; its beauty is superficial. The Macintosh has an interface that has a very direct, visual appeal. The images and systems that the Macintosh presents to the user are very easy to use and manipulate, but the same techniques cannot be used to manipulate the Macintosh itself. The concepts of the Macintosh screen display are not extrapolated into the system itself. This is perhaps necessary, but it is rather unfortunate from the point of view of those who would like to understand and manipulate the system for their own purposes. (The Macapp application development environment represents a major improvement in this respect.)

What is needed is a system that is both easy enough for most end-users to understand (as is the Macintosh window environment) and powerful enough to be used in implementing the system as a whole (as is Smalltalk-85). A semantic database could do just this; it could be used as a basis for a system description that is detailed enough to be useful but simple enough to be manageable. Given the separation of the physical and logical layers of the directory, plus a reasonably powerful query language, much of the business of operating and monitoring a data processing system could easily be described and managed using an SDM.

INTERFACE TO THE SYSTEM

Historically, there have been three main models of the data processing environment as seen by the external user: the file model, the database model, and the semantic model of the system.

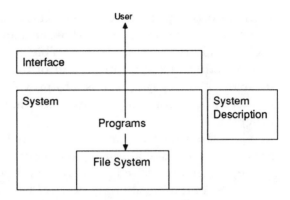

In the file model, the system description is located entirely outside of the system and is not accessible either to the programs running in the system or to the end users. The users' interface to the system is necessarily limited, given that the system description is not available. The interface frequently consists of reports produced in batch mode. Whatever integrity the system has is embedded in the programs. If the programs fail, the system fails.

So far as the end user is concerned, the only redeeming feature of the system is that the interface will probably be (in a batch environment) to some sort of data control clerk. If things go wrong, the clerk will probably be able to take some sort of effective action. If, however, the system does not provide what is required of it, programs will have to be rewritten, a process that can be expected to take a very long time and be somewhat unpredictable in its results.

The second of the three system models, is the database model:

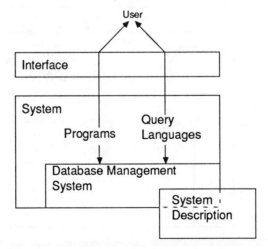

In this case, the system description is at least partially located inside the system, and it may even be a part of the database management system itself. If this is the case, it is possible to increase enormously the sophistication of the interface and of the programs that access the database. A query language is also provided, and it may be used to extract information from the database that is not allowed for by the programs.

It is worth noting that much of the benefit to be derived from such a system (in terms of automatic maintenance of consistency and ease of use) is actually derived more by the programmers than by the end users. The end users are only aware of benefits, if any, in the form of increased responsiveness on the part of the data processing department. It is usually the case that critical, multiuser databases cannot be accessed by the end users using ad hoc query languages because of the complexities of the way that the data has been stored. The query language is likely to allow the user to do all sorts of things that, in terms of the semantics of the data, are quite nonsensical.

In the absence of a full-featured SDM, ad hoc query languages at best can only be used for simple read-only access. Even then, considerable sophistication is likely to be required of the user if the data extracted from the database is not to be meaningless gibberish.

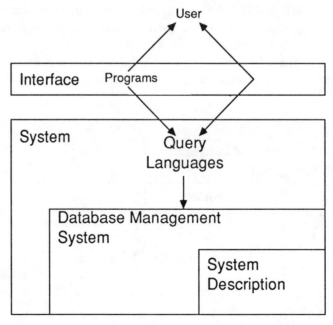

In the semantic system model, the "system" has effectively become the data management system, with its associated query language. Anything else, such as the programs used to access the system, is essentially outside of the system. This is so because the system contains all of the information needed to maintain and understand it.

It does not really matter whether an access to the system originates from a program or from a user; the system knows enough about itself to ensure that the access is reasonable and correct.

Programs cease to be a part of the system and become merely a part of the interface to the system. The proper business of the program then becomes to ensure that the semantics of the system are obscured as little as possible. Programs and the interface generally should be as *transparent* (i.e., unobtrusive and invisible to the user) as possible.

The more the external interface reflects the underlying system, the more transparent is the system, and the easier the system will be to use. Any attempt to hide the complexities of the underlying database will simply result in a reversion to the database model. The programs become a part of the system, and the user is dependent on the programs do what is wanted, rather than being able to do it himself.

The ideal user interface then is a consistent method of looking at data—a mechanism or protocol that either makes the look of the interface predictable, given a knowledge of what it is interfacing to, or makes the underlying system predictable, given a knowledge of the interface.

What is provided is a context within which it is possible for the user to tailor the system to suit himself. In the case of the underlying (internal) system, the context is the SDM. The context of the external system is likely to be more application-specific. In any event, it will consist of a template (or a set of templates) and associated protocols, techniques, and capabilities.

There are examples of such systems. Probably the most sophisticated is the Smalltalk-85 Operating System, where the entire system, right down to the level of the operating system itself, is described in the same terms. Less ambitious examples are the Unix and Pick systems, for which the key to the power and ease of use of the system is the ability of the system to reflect the needs and requirements of the user. The underlying model for the Unix and Pick systems is language based—C for Unix, COBOL for Pick, which is excellent if you happen to be a C or COBOL programmer.

Even given a good semantic database management system (DBMS) and a well-designed database, it is still possible to develop applications that make no sense at all to those who have to use them. A good model of data is crucial at all levels of the system, especially when dealing with systems that have to accommodate a variety of different user requirements. To make a system truly flexible and manageable, the same model has to be used at all levels of the system.

User interfaces then may be assessed (and designed) in terms of the following:

Transparency—the degree to which the underlying semantics of the system are reflected in the interface

Consistency—the extent to which different parts of the system do similar things in a similar way

Simplicity—the number of elements apparent in the system over and above the basic classes and attributes of the system detracts from the simplicity of the system

Complexity—the number and range of ad hoc verification conditions that have to be added to the schema in order to ensure that the data in the database remains consistent.

Commands as Data

In the semantic system model, the system interface must be flexible and easy to use. That is, it must be possible for a user to tailor the interface to the user's own requirements of the system, and the interface must be reasonably easy to use. This contrasts with the database system model, where the user has to rely on a programmer to produce what is wanted. The user must contend with all the attendant problems of the process of dealing with the data processing environment and hope that the end product is moderately easy to use.

Given the semantic system model, how can flexibility and ease of use be provided? Are they even possible to describe? This section looks at computers and data processing environments, with a view to providing answers to these questions.

It could be argued that the file–database–semantic system characterization is too simplistic, inasmuch as it ignores differences among programming languages. LISP might be contrasted with ALGOL, or C with COBOL, the claim being that in both cases, the first language is superior to the second as a basis for a user interface. Therefore, the language might be taken as another dimension in addition to the preceding file–database–semantic distinction.

But is this really the case? The success of Unix as a general-purpose user environment is related to the features of the Unix shell rather than any specific features of C. Other user environments offer considerably more power but at the expense of verbose and complex syntax.

The key feature that makes the Unix shell a viable user interface is its ability to treat commands as data. This allows UNIX, in various ways, to manipulate the commands prior to executing them. Sorensen (1976, p. 76) has said that the "power of recursive productions in a grammar cannot be underplayed" and makes two statements to illustrate the point:

1. Any grammar containing a recursively defined production describes an infinite language (i.e., a language with an infinite number of sentences).

2. Any grammar containing no recursively defined productions describes a finite grammar (i.e., a language with a finite number of sentences).

While the existence of recursion is no guarantee of conciseness, it is a sound starting point for the definition of a powerful language.

Sorensen was talking specifically about grammars that are both used to describe languages and associated with objects such as programs. In such systems, the languages are traditionally essentially passive objects that are acted on by other parts of the system, such as a compiler or an interpreter. The output from the compiler is an object that does not have any significance so far as the compiler or the language are concerned. The system can be depicted as follows:

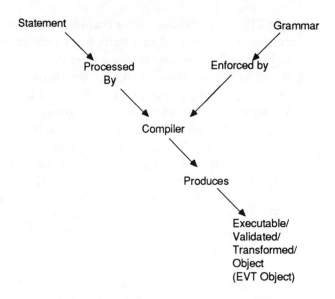

The essential characteristic of the system is that the compiler, the grammar, the statement, and the EVT (executable–validated–transformed) object are all distinct entities. In the type of system considered by Sorensen, it is not usually expected to be the case that a compiler may be a grammar, or that a grammar may be a statement, or that an EVT object may be a compiler. There is, however, no essential reason why at least some of these relationships should not hold.

For example, in the case of the ALGOL compiler written in ALGOL (hereafter referred to as the system ACA), EVT object and the compiler become one and the same thing. That is, the ALGOL compiler is compiling the ALGOL compiler and producing ALGOL! In ACA, the system has a type of recursion available to it that transcends even the recursion implied in a grammar that contains recursive productions. ACA has the ability to redefine itself. The ALGOL compiler in ACA can be used to modify and extend the ALGOL language.

There are, of course, limitations to this. Specifically the ALGOL compiler does not, in and of itself, do anything at all; it only does what it is told to do. However ACA does represent an environment that contains tools that allow the environment itself to be modified by external agencies (i.e., systems programmers). The system ACA can be depicted as follows:

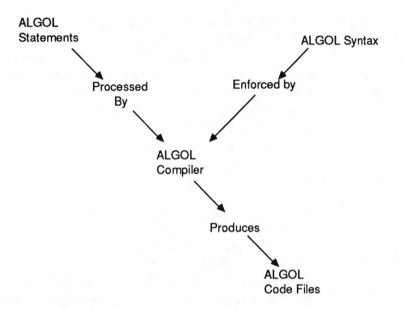

Therefore, systems are conceivable in which the following could occur:

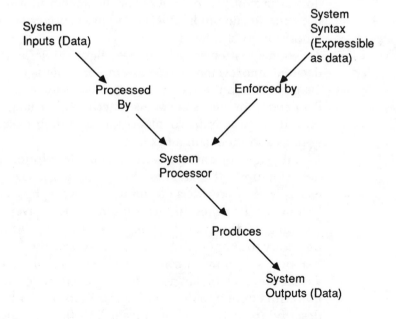

The ability of environments to provide and support tools that may be used to modify the environment is the key to the power of the computer; it is the characteristic that above all else distinguishes the computer from any other cultural artifact. Returning to Sorensen's remarks about recursion, the computer is more than just a grammar that will produce an infinite number of sentences; it is a grammar that can be used to produce an infinite number of grammars.

Evaluating the System

In looking at different data processing systems, key criteria for evaluating the system must be (a) the type of self-modification tools the system supports, and (b) how easy or difficult the tools are to use—what exactly is involved in their use.

The least desirable systems do not provide any mechanism that allow the system to be modified. About the only method of providing such a system is to (a) provide object code only, (b) not allow object code modification, and (c) make the system itself completely rigid. Assembler-language programs are only slightly better than this because they do not permit representation of the system in a format that is both meaningful and modifiable, and such a representation is crucial to the modification of a system.

Systems written in a high-level algorithmic language represent a decided improvement over assembler languages; however, the language in which the system is expressed is still likely to be completely divorced from the system being described. The language will be biased toward the description of algorithms and their execution, not toward systems and their semantics.

Languages oriented toward system description are probably the next step upward. Data description languages (DDLs) are the prime example; they provide a mechanism whereby the characteristics of the system are described in terms intended to convey the structure and meaning of the system rather than the algorithms and processes necessary to support the structure and provide the meaning. Explicit system descriptions in which the system as a whole is encapsulated in a clear and concise language have enormous potential. The system is powerful enough to describe objects in its own environment, so if the description of the system is itself an object in the environment, it becomes possible for the system to assist in the manipulation of itself.

Consider, for example, a data dictionary. The data dictionary is implemented as a database. The data dictionary can contain database descriptions and can validate database descriptions. It follows that the data dictionary can contain at least a partial description of itself and can at least partially validate alterations of itself.

Returning to Unix, recall that Unix allows functions to be set up in such a way that the function can return a command, which will then execute. The function sees the command as a string, and can manipulate it using any of the standard operations used on strings. Unix then allows the user of the system to redefine the system, extending it to support any function the user requires.

The same consideration applies with the semantic end of the file–database–semantic distinction. The difference, however, is that at the semantic end, the system can provide a far more detailed and meaningful description of itself than is possible using database-type systems or Unix-type environments.

It would be inaccurate to say that the language used to implement a system does not matter. Clearly, a system has to have a user environment, and it is important for the user environment to allow the user to tailor the environment to suit himself. But it is also the case that the environment must not obscure the semantics of the underlying system. Just as much as any application running in the environment, the user environment itself must be

- Transparent
- Consistent
- Simple
- No more complex than the underlying application.

Within these constraints, flexibility may be achieved by allowing the user access to tools that can be used to manipulate the interface, allowing the user to shape the system to suit himself.

Ease of Use

A further factor in assessing a system's ability to modify itself is the *type of agencies* (i.e., what level of skill and expertise is possessed by the persons making the changes) that have to be involved in the modification process. Originally, skilled programmers had to be involved who understood the complex languages, algorithms, and processes involved in the description of the system. As more powerful languages become available, and as it becomes possible to capture more of the semantics of the systems as a result of the more powerful languages, the skill requirements become less stringent.

It will eventually be the case that casual users of the system can define reasonably complex operations and arbitrarily complex semantics. Given that it is the end user who is doing the defining, much of the interface-related problems disappear. They are only problems when the interface being designed is an interface to be used by someone other than the designer. At this point, languages such as C or LISP become a useful (but not essential) adjunct to the system; however, it is hoped that it will rarely be necessary to use anything quite so complex as C or LISP.

SOME UNSOLVED PROBLEMS

There are a number of areas that (a) have not been touched on at all in this book, (b) represent problems to which no adequate solutions currently exist, or (c) are the subject of some controversy. Some of them relate to the following:

- Views
- Manipulation of descriptions of abstract types
- Temporal data
- Multiple entity entities
- Reorganization
- Optimization
- Generalized verifies

Views

A *view* is a tailored subset of a database schema. Views are covered in McLeod's version of the SDM by the use of classes and subclasses, but it is not clear that this meets the full CODASYL idea of a subschema. It is not even clear that a view, in the relational sense, is reasonable in the context of an SDM.

There are a couple of issues here. First, if a view is defined on a semantic database schema that consists of a subset of the schema, what are the semantics of the objects in the view? Either they have some semantics, in which case the semantics should be included in the schema. Or they have no semantics, in which case they have no business being in the system in the first place.

A second problem is that views traditionally are associated with security. A view is defined to specify access rights for the user of the view, and users are then limited to using views that confine them to a suitable set of operations. This arrangement has the very unappealing side effect of requiring the introduction of additional named objects into the schema in order to allow for security. This is particularly problematic if the application has a very large number of differing security requirements. The number of names implied may be very large and therefore a source of much confusion.

Manipulation of Descriptions of Abstract Types

It is not clear to what extent the abstract types can be described in the schema. In some scenarios, the entire system ends up being described in the schema; this may be desirable, but it is probably not practical (see particularly, the early versions of Smalltalk for example). The usefulness of abstract types themselves is not in question here, just the extent to which the description of the type can be incorporated into the system.

If the type's description is to be incorporated into the system, because the type will involve generalized algorithms for its implementation, a generalized algorithmic language will have to become a part of the system. This may, in the end, compromise the simplicity and clarity of the system, leading to a regression to the database system model.

Temporal Data

Dealing with different versions of the same thing is not addressed directly by the SDM, and dealing with different states at different moments in time is not addressed at all. There are some obvious ad hoc solutions, most of which very quickly run into severe problems if the application becomes at all complex. It may be possible to provide support for a temporal dimension to the data model, but this is still a very open area.

One promising aspect of the model in regard to time is the concept of the perspective. There is no obvious reason why the perspective should not be extended to encompass time. In this case, the database is viewed via a particular entity in a particular class at a particular time.

Multiple-Entity Entities

The model tends to assume that entities are, in a sense, indivisible, but this is clearly not the case. Almost any conceivable entity consists of component entities, which are not the same as related entities. As we have seen, this can lead to considerable difficulties in some cases.

For example, structures (e.g., a database in a data dictionary) are sometimes a special case of multiple-entity entities, but not always. The problem about structures is that they require a whole class of special operators not really supported by the model but likely to be frequently and heavily used. For example, in a data dictionary context, the model does not support copying, deleting, upgrading, and verifying files, databases, systems, and so on. The SDM does provide a good starting point for understanding and dealing with these problems, but, for the most part, it provides only an outline of a solution.

Reorganization

There seems to be tremendous potential for specialized reorganization capabilities in a semantic database. As there is more information about the semantics of the data present in the system itself, it should be possible to more accurately define legal and illegal schema changes, but this promise remains unfulfilled.

Optimization

Systems based on an SDM also have as-yet-unrealized potential for optimization. At present, optimization tends to depend on techniques developed for other systems (notably relational systems) or simply depend on the optimization capabilities of the underlying DBMS. Good generalized algorithms that use the known semantics of the system to optimize queries prior to execution have yet to be defined (or at least, generally accepted).

Generalized Verifies

Generalized verify operations pose a whole host of problems, mainly associated with efficiency. In theory, the verify mechanism allows an arbitrary condition to be used for the verify condition—that is, any condition expressible in the DML may be used as the verify condition. Consider the following example (the ABS [absolute value function] strips off the negative sign, if present; LSS means "less than")

```
Verify Salary-verify on Employee
        ABS (SUM (salary) / COUNT (employee) – salary)
                   LSS
        SUM (salary) / COUNT (employee) * 0.50
```

This states the very reasonable condition that no employee's salary may exceed the average salary by more than 50%. If the system is very poor, so far as optimization is concerned, it could end up reading the employee file as many as five times in the process of confirming the verify. It is to be hoped that the system can do a little better than this. But it may have to read the whole file at least once, or the system as a whole will have to be smart enough to realize that average salary will have to be computed every time an employee salary is updated in any way whatsoever, and therefore will store and maintain the average value as an optimization.

This sort of thing can very rapidly lead to tremendous complexities in the system and, without some limitations on the conditions that may be used in verifies, it will quickly lead to the system becoming unmanageable.

12

CamDB (Computer-Aided Manufacturing Database)

INTRODUCTION

Computer-aided manufacturing (CAM) is a part of the movement away from the accounting applications that tended to dominate the data processing department in the 1960s and 1970s. Accounting was an excellent application for systems that only supported simple record-based data management facilities. It is a simple process to reduce an accounting system to a set of files, records, and associated processes to maintain them (which is not to say that designing the system in the first place is easy).

Away from the world of accounts, there is a vast range of possible applications for data processing, and CAM is a good example. These kinds of applications are of particular interest in the light of an SDM (semantic data model) because they tend to be much more intractable from a data analysis point of view, and they present the database designer with a far more serious set of problems.

The systems also tend to be on-line, whereas accounting applications can often be quite readily run in batch mode. A couple of hours delay in printing and posting of a bill is of little consequence. A 5-minute delay while 30 tons of molten steel is waiting to be processed can be catastrophic. Given that CAM applications can expect to be on-line, and frequently 24-hour-a-day systems, any number of consequences follow. These points are best illustrated by "Die Nuut Kasteel Staal Werk."

Die Nuut Kasteel Staal Werk

The Nuut Kasteel steel works produces three basic kinds of product:

- Sheet steel, which is produced in various thicknesses in rolls weighing approximately 15 tons each
- Steel wire, produced in various thicknesses in bundles weighing approximately 10 tons each
- Billets, or steel slabs, which are cast blocks of steel, usually intended for further processing by outside specialist steel-processing plants.

The processing of the steel is performed as follows:

1. Iron ore, coal, and so on is input to one of four blast furnaces, which have to be used continually unless shut down for maintenance. The furnace walls are impregnated with various kinds of radioactive substance and burn away as the furnace is used. Prior to the burning away of the last layer (which can be monitored with a Geiger counter), the furnace has to be shut down for maintenance.

2. The molten iron is transported in pots on a standard-gauge railway. There are two pot types, which, when fully loaded, weigh either 80 tons or 50 tons. The pots also require periodic maintenance.

3. The iron is sampled and, if the quality is acceptable, is taken in the pots to the mills for processing.

4. The first step in the processing is common to all product types and consists of turning the iron produced by the blast furnaces into steel of a quality suitable to the product to be produced. The quality of the steel varies across products (e.g., between plate and wire products) and may be very specialized for slabs, requiring the addition of a variety of different types of alloys, depending on the requirements as specified in the customer order.

5. The mills are divided into slab works, wire works, and plate works.

Only the plate works are discussed in this chapter, although the slabbing processes are essentially common to all three.

6. Once a slab has been produced and cast that is a steel of a quality suitable for use in plate making, it has to be homogenized. In homogenization, the slab is kept in a furnace for a few hours to ensure that the slab cools at an even rate. This may take up to 6 hours.

7. Slabs having been homogenized are then checked for any flaws. Flawed parts of the slab are sawed off. Hence, slabs may be of any length.

8. The slabs are then scalped, whereby the external layers of the slab are removed to ensure a consistent finish on the slab prior to further processing. The slab is then further tested, weighed, and graded. This results in a slab that may have considerable variations in length, thickness, weight, and quality prior to being delivered to the plate works. At this stage, if the slab fails to meet specified tolerances for composition and finish, the slab may be scrapped, and subsequently remelted in an electric arc furnace.

9. The slabs are taken to a holding area where they are kept until they can be processed by the appropriate mill. In preparation for the plate works, the slabs are placed in the soaking pits, where they are raised to a temperature suitable for use in the hot mill. There may be up to 20 slabs in the soaking pits at the same time. Once the slab has been brought up to temperature, it has to be left for several hours so that the slab assumes a uniform temperature. The operators have to know which slabs to load, and what temperature they have to reach.

10. Once the slab has been soaked it has to be loaded onto the hot mill, where it will be rolled into plate of the appropriate thickness for the customer's order. The plate steel may have to be further trimmed, depending on the quality of the edge produced by the rolling process.

Perhaps the most interesting aspect of CAM systems is the complex interactions among their various parts. For example, it is highly desirable to be able to backtrack from any point in the process to the original blast furnace batch from which a product was produced. If, at the milling stage, it is discovered that there may be some flaw in the slabs that came from a particular batch, all the slabs from the batch should be examined. Slabs have to be accessible by blast furnace batch.

The calibration of the various instruments and machines used by the processes are frequently critical to the successful performance of the process as a whole. If, for example, temperature monitoring is not being properly performed in the steel-making stage, this may only become evident in an increase in slab faults, which itself may only be detectable using sophisticated statistical analysis of the fault rates on the production line.

STAAL WERKS SCHEMA

The following is a partial schema for the production monitoring system. It is intended to represent the ingredient and sampling information that has to be kept by the system. Location and order information is not represented. There is no representation for information about particular resources, such as pots, blast furnaces, soaking pits, and mills. All of this would be required in the complete schema. The schema is a preliminary version and has a number of problems.

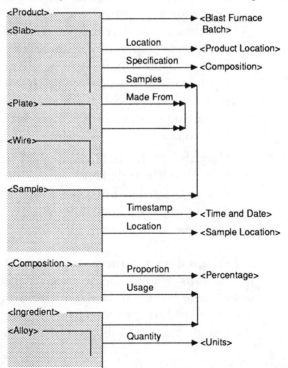

Note that the technique used to identify products is completely ignored. This is as it should be, especially in an application such as this, where identification is a considerable problem in its own right. Having established that products have to be identified, and that it is uncertain how they can be identified, there is no point in pursuing the matter any further while there are other areas of the application that can be further refined. Once other aspects of the application have been clarified, the scope and impact of the product identification problem can be properly assessed and some suitable solution devised. The assumption is that there is a solution—it is just a question of how expensive and how complex it is.

The schema of course is incomplete, both in the sense that it does not provide a complete description of the process and in the sense that it is inaccurate. For example there is a single-valued (SV) relationship, "specification" between "product" and "composition." Composition has an SV relationship to "ingredient." But this implies that a product may only have a single ingredient, which is obviously wrong. Also, the class "sample" is an interesting case: A "sample" has all of the characteristics of a "product," and so, it could be argued that "sample" should be a subclass of "product."

And beyond these kinds of issues are those associated with the information that is simply missing altogether.

How are these issues to be resolved? Obviously, the normal processes of systems analysis have to be invoked. A vital ingredient of any process of systems analysis is some method of expressing the current understanding of the application environment. This understanding has to be communicated to the people (a) who will have to use the application and (b) who currently have to be relied on as the ultimate source of how the application is to function.

The vital difference in the case of an SDM is that there is no translation required between the systems analyst and the application user. It is possible to express the formulation of the application in such a way that it is intelligible to the application user, the systems analyst, and the database management system. This formulation may be used without the need for a translation process between any of the three parties involved. Some massaging of the input and care over the arrangement and presentation may be required, but the differences are purely cosmetic.

It is difficult to overemphasize the importance of this point. Without the requirement for a translation process, a variety of approaches and techniques become possible. Consider for example the use of questionnaires and conferences:

One of the problems about a conference is when to hold it. If it is held at too early a stage in the application development process, it will be a waste of everyone's time. On the other hand, if it is held too late, a great deal of time will be wasted trying to reconcile opinions that are fundamentally different. They can only be reconciled by a face-to-face confrontation or by an executive decision.

Another problem about a conference is whom to ask to attend. It should not be too many people; large conferences are never as effective as small ones. It should not be people who entirely agree with the current understanding of the application; they presumably have nothing to contribute. It should not be people who completely disagree with the current understanding of the application; they should formulate their own understanding and let everyone else argue with it.

The following describes an approach to solving all of these problems in a reliable and determinate fashion. It is not meant to be a description of a complete systems analysis technique. Such a description would require far more discussion than can be provided here. The process described is intended to give some indication of (a) how a suitable data model can be integrated into a systems analysis technique, and (b) how a data model can make a significant difference to the reliability and accuracy of the systems analysis.

The process relies on using repeated cycles of a restricted-format questionnaire. It allows the application design process to be monitored and controlled in such a way that it will converge on a solution based on a consensus, if one exists.

The process involves a series of steps:

Step 1 assumes a questionnaire in the following format:

Name	Ext.
This questionnaire is intended to find out what kinds of things you want the computer to store information about. Please specify the characteristics of the things. Provide , where known, constraints on the form or content of a characteristic, such as a zip code being 5 digits plus 4 digits after a hyphen. A number of other questionnaires will follow this one some time in the next few weeks. The first lines give you an example of the kinds of things you might put in the questionnaire. Do not put anything in you are not sure about. Prefer to leave a thing out.	

Names of things	Names of their characteristics	What sort of thing is the characteristic?

Address	Street
	
	City
	State
	Zip code
		Street number and
		    street name
		City name
		State code
		5-digit number plus 4
		    digits after a hyphen

The questionnaire is deliberately kept very small, with slots for only 4 things on it, each thing having a maximum of 5 characteristics. No more than 10 questionnaires should be given out in this cycle. The reasons for these restrictions will become apparent in a moment.

This is the only step where unstructured input is solicited from the users. In subsequent steps, the input from the previous step is always used in the formulation of the questionnaire.

Step 2 consists of feeding all of the answers into a database. No structure will be implied by the data description at this stage. No equivalences need be established by name between the things and characteristics in the various responses received. This will be done based on subsequent input.

Step 3 requires sending a questionnaire to each respondent. The questionnaire is intended to establish equivalencies between the various responses received and to establish any interrelationships within the responses. The questionnaire is in the following form:

Name	Ext.

This questionnaire is a follow-up to the one you responded to previously. It seeks more information about the things you said you were interested in. It is also trying to find out how the things you are interested in are related to the things other people are interested in.

A number of other questionnaires might follow this one some time in the next few weeks.

1.	Is a \<thing1\> always a \<thing2\>?	Y	N
2.	Is a \<thing1\> always a \<thing2\>?	Y	N

⋮

150. Is a \<thing1\> always a \<thing2\>?	Y	N

Are there any other things you would like to add?

Names of things	Names of their characteristics	What sort of thing is the characteristic?

The questions in this questionnaire are derived as follows: Taking all of the things and all of the characteristic descriptions (i.e., the last column in the previous questionnaire) across all the questionnaires generated, this question is repeated for all possible pairs. Any given questionnaire will have no more than 150 questions. If there are enough respondents available, the questions should be repeated as often as possible.

The 150 questions include the things that the respondent has responded on previously. The 150 questions will also include things from other responses. Accompanying the questionnaire will be a list of valid things, in alphabetical order. Each item in the list will include the name of the person who originally described the thing. In this way, if there is a question as to the interpretation of a thing, it can always be referred back to the originator.

Step 4 reconciles the answers received from Step 3. If the answers do not reconcile—that is, if there are contradictions either within or across responses, go back to Step 3.

Step 5 is required because it is unlikely that Step 4 would completely reconcile the answers being derived from Step 3. Step 4, however, will show a definite pattern, whereby the answers tend to converge on some point beyond which no further improvement is achieved. At this point, it is necessary to call a conference in order to make any further progress. Once a conference has been held, it is then possible to go back to Step 3 and start the cycle again if necessary. The whole process is repeated until such time as a working consensus emerges. The definition of a working consensus is likely to depend on such external factors as time constraints, costs, or executive decision.

Having described the entire process, it may help to return to Step 3; the combinations of pairs can best be illustrated by an example. Here, we assume that the following is one set of responses received on the first round:

Names of things	Names of their characteristics	What sort of thing is the characteristic?
Product	Location Batch Specification Samples	A place A blast furnace batch Mix of ingredients A bit taken out for analysis

Another response could be the following:

Names of things	Names of their characteristics	What sort of thing is the characteristic?
Sample	Source Time Analysis Location	Slab Time when the sample was taken Content of the sample Where the sample is kept

In these two responses, the *things* are as follows:

```
Sample
Time when the sample was taken
Slab
Content of the sample
Where the sample is kept
Product
A place
A bit taken out for analysis
Mix of ingredients
A blast furnace batch
```

The questions include the following:

Is a *product* always a *sample?*

   [y]   [n]

Is a *product* always a *slab?*

   [y]   [n]

Is a *product* always a *time when the sample was taken?*

   [y]   [n]

Is a *product* always a *content of the sample?*

   [y]   [n]

Is a *product* always a location *where the sample is kept?*

   [y]   [n]

Approximately six questions are generated for each thing. A lot of them will be nonsensical; many of them will be quite useful, for example:

Is a *slab* always a *product?*

[y]   [n]

This, combined with "Is a *product* always a *slab?*" establishes "slab" as a subclass of "product." Another couple of questions follow:

Is a *mix of ingredients* always a *content of the sample?*

[y]   [n]

and

Is a *content of the sample* always a *mix of ingredients?*

[y]   [n]

With a bit of luck, the answer to both these questions will be yes, establishing that a mix of ingredients is the same thing as a content of the sample.

At the end of this process, it will be possible to arrange the things into a series of hierarchies. The hierarchies may each have a number of roots, thereby making a forest. Starting at a root, each thing will be connected to another thing by an ISA link, through to the leaves, which will have no such connection to another thing. It is to be expected that cycles will arise, such as the following:

$$A \xrightarrow{\text{ISA}} B \xrightarrow{\text{ISA}} C \xrightarrow{\text{ISA}} A$$

Though it would be a simple matter to spot these situations automatically, they would have to be sorted out manually. An algorithm to find cycles is easy enough to produce. Why the cycle is there in the first place is another matter altogether.

Each thing of course would be characterized by a number of attributes, (generally) the union of all the attributes specified by all of the questionnaires that contained the thing. (Remember that multiple things may have been collapsed into one.) It may be that some of these are still duplicates. Thing A may have attributes from A_1, A_2 ... A_n, as described by Respondents 1 through n (all the A_n's really being the same thing). It is very likely that attribute a_n is the same as attribute a_m, just that the two respondents happen to call it something different. It is also possible of course that some attributes may get lost as a result of different respondents giving different things within the same class the same name. Given that the homonyms must be attributes of the same class for any confusion to arise, loss of attributes seems rather unlikely.

Depending on the complexity of the application being modeled and the patience of the respondents, the process may be repeated several times. On each cycle, each respondent should be given a varying list of questions, the process being repeated until the result becomes stable.

If the result does not stabilize after a chosen number of iterations, call a conference, inviting those who are disagreeing with each other. It is possible from the questionnaires to determine both who disagrees with whom and about what they disagree.

Once agreement has been reached, the schema will almost have been formulated; the remaining tasks being (a) to make the forest hierarchy into a limited collection of trees and (b) to reconcile differing attribute and class names.

This discussion still has not addressed the formulation of the business's data rules. But it has not been entirely left out. Half the problem in formulating the rules of the business is "What are the rules about?" and "To what things do the rules apply?" This question has been answered. Further, once the rules have been formulated, they can be explicitly represented as a part of the system by applying suitable **verify** operations to the schema. Once this has been done, the schema for the database will become a complete description of the business and its rules, or at least as complete a description as it is possible to capture within the limitations of a formal logical system.

Note also that it is possible to deal not just with the design of new systems, but also, and much more importantly, with amendments to old systems. The list of things of interest to the business is encapsulated in the schema. If something has to be added or changed, the questionnaire approach can be used to examine systematically the impact of the addition or change.

The algorithm that is used to produce the Step 3 questionnaires in the process for new design need only be modified slightly to produce a suitable set of questionnaires for a Step 3 process for the addition of a new thing or an amendment to an existing one.

Beyond additions and changes to the schema, the technique can also be used to periodically check the accuracy, completeness, and relevance of the schema. Going through the questionnaires and conferences for such revisions provides not only a check on the schema, but also a check on the adequacy of the understanding of the schema.

All of this is only possible once the representation of the logical structure and content of the system is close enough to the perceptions of those who use the system for little or no translation to be required. An SDM is excellent in this respect.

13

On Piecemeal Engineering

Ivle is bending over something on the floor. Dasd walks in, there is a loud noise—Sproing!

Ivle.	Ach! Siss! Not again. Oh, well. At least I only got to part number 78 this time.
Dasd.	Morning Ivan, Was gibt's?
Ivle.	This thing's giving me a pain in the head, that's what gives.
Dasd.	What thing? All I see are lots of bits. What are they anyway?
Ivle.	Here.

Dasd reads.

The New Miracle Patent **Watch!**

Save $$$$$'s

Assembling it yourself

Only ONE Part to Fix in Place

Only Tool Required is a

Dynamic Entity Allocation Device

Send Money NOW !

While Stocks Last

Dasd. Sounds OK. Mind you, I wouldn't fancy assembling a watch. What's this Dynamic Entity Allocation Device?

Ivle. It's this piece of paper here.

Dasd. What piece of paper?

Ivle. The one you're standing on.

Dasd. Hey. What a huge piece of paper. What are all the squares with the pockets and the numbers?

Ivle. Well there's the problem. What you get with the watch is all the watch parts, each of which has a number. You take each part and put it in the packet on the square with that number, and then you assemble the watch, by starting at Square 1 and working your way upward. The instruction for assembling each part is written in its square.

Dasd. So where's the problem?

Ivle. The stupid watch only has one fixed part and hundreds of moving ones. If you get one part wrong, or you put one part in the wrong place, as soon as you try to do something about it, the whole thing comes to bits and you have to start again.

Pscl enters.

	There are 280 moving parts. I seem to be making a mistake, on average, once every 122 parts. Each time I have to start again, it takes me about 2 1/2 hours to get the parts sorted out—please, Pascal, mind you don't stand on anything—and 45 minutes to assemble the parts again. It's going to take me forever to assemble the stupid thing.
Pscl.	I wouldn't say forever. With a Poisson distribution with 1 error for each 120 parts, I calculate the chances of you completing the watch as approximately 1 in 10 million, that is 1 in 10 million tries. If you persevere, you should be reasonably confident of finishing it in about 3710 years. Provided, of course, you work 24 hours a day, 7 days a week.
Dasd.	Cheer up Ivan. Just imagine that you were trying to reorganize a company with hundreds of employees (talk about moving parts!) or even a whole country with millions of people living in it. It'd be enough to drive you scats.
Pasl.	How can a watch have 280 moving parts anyway. That's ridiculous.
Ivle.	Oh, but it doesn't. The watch itself has only 15 moving parts. The other 265 parts are secondary parts. That is, they are needed at various points in the construction of the watch to make later stages of the construction possible.
Dasd.	Now I've heard everything, the guy who invented your watch was an idiot.
Pscl.	An idiot with great dexterity, mind you—always assuming he ever built one of them himself.
Ivle.	On the contrary, I think the whole arrangement is quite reasonable. Consider how many systems and great organizations have been built on the same assumption. As Hubbard said, "The greatest mistake you can make is to be continually fearing you will make one." Wasn't it you who said "Things are always best from new beginnings"?
Pscl.	No, I did not. I said, "Things are always at their best at the beginning."

Ivle.   Well, it amounts to the same thing. What you are saying is that if a system ceases to do what you want it to do, the best course of action is to tear it all down and start from scratch. As Santayana said,

"To reform means to shatter one form and make another." Fine revolutionary sentiments!

Pscl.   The quote does go on, "but the two sides of this act are not always equally intended, nor equally successful," which I take to imply that you may end up worse off than you were to start with.

Ivle.   Quibbles! Engagement! To take part in the struggle to bring forth the brave new world of the socialist utopia. Do you expect to achieve all this without the odd setback.

Pscl.   The odd one I could cope with, but 10 million?

Ivle rolls up the Dynamic Entity Allocation Device.

Ivle.   Well, I must be off. Bye now.

Ivan departs singing.

My Heart is so sad, My heart is so sad, To

see how the Young hap-py years pass aw-ay. My heart is so

sad, my heart is so sad, for I yearn for my youth to stay.

Dasd.   Schmaltz.

Performance

INTRODUCTION

This chapter is aimed primarily at those who are concerned with the design or maintenance of databases. However, it is also of interest to anyone making extensive use of computers, as it provides a basis for informed decision making with respect to costs and opportunities in the use of data processing systems.

Tuning a computer is a very specialized job and can only be successfully attempted by someone who has an intimate understanding of both the hardware and the software of the machine involved. It is useful, however, to know certain general principles, particularly with respect to database management systems. They are useful on two grounds:

1. You will not learn the principles by studying the hardware and software itself, yet it is essential to be familiar with these principles if you are going to try to tune a system. So even if you know some computer system very well, tuning is a study in its own right.

2. Machines and their performance are such an important part of the everyday working life of a data processing system that it is crucial to have an understanding of the likely performance characteristics of a system.

There is a lot to be learned. Of particular importance are queuing theory and the statistical analysis of large volumes of data. It is not necessary to be able to perform these analyses yourself; there are any number of very good program packages that will do all the statistics for you. What is important is to have an understanding of the basic implications of queuing theory and of the behavior of the basic types of file structures, such as random structures and binary trees. Once these lessons have been grasped you will know what to expect from, and what can be done with, (a) a system you are using, (b) a system that is performing badly, or (c) a system you may be contemplating using.

It is very likely to be the case that if you cannot keep an eye on the performance of the systems for which you are responsible, no one else will either. Therefore, both tuning and systems performance are important for almost anyone who has to depend on or use a computer in the course of their normal work.

This chapter begins by looking at tuning from a general point of view. It then looks at the types of tools and information that might be available in a particular data processing environment. The basic characteristics of the principal types of file structures are described. Where appropriate, statistical techniques that may be used in the analysis of the performance of the file structures are described. Finally, there is a discussion of queuing theory.

TUNING A SYSTEM: THE DESIGNER'S VIEWPOINT

Two conflicting goals face the software and hardware engineers who design the system:

1. The system must be as cheap as possible.
2. The system must be as fast as possible.

These goals, of course, only conflict if fast means expensive, but it usually does. The system designer, in designing the system, will make a series of decisions about cost versus performance, always asking the question "How do I minimize cost and maximize performance?"

One obvious way *not* to do this is to have some component of the system be monstrously expensive and extremely fast relative to other parts of the system. This has two results: (1) there will be less money to spend on other parts of the system, and (2) the fast part of the system will spend most of its time doing nothing (i.e., the money will be wasted anyway!). Clearly, the system designer has to try to balance the various components of the machine. It should be the case that when the machine is working at its maximum capacity, all of the parts of the machine are working at maximum capacity. In this way, nothing is wasted and everything is as cheap as possible.

Machine architectures do differ. Such things as memory access, and the degree of *parallelism* (i.e., trying to do more than one thing at a time) vary tremendously from one machine to the next. Nonetheless, the memory cycle time does not vary that much, and most especially the I/O subsystem structure does not differ very much. This is especially true when looking at medium- to large-scale machines (i.e., anything bigger than a microcomputer ["micro"]).

Obviously, the system designer's aim of balancing the system is bound to become compromised in some situations. A data communications front end that is capable of saturating a small machine may hardly be noticed by a fully configured large one. Similarly, memory that is fast enough to keep a small machine happy will probably not be good enough (unaided) for a bigger one.

So unbalanced configurations are a fact of life (i.e., systems in which some portion of the system is not doing very much while other portions are working at capacity). The software configuration can do a great deal to make matters worse. The placement of files, the way in which memory and I/Os are managed, and the utilization of the CPU can vary enormously, depending on the type of algorithm chosen to implement a program. It is almost always possible to make sacrifices in one area in order to make some gains in other areas (it is also possible of course to make sacrifices that give rise to no benefit at all).

Given the way that the systems have been designed, configured, and set up, the following is inevitable:

- Some parts of the system will be used a lot more than others.

- Slight changes in the configuration, or in the way that the system has been programmed, can result in shifts in this work-load pattern, moving the work from one portion of the system to another.

- In a reasonably well-designed, well-configured, and well-programmed system, relieving an overload in one place is unlikely to lead to anything other than a slight improvement, followed by the discovery of another overload somewhere else.

Each of the preceding points imposes a burden on those that are responsible for setting up and using the system, specifically the following:

- The system must be monitored to detect parts of the system that are overloaded and to find parts of the system that are being underutilized. In a well-managed system, it is no good doing this as an after-the-fact process. Overloads have to be anticipated. If they are not, the user's perception will be of a machine that always has some bit overloaded, and therefore always performs badly.

- The individual responsible for the performance of the system has to be aware of the types of trade-offs that can be made, exchanging increased use of one part of the system for decreased use of some other part. The systems have to be built and run in such a way that it is possible to take advantage of these trade-offs.

- It is necessary that the system be properly designed, configured, and programmed in the first place. If the problem is bad hardware or bad system software design, the only choice available is to buy another machine. But the configuration and the programming of the system are very much the user's responsibility and very much of a continuing process. The demands on the machine will inevitably change over time. Therefore, the way that the machine is programmed, and especially the way that it is configured, must be constantly reevaluated.

The following sections cover system monitoring, performance and trade-offs, and configuring and capacity planning.

SYSTEM MONITORING

Adequate monitoring of the system may involve any number of different sources of information, and there are many different tools available that allow the information to be analyzed.

Sources of Information

Performance-related information may be derived from a number of different sources, at least in a large-scale multiuser system. In a sense, micros are easier to deal with because the performance problem may be confined to something that fits on the top of a desk. On the other hand, micros may present some formidable performance problems. Not being built as multiuser systems (though many these days are multitasking systems) they are unlikely to have the same entry point "hooks," into the systems software, which can be used on larger machines to maintain performance-related information. Most of the remarks regarding information-gathering tools should be taken then as applying to large-scale systems, not to micros, although of course similar problems frequently apply.

The following are cited as examples of the types of information sources that ought to be available on a system:

- System log, maintained by the operating system, containing potentially huge amounts of information related to execution of programs, usage of files, and user-related activity.

- Sampling and system status utilities, which may make use of hooks provided by the operating system, which can be used to access information concerning the current state of the machine. By definition, sampling does not provide a continuous record of what has happened on the machine, but rather gives a snapshot of the machine at some particular moment in time. As such, interpolation may be necessary to get a smooth picture over an extended time period. It may be possible to monitor the system to a very fine level of detail, but this is likely to be prohibitively expensive.

- A database audit trail is maintained by the database management software and should contain time-stamped entries for almost all significant activities on the database. As such, it can be used as a source for a variety of different types of information. For example, amount of time spent in transaction state, number of updates per transaction, and so on.

- The message control system (typically CICS [Central Information Control System] in an IBM environment) maintains audit trails. Statistics may be derived from the audit trail and in turn may be used to derive information about the data communications activity on the system.

Another way of looking at sources of information is to consider both the kinds of things that it may be desirable to monitor and where the relevant information may be found:

Terminal response: No readily available source; there are some devices that allow individual messages to be monitored, but these are so expensive to run that they are usually not used. Intelligent terminals may help.

Line utilization: May be monitored indirectly by looking at messages on a per-line basis.

Memory utilization: Can be looked at in a variety of ways, usually either using information extracted from the system log or sampling via hooks into the operating system.

Processor: Can be monitored using much the same tools as are used for monitoring memory utilization.

I/O subsystem: Has usually been the most complex to monitor; operating system hooks and the system log are the usual primary sources of information, but there are any number of other mechanisms for obtaining information about the I/O subsystem's performance, particularly in a database system.

Monitoring Tools

There are at least four distinct types of monitoring tools likely to be of use in the process of tuning the system:

1. On-line performance
2. Static performance
3. Database performance
4. Static database analysis

ON-LINE PERFORMANCE

An on-line system performance monitor is capable of providing a second-by-second picture of the state of various machine parameters. Of particular importance is the ability to see processor, memory, and I/O utilization, preferably in some sort of graphic display. Also extremely important is being able to see the machine state. If the machine performance degrades periodically because some high-priority process is saturating a critical resource, identifying the culprit can be extremely difficult. It is not unusual for a large machine to be running in excess of 300 separate tasks simultaneously, any one of which may have an adverse impact on the performance of the system.

It is also vitally important to be able to spot hardware failures reliably and quickly. Large machines are very carefully modularized so that failures in one component do not disable the entire machine. In some cases, they may be so insensitive to failure that large portions of the configuration may have to fail before the machine ceases operating altogether. The problem is, however, that the performance very rapidly degrades. If, for example, some of the I/O channels to the disk unit that contains the memory overlay file fail, the whole system will rapidly go idle. Processing units will be suspended, waiting to activate tasks that cannot be activated because I/Os are not completing against the overlay file; the processing on the machine as a whole will rapidly come to a complete halt.

One very important tool here, not directly connected with performance monitoring, is a supervisor program. There are a number of such programs available for most of the large mainframes. Generally, they will ensure that the machine hardware and software configuration is correct. This involves ensuring that all of the disks, memory, processors, and so on are present that ought to be present. It also involves ensuring that programs that ought to be running are running and that nothing is either running when it should not or running at a higher priority than it should. Supervisor programs will also activate jobs that have to be run on a regular basis.

STATIC PERFORMANCE

A static performance monitor is probably the most important tool and should provide the ability to store and retrieve information in a properly featured and documented statistical database. The process of monitoring a system more than justifies the need for such a tool. In the absence of something of the kind, the monitoring and analysis process is likely to be very haphazard.

DATABASE PERFORMANCE

A database performance monitor may be provided as a specialized tool, allowing the performance of the database to be dynamically monitored and altered. In practice, many of the performance-relevant characteristics of a system are likely to be so complex as to be beyond the statistical capabilities of most database administration departments. As a result, the only way to tune the database is to prod it and see what happens. This implies the ability both to prod it and to see it, which is what the database performance monitor is for. Without such a tool, it is unlikely that adequate fine tuning on the system will be possible. It is extremely important.

STATIC DATABASE ANALYSIS

A static database analyzer is necessary to be able to detect situations where the structures that compose the database have become unbalanced. The classic case here is that of random structures and the number of overflow blocks, but most data management systems tend to support a variety of structures that may need readjustment over time.

A PERFORMANCE DATABASE

Listed below is part of the schema implied by a performance monitor. The database may be thought of as being automatically populated by various utilities that may be run as a part of the performance monitoring system.

The following figures obviously represent an ideal case, but it is highly informative in a number of ways. First, this case provides some insight into the immense range of information that has to be maintained if the performance of the system is to be monitored adequately. Second, it illustrates a tantalizing versatility on the part of the semantic data model (SDM). The model has no trouble providing a clear and understandable representation of a very complex data domain; all that remains is to implement it. This, too, need not be very difficult once a suitably structured semantic database management system has been constructed. Unfortunately, this is likely to be quite beyond the resources of most data processing organizations.

The "slice" class is a device for representing time. The entities in the subclass "disk slice" of "slice," represent temporal instances of the entities in the subclass "disk" of "object." The entities in "disk" of "object" each represent a class because they have instances, and only classes can have instances. Although it is not explicitly stated then, there is an ISA relationship between "slice" and "object" indicating, for each given "slice," what it is a "slice" of.

The entities in the "slice" class can also be thought of as samples—that is, snapshots of the state of an entity at a particular instant in time.

The following are examples of some of the types of data that might be derived from the database.

```
Sessions by user code
     From Session Retrieve User code, Start time Order
          BY item 1

Session I/O time
     From Session Retrieve User Code, SUM (I/O Time OF
          Session Tasks)

Average Session Process time by User Code
     From Session Retrieve User code,
     AVERAGE (SUM (Process Time OF Session Tasks))

Sessions by station name
     From Station Retrieve Name, COUNT (Sessions)

Syntaxed compilations by user
     From Compile Retrieve User Code,
     COUNT(Syntax Error COUNT > 0)
     Order BY item 1, item 2

Worst case I/O
     From Task Retrieve Name OF Code File
     where I/O Time = Max (I/O Time)

Worst case memory
     From Slice Retrieve Name OF Code File OF Object
             where
       MAX(Memory Utilization OF Transitive(Last
           slice)) =
       MAX(Memory Utilization)
```

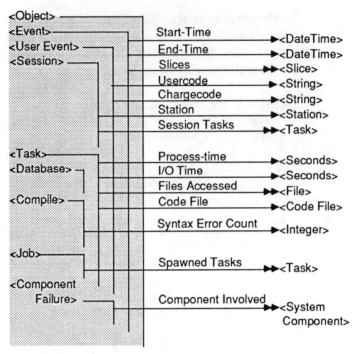

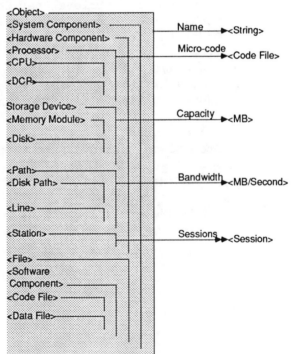

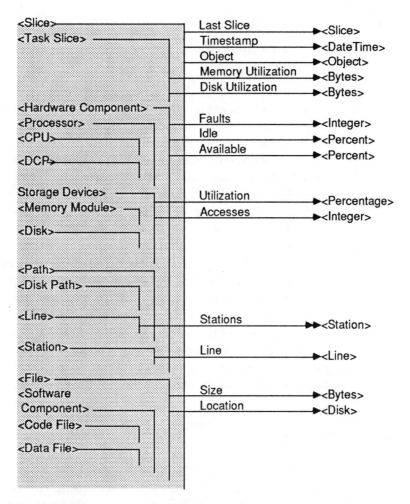

The following are examples of the information that is important to the utilization of the machine as a whole.

Available memory

Memory overlays

Amount idle

I/Os per second

Mix count

Processor overhead

Processor time logged

Task elapsed time

Task I/O time

It is a useful exercise, so far as reviewing information sources is concerned, to look at the performance database from the point of view of how the utilization information could be derived. Much of it is derivable from information already present in the database; some of it would require additional classes or attributes. The information is all just different manifestations of the information that was outlined at the beginning of this chapter, such as sampling data, audit trail, system log extracts, and so on.

It is somewhat unusual to see performance data represented using a database. This is largely, however, due to the inadequacies of the data models that have previously been available for the purpose. The SDM provides a perfectly adequate vehicle for expressing the semantics of a data processing system. There is no reason why it should be limited to the expression of the semantics of a business application.

As is shown in the following section, the process can even be extended beyond the representation of performance data, to the representation of the current state of the system itself.

Database Monitoring

Monitoring a database is one very specialized aspect of monitoring the system as a whole. As with the system itself, the current state of the database is represented here using an SDM diagram, though a significant extension to the model is being introduced. In almost all of the previous database examples the data in the database has represented something else. The entities have not actually been entities at all; they have been representations of entities. With the database monitoring system, the situation is quite different; here, the entities in the database are the things themselves. When the contents of the database are manipulated or examined, it is the things themselves that are being manipulated or examined.

There is no particular reason why a semantic database should not be used in this way in other contexts as well. For example, in controlling an automated assembly line or in monitoring and controlling industrial robots, the same consideration applies. Provided the data model is rich enough to capture the semantics of the system, it can be used to directly control and monitor the system, not merely to represent the behavior of the system secondhand.

As mentioned, the behavior of the database system, considered as a unit, is likely to be extremely complex. It is essential to have both an adequate set of techniques for altering the behavior of the database and an adequate source of information as to the state of the database on a moment-by-moment basis. The database monitoring schema is a subset of the performance monitoring schema presented previously.

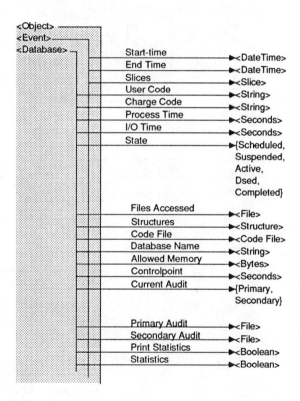

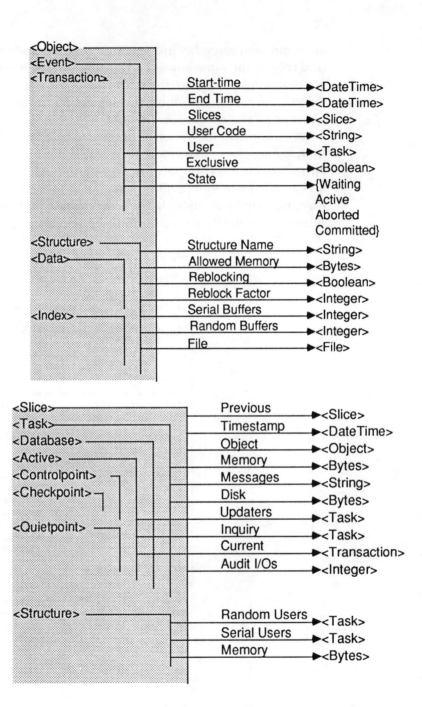

<Object>
<Event>
<Transaction>

Start-time	►<DateTime>
End Time	►<DateTime>
Slices	►<Slice>
User Code	►<String>
User	►<Task>
Exclusive	►<Boolean>
State	►{Waiting Active Aborted Committed}

<Structure>
<Data>

<Index>

Structure Name	►<String>
Allowed Memory	►<Bytes>
Reblocking	►<Boolean>
Reblock Factor	►<Integer>
Serial Buffers	►<Integer>
Random Buffers	►<Integer>
File	►<File>

<Slice>
<Task>
<Database>
<Active>
<Controlpoint>
<Checkpoint>
<Quietpoint>

Previous	►<Slice>
Timestamp	►<DateTime>
Object	►<Object>
Memory	►<Bytes>
Messages	►<String>
Disk	►<Bytes>
Updaters	►<Task>
Inquiry	►<Task>
Current	►<Transaction>
Audit I/Os	►<Integer>

<Structure>

Random Users	►<Task>
Serial Users	►<Task>
Memory	►<Bytes>

Most of the elements of this schema are explained during the course of this chapter. In particular, random and serial users and the structure types are explained in some detail in the discussions of performance trade-offs and the statistical characteristics of the different structure types.

Here are some examples of how the database may be controlled: (1) setting the allowed memory of PartsDB to 600,000 bytes and setting the control-point frequency to 200 seconds—

```
Modify Database (
    Allowed Memory := 600000
    Controlpoint frequency := 200)
    Where Database Name = "PartsDB"
```

or (2) altering the PartsDB Audit file to the secondary audit—

```
Modify Database (
    Current Audit := Secondary)
    Where Database Name = "PartsDB"
```

or (3) decreasing the allowed memory of all databases by 10%—

```
Modify Database (
    Allowed Memory := Allowed Memory * 0.9)
    Where true
```

The examples could be elaborated almost indefinitely, but the last example particularly underlines a very serious problem so far as controlling databases is concerned. It is frequently the case that a large system is running multiple databases simultaneously. At the very least, it is running multiple programs simultaneously. It may be necessary to perform precisely the type of operation indicated by the last **modify**— that is, a change to all of the databases running on the system.

At present, very few mechanisms exist that would allow this to be done conveniently and effectively. Those that do exist (generally in the form of supervisor programs) do not provide a general-purpose language for describing and manipulating the system. They tend to provide specific commands that can only be used to deal with whatever circumstances were envisaged by the designers of the system.

So far as monitoring and controlling tools are concerned, there is little more than cold comfort for those responsible for database performance. The environments in which the database runs tend to be very fragmented, and the facilities available to alter the performance of the database while it is in use are limited and very system-specific, with differing implementations and approaches. There is no unified language for handling the system. With the SDM, however, it is at least possible to represent one's understanding of the information in a rational manner, even if the tools themselves still leave a great deal to be desired.

SYSTEM-RELATED PERFORMANCE TRADE-OFFS

Extracting the maximum possible performance from a database is generally a case of making the best of a bad job (i.e., trading off advantages in one area against disadvantages in some other area). All such design trade-offs have to be considered in terms of the basic resources available on the machine:

I/Os (inputs/outputs)

Memory

Disk space

Processor

The order of importance varies greatly from one machine to the next, and may even vary from one application to the next on the same machine. The characteristics of each of these resources is summarized in what follows.

I/Os (Inputs and Outputs)

The I/O capability of a system is determined by a series of paths. Each path has a *bandwidth*—that is, a maximum amount of data that can be transferred down the path in a given unit of time. Each path also has an upper limit on the number of transfers that can be handled in a unit of time, regardless of the amount of data per transfer. The I/O subsystem can be pictured as a branching tree interconnected with a single root, which is the system main memory, and multiple leaves.

There may be more than one path from the root to a given leaf. The bandwidth for a path varies, depending on how far the path is from the leaves. On a large mainframe, paths near to the root have bandwidths in the order of tens or even hundreds of megabytes per second.

Memory

From a structural point of view, memory tends to be the simplest of the resources. With some older operating systems, memory subsystems have to be established to overcome memory address limitations. These can lead to major complexities but are ignored here. Related to this is the fact that memory historically has been fairly small, both because there was no perceived need for large memories and because memory was very expensive. It is now the case, however, that very large memories are becoming available. It is common, especially with the advent of PS/2, for micros to have more than one megabyte of memory. Large mainframes may have tens or even hundreds of megabytes of memory. It is frequently the case that the system software is several years behind the hardware in taking advantage of the general increases in memory size.

Another related development is the use of structured memories with very high speed cache memory located architecturally close to the central processor. Slower devices are used for main memory. Memory chips are also beginning to appear outside of the central system as intermediate storage areas (e.g., associated with disk controllers and paths to disk and data communications controllers). For the most part, these considerations can be ignored, as it is generally not possible to alter these factors once the system has been installed.

Mass Storage

There are fundamental differences among mass storage devices, based on the way that the data on the device is to be used. At one end of the continuum are data that will be regularly accessed, in a random fashion, as a part of an on-line system. At the other end of the continuum, the data are infrequently accessed, in a serial fashion, by batch processes which may be scheduled so as not to clash with other users of the data.

The on-line system implies random access mass storage devices with read/write capabilities, able to deliver arbitrarily selected data in a very short period of time, generally about 20 to 30 milliseconds. Oddly enough, bandwidth of the data path is usually not an issue. The ability to transfer large volumes of data is not important; the ability to rapidly access small amounts of data is what counts. From a practical point of view, the only devices currently available for this purpose are disks.

The batch system implies serial access; write-once-only devices may be used on the assumption that data, once written, will not be rewritten. Magnetic tapes are the principal medium. They are cheap, and so far as bandwidth is concerned, they are comparable with disks, in some cases even offering a considerable improvement. Batch systems may make use of disks, but they have a quite different requirement so far as accesses are concerned.

The ideal for a batch program is for the system to be able to deliver information in chunks large enough to keep the program constantly busy. As soon as the program finishes dealing with one chunk, the next chunk becomes available. This is possible if the program, or the system, initiates the next I/O operation before it starts dealing with the current buffer. The disk unit, when servicing a batch program, needs to supply information in large contiguous chunks.

This is in direct conflict with the requirements of the on-line program. The pattern of I/O usage on the system then must at best be something of a compromise.

Processor

The central processing unit or CPU, is a single-user device that has to be shared among multiple system users. In the absence of radically new software architectures, the CPU will remain an overriding factor in the performance of the system as a whole.

Where a process may be broken up into a very large number of small, independent processes, it is possible to use a system with multiple CPUs. Such a system may have a very high nominal processor rating. Unfortunately, this processing power is only available currently for a very limited set of applications, mostly in the scientific arena. For normal commercial database applications, a single or limited number of CPUs is unavoidable.

In normal commercial applications, where a multiple processor system is used, the increase in processing power for an additional processor tends to be very small beyond about the fourth processor. The problem is that the processors need to communicate with each other in order to coordinate accesses to whatever resources have to be shared on the system—in the case of a database application, notably, the database itself. It is in this process of communication that the problem lies. Before performing certain kinds of operations (for example, initiating I/Os or allocating memory), the processor has to ask all the other processors if it is OK to do the operation. It has to interrupt the other processors, wait for them to respond, and then carry on. This represents a substantial overhead that increases as the number of processors in the system increases. It is the main reason why current developments in mainframe design tend to focus on large, one- or two-processor systems.

Database-Related Performance Trade-offs

There are a number of miscellaneous considerations that have to be taken into account in a database context:

- Random versus serial users
- Recovery speed
- Abort speed
- Structure overhead
- Ease of reorganization

These are not in any particular order, although the first four can have a drastic impact on performance in the form of perceived response time. The trade-offs implied are summarized in the following subsections.

Random versus Serial Users

Random users require small block-sizes. A random user, by definition, is unlikely to look at more than one record in a block. Every record the block contains beyond the one of interest represents wasted memory and wasted I/O capacity for records that are never looked at. The serial user, on the other hand, looks at every record in a block. The serial user does not want to do more I/Os than necessary, so the block should be as big as possible, within certain limits. Random and serial users are completely at odds with each other so far as their demands on the system are concerned. Some techniques for getting round this problem are discussed later.

Recovery Speed

It is possible to reduce the amount of time it takes to recover a system to an arbitrarily small amount, depending on the frequency with which the database buffers are flushed to disk. A record in the buffers is ordinarily not written to disk on the assumption that if it is altered, the altered image of the record will be written to the audit trail and so may always be recovered from there. If nothing is ever written to disk (everything only being written to the audit trail), it follows that it may take nearly as long to recover the system as it did to do the processing in the first place. On the other hand, however, the system will go very fast because there are only (unavoidable) I/Os to the audit trail and no I/Os to disk. Obviously, there must be a compromise somewhere between (a) the frequency with which the database buffers are written to disk and (b) recovery speed. The less frequently the buffers are written out, the longer the recovery process. The business of writing the buffers to disk is known as a control point.

Abort Speed

An abort is the process of undoing a single transaction. The undo process will involve going back through the audit trail finding all of the things that the transaction did, and reversing them. The basic trade-off here is a somewhat fixed one between the complexity of the audit trail and the speed with which an abort can be performed.

Under some circumstances, the database buffers may not be lost, but it may still be necessary to get the database into a state where no users are in *transaction state* (why will be addressed in the chapter on integrity). This is a *system abort.* Here the main requirement is for a quiet point. This is different from a control point, which usually implies a quiet point. With a *quiet point,* the buffers are not flushed, but all users have to be out of transaction state. A quiet point will still have the considerable overhead of forcing the system to wait until all users are out of transaction state. System aborts may be speeded up at the price of forcing quiet points more frequently.

Structure Overhead

Each additional logical structure tends to add overhead because of the large amounts of data that may have to be maintained by the database in order to manage the structure. A structure here may be either a file or an index. It is not uncommon to find databases with more than 1000 physical structures in them; if each structure requires 300 bytes of information for its management, this means 300,000 bytes just for metadata. This is probably a gross underestimate, as 1000 physical structures may imply in excess of 10,000 to 20,000 items.

Ease of Reorganization

The speed with which a structure can be accessed can often be increased by making the structure more elaborate in various ways. It is also the case that the more complex a structure is, the less flexible it will be. So it may be possible to design a very complex and very efficient database, but if the logical structure of the database changes, the ramifications, so far as accessing algorithms and protocols are concerned, may be extensive.

OPERATION-RELATED PERFORMANCE TRADE-OFFS

In designing a database system, both database-related and system-related trade-offs must be taken into account. The individual requirements of a given database and of the system as a whole have to be considered in determining what is an appropriate balance.

In addition to the system- and database-related trade-offs for a particular database (and often even for a particular structure), it is important to consider the performance implications for the usual database operations. Once again, trade-offs are common. Improvements in one area often lead to a loss of performance in others. These areas include trade-offs for record

- Insertion
- Deletion
- Modification
- Access

The various techniques available for implementing a relationship, for example, can only be fully assessed in the light of these design trade-offs. It is often the case that some approach will only be preferable to another in the light of some specific trade-off. It is also often the case that a structure that performs extremely well in some respect is prohibitively bad in some other, meaning that some middle-of-the-road approach has to be adopted.

The operation-related trade-offs are usually very system-specific. Typical of the kind of issue that is to be found in this area is space allocation. When inserting a new record, the system has to be able to find a slot for the record without having to spend too much time looking for one. One obvious strategy is to simply stick the record on the end of the file, but then as records are deleted, the file will come to have an enormous amount of wasted space in it. So it becomes necessary to make **delete** more expensive by requiring the **delete** operation to maintain some sort of list of available space.

Another common trade-off is speed of access versus deletion and insertion cost and space utilization. The ideal case is for access to be via an index of some sort. An index implies an additional file, which both requires some space (in memory and on disk) and requires some sort of maintenance. Every time a record is inserted into the file, or deleted from the file, all of the indexes that span the file have to be updated as well. So a record insertion or deletion may become an operation on many different files just so that accesses can go a bit faster. It is not uncommon to find systems that have an index that is accessed once a month or so, by a program that could quite readily be run as a batch process. In this case, the index is a complete waste of time and space.

When designing a database, it is necessary to bear all of these factors constantly in mind. The choice of structure type will have a direct, and in some cases dramatic, impact on the performance of certain types of operations. When the database is designed in the first place, and every time it changes in any way, all of this has to be reevaluated.

IMPLICATIONS

The more complex the database structures used, the more difficult it is to write programs to access the database. Furthermore, the database will be less flexible and more difficult to manage. A lot of the design strategy therefore depends on the expertise of the individuals likely to access the database. In the absence of an SDM, if all the programmers are super smart and highly experienced, do whatever you like; otherwise, watch it!

Probably the best strategy for most data processing installations is to stick to flat files with foreign keys and make 100% certain that everyone understands these ideas (especially 1:M and M:M relationships).

PERFORMANCE-RELATED DATABASE CHARACTERISTICS

Various aspects of the physical specification of a database are purely performance related and have little or nothing to do with data modeling. They come under two general headings; data compaction and physical options.

Data Compaction

A number of possible options may allow for automatic data compaction. The options available will be very system-specific. There is, of course, a major trade-off between processor time and space utilization. Something that is frequently overlooked in this respect is memory utilization. As the records are compacted, not only do they use less space on disk, but they are also likely to use less space in the database buffers. This is often a far more important consideration than the disk space saved by the record compaction.

Data compaction has had a number of pernicious effects on the logical structure of the database. In many cases, the lack of good compaction capabilities has led to size specifications in the database that are not derived from the logical characteristics of the data, but rather are associated with the physical constraints on the way that the data has to be stored. This is particularly evident with unstructured alphanumeric descriptions, which, in programming terms, are probably unbounded strings of characters. So far as the database is concerned, some upper bound on the size will have to be declared, with the size frequently being a poor compromise between the space wasted in the average case, which may be very small, and the difficulties in dealing with the exceptional case, which may be very large.

Physical Options

A number of aspects to the physical database have to be specified as a part of the process of specifying the database as a whole. Here, the discussion is somewhat hampered by a lack of standardization in the terminology. The following terms have a special meaning here, and a familiarity with the meaning should be acquired from the glossary, if necessary, before reading the section.

- Buffers
- Block and block size
- Table and table size
- Record size
- Cylinder and track size
- Modulus
- Population
- Load factor

Various physical structure options may have to be specified for each structure or file type. The options that may be specified will vary from type to type. The main possible options types are as follows:

Block level integrity checks

File physical location information

POPULATION = <integer>: This provides an upper limit on the number of records that can be stored in the structure. It is likely to be used at initialization time in determining sizes for tables needed to maintain the structure.

REBLOCK = TRUE/FALSE: If true is specified, this allows different block sizes to be specified for random versus serial users—an essential feature that is discussed later in this chapter.

REBLOCKFACTOR = <integer>: The integer indicates the size of the block to be allocated for serial users, in blocksize units.

AREAS = <integer>: Some mechanism is needed to allow for the specification of the total amount of space to be allocated on disk. This can be computed from the population and the area size.

AREASIZE = <integer>: The size of each area allocated on disk is the unit in which disk areas are allocated. The term, though not the concept, is somewhat system-specific. If there are a lot of mutually prime area sizes, the disk will, after a time become checkerboarded. That is, a number of areas will not be in use on the disk, but they are not of a size likely to be requested by users of the disk.

BLOCKSIZE = <integer>: This is the basic unit of I/O, the minimum amount of information that can be read from the file in a single I/O. It should be small for random users and large for serial users.

BUFFERS = <integer> PER USER + <integer> PER USER . . . . : This is the number of memory buffers that are allocated to the file by the data management system. Obviously the more buffers that can be allocated to the file, the faster the access to the file is likely to be. It is highly desirable to be able to bias the memory allocation toward those structures that are critical or likely to be heavily used. It is also highly desirable to be able to differentiate between random and serial users, allocating a basic set of buffers for use by random users, plus additional buffers for those accessing the structure serially.

LOADFACTOR: The load factor indicates the way that index-sequential structures are to be loaded.

MODULUS: Determines the number of base blocks in a random structure. This is further elaborated subsequently.

TABLESIZE: The equivalent of block size for an index.

Given the complexity of the structural physical options, it is essential to be able to specify global defaults. It is also essential that altering the structural characteristics not be too difficult. Specifically, where possible, alterations should not require the database to be taken down.

Basic Access Types

Before describing the specification of the physical structure parameters, it is advisable to look at the basic features of the various structure types and the methods of accessing them. If the value for one of the attributes of a record is known, and if the record happens to be one of a number of records held in a file, there are only three possible ways of accessing the records. The assumption is that the file itself can be accessed by a **read** operation that can specify the file's relative record number for the record to be read. The read will be something like

$$\mathrm{READ}(n)$$

where n is the number of the record to be read. There are three fundamentally different methods of accessing such a file.

METHOD 1

Start at the beginning, and read each record in the file until either the target record is located or the end of the file is reached. This is *sequential access*. A file accessed in this way is sometimes referred to as a sequential-access method file, or SAM file. Generally, the cost of accessing the file, where a record is always found, is reckoned as

$$n / 2$$

I/Os, where n is the number of blocks in the file. The reasoning is that if the records found are randomly distributed across the file, the average case will find the record in the middle of the file. Therefore, the number of records that have to be accessed is, on average, half the records present in the file.

A very important corollary of this is that if a record is not always found, the average cost of the access goes up. Where a record is not found, all of the records in the file will have to be accessed. For example, if three out of every four accesses find nothing, the cost will be

$$7 n / 8$$

Generally speaking, as the proportion of unsuccessful accesses increases, the average cost of accessing the file becomes the cost of simply not finding anything, which itself represents a worst possible case.

METHOD 2

Assuming that the records in the file are in some sort of order, and the value being searched for is a value for one of the attributes on which the records are ordered, the accessing process successively partitions the file until either the record is found or no more partitions are possible. The approach here is to successively divide up the file. Given that the file is ordered, it is possible to determine, at each division, which portion of the file might contain the record being sought. This process is continued until either the record is found or the portion of the file to be divided consists of a single record—that is, it cannot be divided any further! For example, suppose the file consists of the following:

Record number	Attribute value
1	2
2	3
3	5
4	7
5	11
6	13
7	17
8	19
9	23
10	29
11	31
12	37
13	41
14	43
15	47
16	53

In this example, we want to know if there is a record in the file with the number 11 as its attribute value. The search process will involve the following steps:

Search Step	Record Ranges	Attribute Found
1	1–8 and 9–16	19

The attribute found is larger than the attribute being searched for, therefore the record, if it is in the file, will be in the lower record range—that is, records 1–8. The next partition gives the following:

2	1–4 and 5–8	7

The attribute found is smaller than the attribute being searched for, therefore the record, if in the file, will be in the record range 5–8.

3	5–6 and 7–8	13

The attribute found is larger again; look in the lower record range.

4	5 and 6	11

This time, we found it!

There are numerous other ordering and partitioning techniques, but this suffices to give an idea of the general characteristics of this method of accessing records in a file. For reasons that become apparent later in this chapter, the cost of accessing a record in this type of file is generally reckoned as n I/O operations where

$$2^n$$

Is the first power of 2 greater than or equal to the number of records in the file. In the foregoing file search, the number of records in the file was 16; therefore the number of accesses required was 4, 2^4 being equal to 16. If the file had contained 250 records, the number of accesses would have been 2^8, which equals 256, the next power of 2 after 250.

METHOD 3

Random access to a file is possible when the location of the records in the file is determined by the value of an attribute of the record type that the file contains. How this file location is derived from the attribute value does not really matter (for the moment anyway); the main point is that there is some kind of function (a) that may be applied to the attribute value, and (b) that will return the address of the record containing the attribute value if the record happens to be present in the file.

Using the same set of records as was used for Method 2, the function used will be DIVIDE-BY-2(x), which adds 1 to x, divides the result by two, and returns this value. DIVIDE-BY-2 will be applied to each of the attribute values to determine the relative record number in the file of the associated record, giving the following record distribution:

Record number	Attribute value
1	2
2	3
3	5
4	7
6	11
7	13
9	17
10	19
12	23
15	29
16	31
19	37
21	41
22	43
24	47
27	53

The attribute values are still in order in the file. This is unusual and would not normally be the case with the types of functions (known as "hashing functions" or "hashing algorithms") actually used by data management systems. Also, there are *gaps* (unused records in the file), indicating an uneven distribution of the records over the available slots in the file. This is not unusual, although hashing algorithms are usually quite smart and do not bunch records or leave large gaps.

A different hashing function, BEETHOVENS-AGE-WHEN-HE-PUBLISHED-IT, assumes that its parameter is the opus number of a piece of music by Beethoven and returns Beethoven's age when he first published the piece.

Record number	Attribute value	
	41	there is no opus 41
26	2	
26	3	
27	5	
28	7	
29	11	
29	13	
31	17	
31	19	
31	23	
32	43	
33	29	
33	31	
35	37	
35	47	
35	53	

We can assume that in the absence of any relevant date, the function just places the record in the first slot in the file. The records are now no longer in order; also, more than one record is being allocated to a particular slot. This is fine, given that a slot is not just a single record, but a whole block, potentially containing more than one record. If however, a larger number of records than the number of records in a block, gets allocated to a slot, then an overflow block will have to be allocated. At this point, access to the file for this particular hashing value becomes sequential, not random. That is, all of the blocks for that hash value will have to be searched using method 1, which is inherently expensive.

Statistical techniques are available for determining the cost of an access to a random structure. These are moderately complicated, however, and they are described in some detail in the subsection, "File Physical Parameters."

Basic Structure Types

Accesses may be either to a file or to an index. An *index* is a file that contains key values plus pointers to another file. In this way, it is possible both to have random access via two quite different keys to the same file, and to apparently maintain the same file in two different orders, by having two different sorted indexes on it. It should be the case that there are no particular limits either on the *number* of indexes permitted on a file, or on the *types* of indexes and files that may be mixed in this way.

For most purposes, there are only four structure types to consider; they are directly related to the three access types:

Sequential: may be expected to allow moderately efficient usage of
> disk space and has good insertion and deletion characteristics.
> Any performance problems will probably be with associated
> indexes rather than with the files. The files can only be ac-
> cessed sequentially.

Random: may be used for files as well as indexes; the key must distri-
> bute the records evenly across the file. When some block in the
> file becomes full, if the hashing algorithm allocates a record to
> the full block, an overflow block has to be generated. There
> should be too many overflow blocks, as this implies multiple I/
> Os to access any records that happen to be located in the
> block.

Direct (actually a type of random structure): requires the existence of
> a suitable key value. It can only be used where it is possible to
> directly compute the record address from a key value. The file
> is logically split into record slots; a record with a key value of 11
> goes in slot number 11, 15 into slot 15; generally, a record with
> key value n goes into slot n. The data management system can
> directly compute the block to be read from the key value of the
> record being accessed; there is no likelihood of having to do
> additional I/Os. Also, insertion and deletion tend to be cheap.
> It is very fast but not always possible.

Index-sequential: probably used only for indexes. It can be very
> inefficient to use an index-sequential index instead of doing a
> *sort*, where approximately one record per block of the file is
> being touched. Sorting should be performed, at least partially,
> in memory (if the algorithm used is any good at all), whereas
> reading for indexes necessarily involves I/Os, and I/Os tend to
> be orders of magnitude more expensive than memory accesses.
> Accesses to a file via an index (a) inevitably makes the file

accesses random (why else go via the index?), (b) at least involves the extra I/Os to the index, and (c) probably also involves reading the same block of the file several times. Indexes may need rebalancing occasionally, depending on the implementation.

In assessing which of the various structure types are suitable for a given application, a number of issues, other than the straightforward structure characteristics, have to be borne in mind, notably the following:

- The extent to which reorganization may be used to compensate for some deficiency of the structure (e.g., getting rid of overflow blocks in random files; this is covered in the section, "Reorganization Capabilities")
- The extent to which the structure is appropriate
- The type of accesses to be performed (some of these issues have already been touched on; some fairly complex conditions apply to serial access and binary searching; these are discussed in the section on "Efficiency Considerations").

Reorganization Capabilities

Reorganization is likely to offer certain specific capabilities, some of which are aimed at changing the actual record descriptions, and many of which are aimed at garbage collection, or reordering, which allows structures to be adjusted and tuned over time.

The basic reorganization operations may be summarized as follows:

- Reorganize a file so that the order of the records reflects the order of some specified index. This can make serial access via the index more efficient. (If you must do it, you may as well do it efficiently!)
- Consolidate deleted and unused space.
- Generate indexes and automatic partial indexes.
- Balance tables and the distribution of records over coarse and fine tables.
- Change the physical attributes of structures such as, AREAS,

POPULATION, MODULUS, and LOADFACTOR.

- Change a record description.
- Change key, key data, ASCENDING–DESCENDING, and DUPLI-CATES clauses for indexes and partial indexes. The *where* clause for an automatic partial index may also be changed.

Efficiency Considerations

So far as index-sequential indexes are concerned (depending on the optimization strategy), it is likely that certain conditions will have to be adhered to if any binary search is desired (even a partial one). In this, the query is not completely evaluated prior to returning a result to the user. This is certainly the case with most CODASYL or CODASYL-like databases. The conditions are as follows:

- The key items specified must include the highest-order key, and no key items may be omitted between the most and the least significant key used.
- All key conditions on individual key items are connected by AND.
- Except for the least significant key item, all key conditions are in the following form:

<key item> = <expression>

- The relation specified for the least significant key condition may also be significant; for example, one of the following forms may be required (EQL is "equals"):

Find Type	Final Key	Relation
Next	Ascending	EQL, GTR, GEQ
Next	Descending	EQL, LSS, LEQ
Prior	Ascending	EQL, LSS, LEQ
Prior	Descending	EQL, GTR, GEQ

The circumstances under which a system will perform a binary search are likely to be very specific to the system itself. They are, however, extremely important so far as the system performance is concerned. If the system makes widespread use of index-sequential, binary-tree-based structures, any processes that perform random searches in the expectation of using such a structure must be aware of these rules.

This is an unfortunate feature so far as the ad hoc user is concerned, but it should still be taken into account. Consider the following example. A file has a million records in it; each file block contains 100 records (there are 10,000 blocks in the file). A block access requires an I/O taking 0.003 seconds. Accessing a record by reading sequentially through the file may then take as long as 300 seconds, 5 minutes I/O time, and a much greater elapsed time. If the block is accessed using the binary search technique, it will take approximately 14 I/Os, or 0.05 seconds. Therefore, 100 users would require, between them, no more than 5 seconds I/O time, as opposed to over 9 hours for 100 serial users. In practice, the contrast would, if anything be even greater than this.

Some systems allow additional information to be kept in the index tables, which may be accessed without accessing the file spanned by the index. This key data can represent a considerable optimization for accesses that do not require any more than a small subset of the data in the record for the file.

It is frequently the case that access via an index, where a substantial portion of the blocks in the file are being touched, is a lot less efficient than accessing via the file directly. A result equivalent to accessing via the index may be achieved by a direct access via the file, followed by a sort to get the records into the order provided by the index. Effectively, indexes should never be used simply to order a file.

This is the case even in a system that does not distinguish between serial and random users. Assuming that the system does make such a distinction, the performance difference between the two approaches (i.e., reading and sorting versus access via an index) can be quite dramatic. The reason this is the case is associated with the way that the system handles serial versus random users. This in turn is affected by reblocking and read-ahead features (described subsequently).

Reblocking results in a large block being used when performing I/Os for serial users. The normal, presumably smaller, block is used for random users. Users are assumed to be random.

Reblocking occurs when the following happens:

- REBLOCK is enabled for the system.

- REBLOCK is true for the particular structure at run-time (this also implies that the buffers for the structure intended for serial users must be greater than or equal to 2).

- The user program accesses the particular structure sequentially (this is automatically detected by the system software).

Reblocking is also initiated by the use of FIND, LOCK, or DELETE. The relevant structure attributes are REBLOCK and REBLOCKFAC-TOR:

- REBLOCK may be true or false and may be set or reset for a particular structure.

- REBLOCKFACTOR provides the number of block-size blocks to use as a (larger) serial user block, sometimes referred to as a "big block."

Another feature associated with the distinction between serial and random users is read-ahead. *Read-ahead* requires the system to recognize that a user is reading sequentially through a structure. The system anticipates the next access by initiating a **read** on the structure before it is requested. Given that a proportion of the users of a database are likely to be serial users, and given that such usage is likely to be by batch programs that access very large portions of the database, the read-ahead feature can be vital to the overall performance of the system.

Read-ahead is activated if a program does a predetermined number of serial accesses in succession. An access is considered to be serial if it accesses either the same block as the previous access, or a logically adjacent block. Read-ahead is terminated after a predetermined number of random accesses. If a program changes state more than once, the system will make it more difficult for subsequent state changes to take place.

In determining the block size for a structure, particularly either random structures or index-sequential structures that are to be accessed randomly, the following must then be taken into account:

- Large block sizes are unlikely to benefit random users and will probably just result in substantial amounts of wasted space in the database buffers (i.e., the presence of a large number of records in memory that will never be accessed).

- Reblocking may be used to accommodate the needs of serial users.

- It is never possible to take a uniform approach to the entire database. In particular, the strategies required for indexes and files will differ markedly. With indexes, it may be the case that it is worth the trouble of allocating large block sizes and trying to keep all, or at least a large part of the structure in memory.

It should be remembered that serial access via an index usually implies random access to the file (unless the file's records happen to be in the same order as the index), but the system may, when accessing via an index, do read-aheads on the index while not doing read-aheads on the file.

In the case of serial users, allocating more memory beyond a certain point will not be of any benefit. This amounts to saying that there is an optimal REBLOCKFACTOR for serial users, based on the length of time that the user takes to process a single block. Assuming that read-ahead is in operation, REBLOCKFACTOR should be set so that when the user completes processing for block n, block $n+1$ has just been read in. There is no point, however, in reading in block $n+1$ if the user is going to be preoccupied with block n for milliseconds to come. An appropriate value for REBLOCKFACTOR can only be determined experimentally.

It is inevitably the case that, in the absence of the reblock and read-ahead features, if a database is accessed simultaneously by both random and serial users, the system will perform badly for one or the other class of users.

FILE PHYSICAL PARAMETERS

Various types of file parameters will have to be specified as a part of the process of establishing the database. For most file types, establishing appropriate parameter values is fairly simple. Some simple statistical techniques may be used for choosing physical parameters for random structures.

Given that a database is a multiuser system, the placement of portions of files is not considered. The allocation of files to particular physical locations on a disk unit is only likely to be of benefit when there is a single user of the unit. File allocation at this level is usually justified in terms of avoiding unnecessary seek-time on the disk's read heads. Clearly, if there is an arbitrary mix of requests likely to be addressed to

the disk unit, the position of the read heads becomes quite unpredictable, and the chore of specifying cylinder-and-track-level file locations
is quite unjustifiable.

AREAS, or the total number of physical disk areas allocated to a file,
should not be particularly important, as it should be a relatively trivial
matter to change the population for a structure. At the most, the
change may require a file-format reorganization, and it should not
affect any users of the system (other than possibly making the system
unavailable for the period of the reorganization).

AREASIZE can be important as a result of the fact that the disk is
allocated in units of AREASIZE. If there are a large number of different
and mutually prime AREASIZEs being used by different users of the
system, after a while, the disk will tend to become checkerboarded—
that is, there will be lots of areas of a size that no one can use. This is not
very serious if a disk SQUASH can be done on-line.

A disk SQUASH moves the areas allocated to files located on the disk
in such a way that all file areas become contiguous. After the SQUASH,
ideally, the disk is divided into one in-use region and one available
region. AREASIZE should be considered carefully, however, where
structures are especially volatile. SQUASH is inevitably very expensive
business in terms of I/Os.

Minimum disk allocation and transfer unit should of course be
considered when BLOCKSIZEs are allocated. Throughout the following discussion, this is assumed to be 256 bytes; this being the case, block
sizes that are not multiples of 256 bytes (especially small block sizes)
may represent a serious waste of I/O capacity.

Random Files

A random structure that has been in use for some time will have two
types of block in it: base blocks and overflow blocks. Recall that the
BEETHOVENS-AGE-WHEN-HE-PUBLISHED-IT function may be used
to determine the location of any record, where the relevant attribute
from the record is used as the parameter to the function. The function
provides a block number in which the record is to be located. It may be
the case that a number of different records will all be allocated to the
same block—that is, to the same base block. When the block becomes
full, the system has to make additional space available in the same
logical "slot," and it does this by allocating an overflow block. The

overflow block is reached by following a pointer located in the original base block. So if the file is being searched and a block with an overflow block is encountered, both the block and the overflow block will have to be examined for candidate records. That is, extra I/Os have to be performed as a result of the presence of the overflow block.

In the case of random files, it is very important, in the interests of efficiency, to be able to predict the number of overflow blocks that are likely to be created. The calculations to achieve this require the use of the cumulative Poisson probability function. If tables are being used, the normal distribution may have to be used for blocks that contain a large number of records.

The following discussion assumes use of the program "Fisher" to generate a table giving the number of overflow blocks versus the average number of records per block for the block size chosen (this essentially is what has to be done with the cumulative Poisson probability function tables). Fisher actually uses an expansion for the Poisson distribution, so it can save some legwork looking things up in tables.

The *modulus* dictates the number of base blocks, and it is safest to round it up to the nearest prime number. It is important not to use even values for the modulus, as most hashing algorithms behave badly with an even modulus. In this respect, powers of 2 represent a worst possible case. There are a variety of other recommendations for the selection of a modulus value (e.g., odd powers of a prime number; prime numbers alone however, are generally reckoned to be quite sufficient).

A first approximation for the value for the modulus can be derived from the file population divided by the expected number of records per block. As is shown here, this is only an approximation. It pays to try a number of different block-size–modulus combinations. The actual number of blocks in the file is derived from the number of base blocks plus the number of overflow blocks. Both of these values are given in the table supplied by Fisher. The way in which space on disk is allocated is a system-specific task and should take into account the normal constraints on file design.

EXAMPLE 1

In this example, a random file is to contain 20,000 records of up to 180 bytes each, and the required block size is approximately 3000 bytes. (POPULATION = 20,000, record-size = 180, Approximate block size is 3000 bytes. Possible block sizes around 3000 bytes are, 2520, 2880, and

3240, indicating a block size of 16, 14, or 8 records per block.

The program, executed for the values 20000, 8 (i.e., 20,000 records, with 8 records per block), gives the following table:

```
POPULATION = 20000
NUMBER OF   :RECORDS    :PROBABILITY OF   :NUMBER OF   :WASTED
BASE BLOCKS :PER BLOCK  :AN OVERFLOW      :OVERFLOWS   :SPACE (%)
   2500         8          0.399             998         28.53
   2858         7          0.265             758         30.86
   3334         6          0.149             497         34.74
   4000         5          0.062             251         41.18
   5000         4          0.018              93         50.90
   6667         3          0.002              18         62.60
```

If it is desirable that overflow blocks should not occur in more than 10% of the cases, there should be 5 records per block.

Therefore, the number of base blocks is 4000. 4001 is the nearest prime number. The total number of blocks that will be used by the file, when the file is full, is 4250.

One undesirable aspect of the preceding solution is the amount of wasted space implied by the chosen parameters. It is instructive to look at other possible block sizes, comparing, for example, similar levels of probability, so far as overflow blocks are concerned, with the amount of wasted space. Taking a block size of 20 records:

```
POPULATION = 20000
NUMBER OF   :RECORDS    :PROBABILITY OF   :NUMBER OF   :WASTED
BASE BLOCKS :PER BLOCK  :AN OVERFLOW      :OVERFLOWS   :SPACE (%)
   1000        20          0.427             427         29.94
   1053        19          0.340             359         29.18
   1112        18          0.258             288         28.57
   1177        17          0.185             219         28.34
   1250        16          0.118             148         28.48
   1334        15          0.071              96         30.05
   1429        14          0.038              55         32.62
   1539        13          0.017              27         36.13
   1667        12          0.005               9         40.34
```

Using an average number of records per block of 15 gives a probability of .071 and 30% wasted space.

Or, it is interesting to ask, "What does the block size have to be to reduce the wasted space to 25% for the same level of probability of an overflow block?" The answer is about 35 records per block, as in the following:

```
POPULATION = 20000
NUMBER OF    :RECORDS      :PROBABILITY OF    :NUMBER OF    :WASTED
BASE BLOCKS  :PER BLOCK    :AN OVERFLOW       :OVERFLOWS    :SPACE (%)
    572          35           0.434              248          30.33
    589          34           0.368              217          29.10
    607          33           0.304              185          27.84
    625          32           0.244              153          26.55
    646          31           0.190              123          25.68
    667          30           0.142               95          25.01
    690          29           0.095               66          24.39
    715          28           0.063               45          24.82
    741          27           0.038               28          25.73
    770          26           0.020               16          27.26
    800          25           0.007                6          29.13
```

A block size of 35 records means a block size in bytes of

$$35 * 256 = 12600$$

which is far too large for a random structure.

The major trade-off then is the probability of encountering an overflow versus wasted space. This may be illustrated graphically for the situation of 8 records per block as follows:

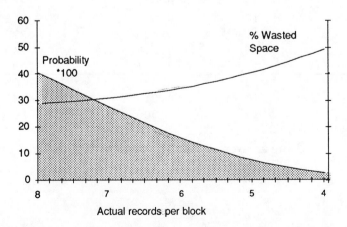

Choosing anything less than an average of 5 records per block will lead to an increase in the amount of wasted space, even though it leads to a decrease in the probability of overflow blocks.

EXAMPLE 2

A random file is to contain 100,000 records of length 480 bytes, and the required block size is approximately 6000 bytes, suggesting a block size of 6720 bytes and a blocking factor equal to 14. Therefore, the program is run with the values 100000, 14 and gives the following table:

```
POPULATION = 100000
```

NUMBER OF BASE BLOCKS	:RECORDS :PER BLOCK	:PROBABILITY OF :AN OVERFLOW	:NUMBER OF :OVERFLOWS	:WASTED :SPACE (%)
7143	14	0.420	3002	29.59
7693	13	0.317	2441	29.51
8334	12	0.216	2563	29.53
9091	11	0.136	1242	30.87
10000	10	0.076	763	33.63
11112	9	0.036	402	37.96
12500	8	0.009	113	43.36

This indicates a value of 10 records per block if it is desirable that overflow blocks should not occur in more than 10% of the cases.

Graphically, the relationship between wasted space (as a percentage) and the probability of encountering an overflow block is the following:

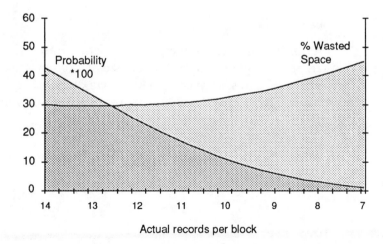

Again, any decrease in probability can only be had at the cost of an increase in the amount of wasted space.

The number of base blocks indicated is 10000, so a modulus of 10007 may be used, this being the nearest prime number. The total number of blocks is given as the number of base blocks plus the number of overflow blocks, or 10763.

Random Indexes

Random indexes provide reasonably efficient random access to records in the associated file, but it is usually the case that random indexes should not be used if sequential access to the records is also required. And, with random files, the modulus used should not be an even number.

The Fisher program may be used to generate tables indicating the probability of an overflow table (in an index, *blocks* are referred to as *tables*) for a table of a given size. Choose a table size that reduces the likelihood of an overflow to an acceptable level. The number of tables (blocks) may be read from the table produced by the program. In dealing with indexes, the number of slots (*slots* being a synonym for *records*) per table may be large, in which case the normal distribution may be used as an approximation for the Poisson distribution.

Fisher must be executed on a machine with a very large word size for slots for each table larger than 50. The tables used here were generated on a machine supporting a 96-bit floating-point real number.

EXAMPLE 3

A random index is to reference a file containing (a) 20,000 records (b) an approximate required block size of 7100 bytes, and (c) a table slot size of 36 bytes, suggesting a table size of 7128 bytes with 198 slots per block. Fisher, given 20000, 198, returns the following table:

```
POPULATION   = 20000
NUMBER OF    :RECORDS      :PROBABILITY OF     :NUMBER OF    :WASTED
BASE BLOCKS  :PER BLOCK    :AN OVERFLOW        :OVERFLOWS    :SPACE (%)
   102          198           0.415               42          30.06
   103          196           0.360               37          27.91
   104          194           0.306               32          25.63
   105          192           0.253               27          23.27
   106          190           0.195               21          20.32
   107          188           0.151               16          17.98
   108          186           0.110               12          15.80
   109          184           0.075                8          13.84
   110          182           0.045                5          12.16
   112          180           0.020                2          11.61
   113          178           0.008                1          11.37
```

Assuming that it is desirable that there should be no more than 1 in 10 tables (blocks) with overflows, a value for slots per table (records per block) of 184 is indicated. This however is not the optimal choice. The amount of wasted space is minimized at 178 slots per table, with the added bonus of a decreased probability of overflow blocks.

A more complete table follows:

```
POPULATION   = 20000
NUMBER OF    :RECORDS      :PROBABILITY OF     :NUMBER OF    :WASTED
BASE BLOCKS  :PER BLOCK    :AN OVERFLOW        :OVERFLOWS    :SPACE (%)
   102          198           0.415               42          30.06
   103          196.02        0.360               37          27.93
   104          194.04        0.306               32          25.67
   105          192.06        0.254               27          23.33
   106          190.08        0.206               22          20.99
   107          188.1         0.152               16          18.07
   108          186.12        0.112               12          15.89
   109          184.14        0.076                8          13.92
   110          182.16        0.046                5          12.22
   111          180.18        0.020                2          10.85
   113          178.2         0                    1          11.38
   114          176.22        0                    1          12.00
   115          174.24        0                    0          12.62
   117          172.26        0                    0          14.00
   118          170.28        0                    0          14.64
   119          168.3         0                    0          15.28
   121          166.32        0                    0          16.63
   122          164.34        0                    0          17.28
```

This table illustrates the fact that there is at least one point where the amount of space wasted is at a minimum (180.18). If this point is at a level lower than the level of probability you take as acceptable, then the minimum space wasted should be taken as dictating the number of slots per table (or records per block).

The situation can be depicted graphically:

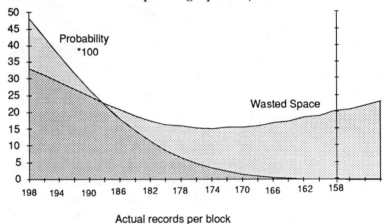

Actual records per block

Index-Sequential Indexes

A search strategy has already been illustrated that makes use of the fact that a collection of records is maintained in some sort of order. Index-sequential structures are a refinement of this type of technique. In an index-sequential structure, the data is maintained in a series of tables in such a way that the location of a record with some given attribute value can always be allocated to a particular table below the current table in the hierarchy. It is easiest to illustrate the idea with an example.

Assume that the index key is "name," and the following is the collection of names:

Auth, Cmmn, Dasd, Desc, Gola, Ivle, Meph

Putting this information into a file spanned by an index with a table size of three entries per table gives, after some operations on the file, the following record distributions:

```
Index                                        File

Coarse/              Fine Table              1   Gola
Root Table                                   2   <empty>
                                             3   Cmmn
                     Table 2.1               4   <empty>
                        Auth 6               5   Dasd
                        <empty>              6   Auth
                        Cmmn 3               7   <empty>
                                             8   Meph
                                             9   Desc
Table 1.1            Table 2.2               10  <empty>
   Cmmn  2.1            Dasd 5               11  Ivle
   Gola  2.2            Desc  9
   Meph  2.3            Gola  1


                     Table 2.3
                        Ivle   11
                        Meph  8
```

The index has exactly one root table. Below the root table are coarse tables if the index has more than two levels, or fine tables if the index only has two levels, as with the preceding example. The fine tables point into the file. The root and coarse tables point to other tables. In the case of the root and coarse tables, each entry in the table points to a table in such a way that all of the entries in the table pointed to are less than or equal to the pointing entry. So, for example, in Table 1.1, Meph points to Table 2.3, which contains entries for Meph and Ivle.

For example, if using this arrangement and the table size is 100 slots, the root table can address 100 tables, and each of these can address 100 tables, and so on. So if the number of levels of table in the index is n, and the number of slots in a table is S, the number of slots in the fine tables is given by

$$S^n$$

Or 100 cubed in the example given, or one million. Because only three levels of tables are required here to address one million records, it may be possible to keep both the root table and all of the coarse tables in memory all of the time. If this can be done, it means that a record in the file can be accessed at the cost of the single I/O operation required to access the fine table, plus the I/O operation required to access the file itself.

While it is unlikely that the direct single I/O access possible with a random structure will be achieved, so long as the number of levels of tables can be constrained to no more than three levels (preferably), the index-sequential structure does offer a solid compromise. It will generally perform reasonably well over long periods of time where the random structure may start getting overflows. Note also that the random structure requires all of the space for the file to be allocated either as soon as the file is established or very soon thereafter, whereas the index-sequential structure will generally only allocate space as it is required.

Index-sequential structure is also very flexible so far as accessing is concerned. It allows efficient sequential and random access to the records in the spanned file.

The LOADFACTOR specified with the structure will control the way that new tables are produced. When an entry is to be placed into a table that is full, the table will be split, and an additional entry will be generated in the next table up the hierarchy. The table will either be split at the location of the new entry, or, if this would result in either table being more than LOADFACTOR % full, the table will be split so that neither is more than LOADFACTOR % full. As a result, when a structure is loaded sequentially, on average, the tables in the structure will be LOADFACTOR % full at the end of the load. Given that table splitting is a rather expensive process or potentially wasteful of space, at load time a LOADFACTOR value should be chosen that is appropriate for the likely future behavior of the structure.

A low LOADFACTOR may result in more fine tables, which in turn may lead to more coarse tables and more levels in the structure as a whole. If the number of levels is large, the probability of having to do more than one I/O on the index tables is increased.

The following will determine the physical parameters for an index sequential file.

1. Obtain the slot size.

2. Decide on the LOADFACTOR.

    a. If the initial load is to be in ascending or descending order and there is to be little subsequent activity, choose a high value for LOADFACTOR (e.g., 90%).

b. If the initial load is to be in ascending or descending order, and substantial activity is expected later, choose a moderate value for LOADFACTOR (e.g., 70%).

c. If the initial load is to be in arbitrary order, take LOADFACTOR to be 50%.

3. Evaluate the number of slots *(n)* per table based on two levels of index tables. Note the following:

$$n = (\text{POPULATION}^{1/k}) / L \qquad (\text{approx.})$$

where k is the number of table levels

and $L = $ LOADFACTOR / 100.

4. Determine the physical table size, using:

$$\text{tablesize} = n \times \text{slot-size} + D$$

where D is a factor to allow for additional table space that has to be allocated for system use. This type of space is required on most systems and will be wholly system-dependent. If physical table size is too large, repeat the calculation with an increased number of levels of tables.

5. Adjust the number of slots per table (slightly!) to reduce the amount of wasted space per block.

6. Determine the number of blocks, using the following equation:

$$\text{Number of blocks} = (((L * n)^k) - 1) / (L * n - 1)$$

EXAMPLE 4

A disjoint index of index-sequential type is to reference a file containing 100,000 records. The initial load is to be in arbitrary order, based on a key item of length 30 bytes (POPULATION = 100,000, slot-size = 30). Take LOADFACTOR as 50%. Number of slots n per table based on two levels is given by the following equation:

$$
\begin{aligned}
n \quad &= (\text{POPULATION}^{1/k}) / L \\
&= (100{,}000^{1/2}) / 0.5 \\
&= 632
\end{aligned}
$$

Table size is given by figuring in slot size:

$$\text{tablesize} = n \ \times \ \text{slot-size}$$
$$= 632 \times 30$$
$$= 18960$$

In order to reduce such a large table size, we can try three levels of tables. Number of slots (n) per table based on three levels is given as follows:

$$n = (\text{POPULATION}^{1/k}) \ / \ L$$
$$= (100,000 ** {}^{1/3}) \ / \ 0.5$$
$$= 93$$

Table size is now given by the following equation:

$$\text{tablesize} = n \times \text{slot-size}$$
$$= 93 \times 30$$
$$= 2790$$

Increasing the number of table levels to three has significantly reduced the size of each table, but, of course, one additional disk access may be required to retrieve a data set record.

Possible table (block) sizes around 2790 bytes follow:

block size	amount of wasted space per block
93 x 30	90 bytes
94 x 30	60 bytes
95 x 30	30 word
96 x 30	0 bytes

This suggests an optimal table (block) size of 2880 bytes and 96 slots per table. Number of blocks (B) is given by:

$$B = (((L * n)^k) - 1) \, / \, (L*n - 1)$$
$$= ((0.5 \times 96)^3 - 1) \, / \, (0.5 \times 96 - 1)$$
$$= 2350 \quad \text{(approx.)}$$

Fisher

This is the program used to produce the tables used in the text for random structures. The PROBABILITY function is based on an evaluation of the following formula:

$$e^{-z}(1 + 2^z \, / \, 2! + 3^z \, / \, 3! + 4^z \, / \, 4! \ldots)$$

Or

$$e^{-z} \sum (r^z \, / \, r!)$$

Where z is the average number of records per block, and r takes successive values from the number of records per block plus one. The calculation of the successive terms in the expansion terminates when the value is sufficiently small as to be insignificant. Insignificance is defined as either no longer producing an overflow block, or producing an additional probability of an overflow block of less than $1/100$.

```
Fisher
Constant
     e                = 2.7182818284;

Var
     Line             : String(1..80);
     Population,
     Actual_records_per_block
     Records_per_block: 1..MaxInteger;
     P                : Real;

Integer Function Blocks;
     Begin
     Blocks :=
          Integer((Population-1)DIV
             Actual_Records_Per_Block+1) ;
     End;
```

```
Write_a_Line;
     Begin
     Writeln(line) ;
     line := repeat(" ",80) ;
     End;
Real Function Factorial(N:Real);
      Begin
     Var
          Accumulator: Real;
     Accumulator :=1;
     For N :=N Down to 1 Do
          Accumulator := Accumulator*N;
     Factorial := Accumulator;
     End;

Real Function Probability;
     Var
          P,
          Local_Actual,
          Local_Per_Block: Real;
Begin
Local_Actual := Actual_Records_Per_Block;
Local_Per_Block := Records_Per_block;
Do   Begin
     Records_Per_Block := Records_Per_Block + 1;
     P := (Local_Actual**Local_Per_Block/
          Factorial (Local_Per_Block))/e**Local_Actual;
     Probability := *+P;
     End Until
     P * Population < 1 OR
     P < 1/100;
End;

Begin
Do   Begin
     Readln(Population,Records_per_block);
     If Records_Per_Block < 1 Then
          Writeln("Records Per Block must be
             greater than 1")
     Else
          Begin
          Actual_Records_Per_Block := Records_Per_Block;
          Line :=
```

```
                              "Population = ",
                              String(Population,*);
                    Write_a_Line;
                    Line :=
          "NUMBER OF:RECORDS :PROBABILITY OF :NUMBER OF :WASTED";
                    Write-a-Line;
                    Line :=
          "BASE BLOCKS:PER BLOCK :AN OVERFLOW      :OVERFLOWS
                    :SPACE(%)";
                    Write_a_Line;
                    Do    Begin
                          P := Probability(
                                  Actual_Records_Per_Block,
                                  Records_Per_Block);
                          Line :=
                                Repeat (" ",2),
                                String(Blocks,6),
                                Repeat(" ",5),
                                String(Actual_Records_Per_Block,8),
                                Repeat(" ",10),
                                String(P,5),
                                Repeat(" ",10),
                                String(Integer(Blocks * P),8),
                                Repeat(" ",5),
                                String(
                                    (1-(Population/
                                    (Records_Per_Block*
                                    (Blocks+Blocks*P))))*100,5),
                                Repeat(" ",16);
                          Write_a_Line;
                          (* Decrease the avg/block by 1% each
                             time round*)
                          Actual_Records_Per_Block :=
                                Actual_Records_Per_Block
                                Max(Integer(Records_Per_Block*.01)
                                  ,1);
                          End UNTIL
                                Actual_Records_Per_Block LEQ 0 OR
                                P * Population < 1 OR
                                P < 1/100;
                    End;
              End;
         End;
```

CONFIGURING AND CAPACITY PLANNING

The question that the user always asks is "Why can't we use 100% of a system's capacity?"

The answer is to be found in queuing theory. Consider, for example, a situation where there is 1 terminal available for 8 hours a day. There are 10 programmers who each use the terminal once a day for 30 minutes. The rather unhappy results are as follows:

Terminal utilization is	63%
Average wait time for the terminal is	50 minutes
Average number of programmers waiting for the terminal is	1.04

The programmer asks, "Why don't we buy another terminal so I don't have to wait 50 minutes when I want to use one? This wait time of 50 minutes represents appalling waste." With 10 programmers, each waiting for an average of 50 minutes per day for the terminal, no less than 8 hours is being wasted every day because of wait time for the terminal!

The manager, of course, asks, "Why aren't we fully utilizing the terminal? It's idle over 1/3 of the time!"

The manager ought to learn a little about queuing theory, buy another terminal, and get rid of one of the programmers.

Queuing Systems

A queuing system is any system where customers arrive, hang around for a while, then leave. As Leonard Kleinrock said, "Life is a queuing system."

A little background information:

1910: A. K. Erlang develops basic foundations, which are applied to telephony

1920: Application of Erlang's results

1930: Feller develops the mathematical foundations of the subject

1940: Operations research becomes fashionable, and it attempts to use queuing theory, but the problems are intractable

Rebirth of queuing theory

1950: Early computer systems

1960: With time sharing, queues become a major aspect of the system

1970: Computer networks and complex systems— queuing theory becomes a pressing problem

Queuing theory analyzes systems that use queues to control resource utilization. It is grounded in the general field of probability theory and makes use of

- Arrival patterns
- Service requirements

Queuing theory may be used to determine

- Resource utilization
- Average number of waiting users
- Average wait time

Queuing theory starts with a simplest case, consisting of

- A single queue
- A single server
- A Poisson arrival process
- Exponential service-time distribution

This is essentially the case that was presented at the beginning of the discussion, where:

- All programmers have to wait for the same terminal.
- There is only one terminal.

- The programmers are expected to arrive in a random way.

Given that the arrival process is random, it is predictable how often, on average, there will more than one programmer arriving in the queue at the same time. This may be predicted using something we have already encountered: the Poisson probability function.

It is assumed that things get worse in an exponential fashion. That is, a point will be reached where things become so bad that nothing more can be obtained from the system. If the manager keeps hiring programmers without buying terminals, eventually no extra work will be done by a new programmer; the new programmer will just join a queue.

Utilization is an important concept in the theory. *Utilization* is defined as the fraction of time a resource is busy.

The major result of queuing theory is the idea of the stretch factor. The stretch factor may be stated as follows:

$$\text{stretch factor} = 1 \,/\, (1 - \text{utilization})$$

This may be interpreted as saying that, as utilization approaches 100% (in terms of a fraction, as it becomes nearer to 1/1 or .9999999999999), the stretch factor will become very large. This can be illustrated as follows:

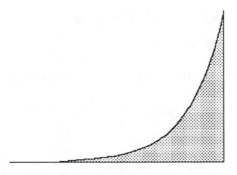

The impact of the stretch factor can be seen in the formulas for the average number of customers in the queue ("Little's Law") and for the total system time. For the average number of customers in the queue:

| Average number of customers in queue | = | stretch factor X utilization |

The total system time is the average amount of time a user spends waiting for and using a resource:

| Total system time | = | stretch factor | X | average service time |

Returning to the example of the 10 programmers and the one terminal, terminal utilization is given by the following:

Busy time   =   10 programmers (0.5 hours per programmer / 8 hours)

Elapsed time =   0.625

Stretch factor:

$$1 \text{ / utilization} = 1 \text{ / } (0.625) = 2.67$$

Average number waiting for or using a terminal:

$$\text{Utilization X stretch factor} = 0.625 \text{ X } 2.67 = 1.67$$

Average time waiting for or using a terminal

$$\text{Session time X stretch factor} = 30 \text{ X } 2.67 = 80 \text{ minutes}$$

Given that each programmer spends 30 minutes using the terminal, 50 minutes must be spent waiting for the terminal.

In a different example, given a system with two queues and two transaction processors where the transaction and their associated transaction processors have the following characteristics:

$$\text{Average time in transaction processor} = 0.5 \text{ seconds}$$

$$\text{Transaction processor utilization} = 0.5$$

Each queue with its transaction processor can be analyzed as a separate system, giving the following:

$$\text{Expected total transaction time} = 0.5 \; / \; (1 - 0.5)$$

$$= 1.0$$

If, however, there are two transaction processors with a single queue, processing the same type of transaction at a rate of two transactions per second, then:

Average time in transaction processor = 0.5 seconds

Transaction processor utilization   = 0.5

At this point, the mathematics becomes considerably more complex because account has to be taken of the fact that although there is still the same amount of work going on in the system as a whole, there is only a single queue being used to service the requests. The previous analysis was based on a single server system; here, we are dealing with multi-server systems. What has to be taken into account is the probability of someone arriving and finding both servers busy, as opposed to the previous situation where the probability involved only a single server. In this case,

$$\text{Expected total transaction time} = 0.67$$

That is a 30% improvement, simply by feeding everything through a single queue.

What this amounts to is that, given the same workload and the same number of servers, the stretch factor decreases as the number of queues decreases; the relationship, however, is not linear.

Bottlenecks

The system component with the highest utilization is the bottleneck component. "System component" may be either software or hardware, something like a disk drive, a program, or a processor.

What any system is likely to consist of is a series of queues. Queuing theory may be used to understand the behavior of the system as a whole. In particular, the stretch factor means that as some bottleneck component approaches 100% utilization, the utilization of the system as a whole is going to degrade toward zero.

This is rather an odd statement—that the utilization degrades toward zero as the system becomes overloaded, but it is very characteristic of large multiuser machines. Where some critical component of the system has become overloaded due to a component failure of some sort, there will be lots of memory available, the processor will be idle, disk paths will be practically unused, the machine will apparently be doing nothing, yet the response times will be terrible. Under these circumstances, good sources of information about the system are vital, both in the long term, for dealing with overloads that happen as the workload of the system generally increases, and in the short term, where the performance of some component degrades and slows down the whole system.

The aforementioned system-monitoring tools may be used to obtain the information needed to estimate the queuing characteristics of the components of the system. Analyzing the system in terms of queues is a fairly skilled and specialized business however, and it may make use of specialized packages (such as Capacity-Q) in analyzing the data.

Implications for Capacity Management

The most significant implications of all this are those for capacity planning and management. Given that the total capacity of all of the crucial elements of the system can be estimated, and the actual utilization rates can be measured, it is possible to use queuing theory to anticipate degradations in performance before they actually happen.

Utilization significantly affects user service levels. The concepts of utilization and stretch factors provide a nontechnical picture of system loading, and they can be used as a means of justifying increases in capacity at a point where such increases are needed but the system is still performing fairly well.

Some guidelines:

Absolute capacity is the total amount of resource actually "sitting on the floor."

Available capacity is the capacity available to the user after the operating overhead is subtracted. Typical figures here might be:

CPU   80–85% of absolute capacity

Memory   under 75% of absolute capacity

Of course, these vary depending on circumstances. The memory figure, for example, applies to a machine configured with a small amount of memory (for a mainframe, under 6 megabytes).

Wasted capacity is typically in the region of 5–10% of system capacity. At issue here are such things as scheduling problems, program reruns, equipment downtime.

Reserve capacity is the amount allocated to maintain acceptable response times during periods of peak demand. Typically, this will be in the region of 15–30% of system capacity (although for many subsystems, disks, for example, 15% would be far too low).

Usable capacity then is

Absolute capacity – (overhead + wasted capacity + reserve capacity)

This may be represented diagrammatically as:

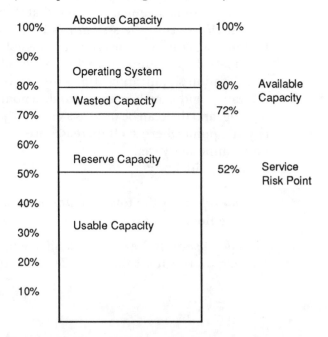

So far as capacity management is concerned, the capacity actually used has to be constantly monitored. If it starts going over the service risk point, then it is time to think about reconfiguring, reprogramming, or expanding the system.

Queuing Theory and Disk Subsystems

As a further illustration of the implications of queuing theory, the following is drawn from guidelines for configuring IBM MVS systems:

1. Generally, channel utilization in direct access storage devices (DASDs) should not exceed 35% for on-line applications or 40% for batch.
2. Individual DASD utilizations should not exceed 35%.
3. Average arm seek-time on a DASD should not exceed 50 cylinders.
4. No block size for either tape or disk should be less than 4000 bytes.

Points 1 and 2 are direct consequences of queuing theory, and 3 and 4 may also be derived from the theory. These are, of course, based on a DASD that has a large capacity relative to the number of "heads" that may be used to access it.

The guidelines also do not apply to on-line database usage of files. As mentioned in the discussion of random structures, 4000 bytes as a block size for a random file may be too large, not because of considerations related to the disk subsystem, but because of the fact that memory is being wasted, particularly if the database happens to support reblocking and a distinction between random and serial users.

Similarly, so far as arm seek-time is concerned, in many cases, very little can be done to minimize the arm movement on a particular pack, unless of course the usage of the pack is restricted to no more than 50 cylinders!

A warning: simple queuing theory analysis may be invalidated by any of the following:

- Priority handling
- Nonexponential distribution of service times
- Non-Poisson arrival process
- Complex interactions among the queuing elements.

≡≡ 15

On Matters of Scale

Author reads; Mephisto looks out the window.

Dear Author,

I had the strangest dream last night. I dreamt our friend Isaac Newton was a cat. Terrible the things people do to domestic animals you know. Anyway, the strange thing about the dream was how everything was really something other than what it seemed, and how everything had a size appropriate to what it was, not to what it seemed to be. There was Mr. Newton (the cat), weighing 70 kilos and looking very English. There were a whole host of things coming and going all the time, mostly in the form of animals. The dream came to an end when I saw this huge hair, shed by a passing mouse, but the mouse was actually the moon!

Funny though, thinking about it afterward, how did I know that the moon mouse was a mouse? I was quite close to it, so how could I see all of it? After all, it must have been over 3400 kilometers long (not including the tail). Come to that, the hair should have been a couple hundred meters thick. Recognizing my moon mouse would be like trying to recognize an elephant when only allowed to see one square centimeter of it at a time. Dreams do play strange tricks on the mind. This dream didn't even make sense in its own terms, as it got its scales all wrong.

Much of the business of making sense of things seems to be tied up with what can be taken in at a glance. A glance, of course, may be a glance of the eye or a glance of the mind. There are definite physiological limits to what we can do in this respect; for example, without actually counting them, how many words are there on this line? What about this line then?
Well, then, this one?
Or this one?
This?

Seven seems to be about the upper limit to what we can comfortably take in. How then, I ask myself, do we ever manage to understand a book? If we can't manage more than 7 words at a time, how do we cope with a 150,000? A very serious problem, both for writers and readers! The answer seems to lie in the groupings of things that we glance at.

A book could, with some advantage, limit the contents of any portion of itself, taken in isolation, to no more than the number of elements that can be taken in at a glance (of some sort). The book can then grow in the realms of the mind. Starting from a general table of contents, proceeding to the detailed contents for each section, and then down to the actual contents of individual paragraphs and sentences. More than just this is required. If something can be glanced at, it must have some sort of coherence to it. Grouping things physically, as with the words in a line, is one way of doing it. More usefully, in a large complex object like a book, things can be caused to appear to be a group by making them look the same, or putting them in the same style, or giving them the same content. Once they hang together in the mind, once they can be glanced at, they can be taken in and understood.

My moon mouse dream must have been playing around with some such faculty, I suppose.

Happy Dreams

Your Friend Blaise.

Auth writes, Mephisto looks over his shoulder.

Dear Pascal,

As you say, poor Mr. Newton.

I liked the idea of your 3000 kilometer Mouse. Your symbolism is a little off, though. The Mouse belongs to Apollo, so it would have been more appropriate for your mouse to have been the sun. A pig would have been better—pigs go with the moon and with Isis, the goddess of the moon. I don't suppose a 3000 kilometer pig would be any easier to take in than the mouse. But, of course, the sun mouse would be several orders of magnitude bigger even than the pig—1.3 million Kilometers. I wonder how long its tail would be!

As to realizing that your moon was a mouse and not a pig, it is extraordinary how often we assume that we understand things or have to come to grips with things that are just as distant from us in size as the moon mouse. Take, for example, the government of a country, or even a large corporation. If there is to be some single intelligence directing and understanding the behavior of the thing, how is this intelligence to cope? What, for example, if the chief executive officer (CEO) has to authorize every interdepartmental employee move, and there happen to be 100,000 employees. The poor old CEO is dealing with a moon mouse at the level of a centimeter at a time and doesn't have a hope of coming to grips with the organization as a whole (except in his dreams!).

Here's another good moon mouse for you: The Bomb. Hofstadter, in his metamagical themas quotes the story of the man unconcerned about the size of nuclear weapons. After all, the story goes, the largest conventional weapons are only 25 times smaller than the smallest nuclear ones. That is 20 tons of TNT, versus 500 tons. But as Hofstadter points out, the typical nuclear weapon is actually 50,000 times bigger than the largest conventional weapons, and closer to a million times bigger than the typical conventional weapon. We are reduced to talking in units of world wars, a "moderate"-sized weapon being taken as equivalent to all the physical destruction of World War II. Whole worlds of destruction encompassed by one small glance.

Here, I think we must be living in a nightmare. How else can we believe that we really understand such things?

Sorry about that. I had it in mind to tell you the story of one of Dasd's relatives. Cafs, who went crazy about books and decided to become a librarian. We ended up having to put the poor soul in a nut house for a while. What happened was this: Cafs applied for all sorts of jobs at libraries of any kind; it didn't really matter what. Eventually, oh joy! Oh rapture! Cafs got this job at a local county library—not a very big one, but a real library all the same.

Well, everything went fine for the first few days, but then we noticed that our budding new librarian was beginning to wilt badly. Nobody could figure out why until we realized that books were popping up all over the place. The librarian was trying to read the entire library! Getting back to your 7-word limit, this poor soul was trying to absorb whole pages, 500 words to the page; whole books, 150,000 words to the book; whole shelves, 150 million words to the shelf; whole stacks, 900 million words to the stack. No wonder Cafs went crazy. What cured it all in the end was this doctor who drew a picture—a series of concentric squares, 1 millimeter for a word, and so on up to 3 football fields for the stack, and a whole city for the entire library. When the budding librarian realized the true scale of things, sanity returned—to some extent anyway.

Mind you, don't we all have a problem then? Haven't we created something bigger than ourselves? Made our own moon mouse, in fact a whole herd of them, filling up our libraries, pouring out in the technical journals all the time?

It's no good asking who reads all that stuff; nobody does. It's as much beyond our control, and beyond our comprehension, as is the world around us.

Moon mice are like real mice; they breed like mad. We ourselves get so used to them that we think we can handle them as easily as real mice. It doesn't matter how small a part of a thing we can see at a glance, we think that if we have enough time and energy, we can get right round it in the end. As Newton said, it's "by acts of faith that we come to know the world." We sure as heck don't get there just by looking at it.

But it's amazing what you can squeeze into a small space if you really try, or if you're really lucky. For example, a wonderful short poem, called "Matina," is about the rising of the sun. It means "I fill myself with the light of the immense." (You pronounce both m's in the second line.)

> M'illumino
> D'immenso

The whole of the rising sun in two lines of Italian. Wonderful!

Well that's it for now. See you at next week's debate—on pole reversals, isn't it?—whatever that is!

Meph. Hang on a minute. What on earth was the point of all that?

Auth. I had it in mind to mention a bit about the different sizes of things in a data processing environment.

Meph. What's that got to do with anything?

Auth. Same idea as the librarian's mental cure; when we deal with a big database, we are in much the same position as the person studying the elephant through a centimeter window, or the librarian trying to read a whole library. All you can usually see of a database is a screenful of information, maybe 1000 characters. Now, the database system in memory may use up to 1 million characters worth of space, and databases of a 1000 million characters are not that uncommon these days. That's only 4 full medium-sized disks. That matches up very nicely with the moon mouse. If you take Pascal's dream, the smallest unit (the Moon Mouse) is several orders of magnitude bigger than Pascal is. Given this, the memory (the Sun Mouse), several orders of magnitude bigger still, is the disk units. Here we find ourselves, sitting in front of a terminal, trying to find our way round the sun, a centimeter at a time. We must be crazy. Crazy to even try and do it without thinking about it pretty carefully first.

Meph.   So we need data models, I suppose?

Auth.   Precisely my point!

Meph.   A bit obscure, if you ask me.

Auth.   O.K. Well, I'd better finish this letter.

16

Integrity

INTRODUCTION

Database integrity is concerned with ensuring that the data in the database is correct. It must be correct in terms of certain explicit and implicit rules about the database. These rules specify acceptable and unacceptable database states. For example, given the rule that every entry in an index must have a corresponding entry in the file spanned by the index, it must not be the case that an index has an entry in it where there is no corresponding record in the file. Or, if there is a rule that says that every department must have a manager, it must not be the case that there is a department that does not have a manager.

The end user becomes aware of integrity in several ways:

1. When the user breaks a rule, the system returns an error message and ignores the invalid command.

2. There are many situations where the integrity constraints imply a structure to the data. For example, in the case of departments requiring managers, the user has to be aware of the fact that the department manager must be present in the database before the department is established.

The integrity rules act as constraints on the types of operations that may be performed by the end user.

Another and rather more obscure manifestation of integrity is where a number of users are all operating on the same set of data. Here, it is up to the system to ensure that people do not tread on each other's data or data operations. The system has a variety of mechanisms for achieving this. At times, these mechanisms have the effect of making it impossible to complete an update, or they may specify a certain way that updates be performed.

Therefore, for these and other reasons, it is essential for end users to have some understanding of the implications of maintaining the integrity of the database. Needless to say, it is essential for the database programmer and administrator to have a thorough grasp of the concepts addressed in this chapter. The database designer is also affected, but only where the database has to deal with complex multientity objects, or where changes have to be performed on the database that span long periods of time. (A long time here is measured in terms of the shortest transaction on the system—on a heavily used system, anything more than 100 times longer than the shortest transaction is a long time—the reason for this definition will become apparent in due course.)

The chapter begins with a general discussion of integrity in the database context. Next, transactions and locking are described, followed by the implications of maintaining integrity so far as programming is concerned. Finally, the basic integrity-related functions of a database management system are described.

INTEGRITY

The database mapping hierarchy represents a picture of some of the levels of information present in a database system. The top level is the most abstract and is not actually found in most database systems currently available. The lower levels represent operations and data structures that are closer and closer to the hardware, and as such are less likely to be meaningful to an end user.

Database Mapping Hierarchy

Access Methods

1.	Saying what you want, rather than how to go about getting it.
2.	Programs doing Finds, Stores, Deletes, and so on. The programmer as navigator.
3.	Manipulating variables internal to the data management software. Making sure programs do not mess things up.
4.	Lower-level data management variables, looking after the buffers
5.	Operating system file management

The SDM (semantic data model) is intended to address the integrity of the topmost layer of the hierarchy. It provides a means of specifying, in detail, what are acceptable database states, so far as the entities that compose the database are concerned. Essentially, any discussion of data modeling is really a discussion of integrity. There are, though, different types of integrity at different levels of the system. Much of the discussion of the implementation of the SDM is concerned with just these issues—that is, how to derive a physical representation of the logical schema that is correct and manageable.

There are a variety of integrity-related concerns that emerge both at this and at lower layers of the system. These fall into two areas:

1. Processes that access the database must follow certain program-

ming-related protocols. These protocols must be followed if the database is to be kept consistent, and if the processes are to see correctly the data in the database. These protocols are discussed later in this chapter.

2. Recovery-related functions must be performed either by the database or as a part of the process of running the database. These must be performed in order to ensure that the database has a reasonable chance of surviving any sort of failure in the data processing system. A database here is considered to have survived if it can be made usable after the failure. A substantial part of the code comprising the database management system, at the physical level, is likely to be concerned with just the recovery-related functions.

RECOVERY

Database recovery has to be able to deal with a variety of different types of failure, at a minimum:

- Transaction failure
- System failure
- Media failure

The implications of these may vary from the trivial to the catastrophic. Particularly deadly are combinations of failures. The system is usually built on the assumption that only parts of the system will become irreparably unusable. If, for example, several disk units are lost simultaneously, substantial amounts of data may be irretrievably lost. To deal with all this, there are essentially two types of database recovery mechanism: crash and archive recovery.

Archive recovery equates to *dump recovery*—that is, recovery from a previously saved, complete copy of the database. The database is *dumped* (i.e., saved off of the system's storage device) on a periodic basis, usually to magnetic tape. The dump is kept in a safe place. If the database is lost, it can be reestablished using the last dump. Actually, a lot more is involved than just this because it is desirable to recover not just to the last dump, but also to the last processed update. The mechanisms used to accomplish this assume an archive dump, but they require additional operations.

Crash recoveries are likely to include a number of different types, depending on the type of crash:

- Software or network failure, in which the contents of memory are not lost

- System failure, in which memory is lost

- Media failure

- Localized media failure, in which case a relatively minor recovery operation may be implied

- Widespread media failure, requiring a full dump recovery.

These various recovery types will be provided by the use of a combination of four basic recovery-related operations:

Transaction undo: whereby it is possible to undo the effects of a single transaction. This may be done without affecting any transactions, either processed concurrently with it or before it. It is not, however, possible to undo a transaction without the possibility of affecting transactions processed after it.

Global undo: allowing the entire database to be taken back in time. This will be either to some specified moment in time, or to a point prior to the execution of some program. It implies that *all* of the work performed against the database during the relevant period is discarded.

Partial redo: whereby some portion of the database files may be reconstructed. This is not usually transaction-related, but is rather aimed at fixing localized media failures.

Global redo or *dump recovery*: whereby the database may be brought forward in time from some previous dump, reapplying whatever changes have been made to the database in the period since the dump.

These operations are all based on the assumption that updates (and inquiries) are delivered to the system as a series of transactions. The transactions will be recorded in a special file called the audit trail. All the operations are only rendered possible by utilizing the information present in the audit trail. If the audit trail is lost or, for some reason, cannot be used, none of the aforementioned operations will be possible.

The assumption is made here that in the absence of a transaction-processing protocol, the integrity of the database is undefined. It is only on the basis of a transaction-processing protocol that even the integrity of a single-user database can be properly defined. In practice, this assumption is justified for almost all currently available database management systems.

TRANSACTIONS

A transaction is an atomic unit of work so far as the system is concerned. It either *completely happens* or it *does not happen* at all. A transaction is bracketed by a **begin**, followed either by a **commit** or an **abort**. At any point prior to the **commit**, if the transaction does an **abort**, it will completely disappear. That is, any of the changes effected by the transaction on the database will completely disappear.

Transactions and Consistency

A database system embodies a number of rules or assertions, for example:

- A manager may not manage a nonexistent department.

- A department must have a manager.

A database may be said to be consistent if all the data in it obeys all of the applicable rules (i.e., is semantically correct).

In some cases, the database may become temporarily inconsistent in order to transform it to some new consistent state. A sequence of updates that takes the database from one consistent state to another is a transaction. As such, the transaction must either fully complete or not affect the database at all. The transaction must be atomic.

For example, if we have a system that has to obey the preceding rules regarding managers, the system may be represented by a set of tables. One table is for departments, and one table is for managers:

Department

Department Number	Department Name	Department Manager
1001	Pragmatists	1234
1000	Idealists	3211
1002	Advocates	4321

Managers

Employee Number	Manager Name
1234	I.Newton
4321	D.Mephisto
3211	G.Leibniz

Further, it is only possible to change the tables one row at a time. That is, it is not possible to specify a whole series of changes, all of which will take place simultaneously.

If we are to make Mephisto the manager of both the "idealists" and the "advocates" (the rules say nothing about a manager managing more than one department), the changes must take place as follows. We begin by changing the current manager, giving the following set of tables:

Department

Department Number	Department Name	Department Manager
1001	Pragmatists	1234
1000	Idealists	3211
1002	Advocates	4321

Managers

Employee Number	Manager Name
1234	I.Newton
4321	D.Mephisto

Leibniz has ceased to be a manager, so the only thing to do is to remove him from the manager table altogether. The next step is to change the DEPARTMENT MANAGER entry for IDEALISTS to 4321. But consider the state of the tables at this particular point in time. That is after demoting Leibniz, but before effecting Mephisto's takeover: IDEALISTS have a manager who is not a DEPARTMENT MANAGER. The database is in an inconsistent state. This is so in two quite distinct senses:

1. If for some reason, such as a system failure, the rest of the transaction should fail to complete, the next time someone looked at the database, they would see this anomalous situation. Worse still:

2. If someone happens to look at the database at this particular instant in time (i.e., before the transaction goes on to the next step), they will also see the database in an inconsistent state (even if the state does only last for a nanosecond).

The **begin** transaction, **commit**, **end** transaction, and **abort** mechanism is intended to deal mainly (though not entirely) with the first problem. Another mechanism, *locking*, has to be used to deal with the second.

Locking and Consistency

The system has to support various types of **lock**, given that there are both

1. Concurrent operations rather than serial operations within the system, and

2. Concurrency of various types existing at different levels of the system.

Locking is the mechanism used to isolate the transaction, preventing other users from seeing the database as reflecting changes made by the transaction prior to its completion. After the transaction's **begin** point and prior to the completion of the transaction (i.e., **commit**), the database is assumed to be in an inconsistent state.

Consistency and Update Anomalies

Given that a transaction is by definition "undoable" prior to **commit**, it is not only necessary to protect other transactions against inconsistent data, but also to protect them against data that may subsequently disappear.

For example, in the process of demoting Leibniz and making Mephisto the IDEALIST MANAGER, it is possible for the process to be aborted at the stage where Leibniz has been demoted, but Mephisto is still only an ADVOCATE MANAGER. In this case, so far as the system is concerned, none of it ever happened. There is a double jeopardy for someone examining either table during this process then; they may not only see something that is not consistent, they may see something that is not there at all! They have seen something that is subsequently going to disappear, something that, so far as the system is concerned, never happened.

There are several distinct types of situations where invalid results may arise from transaction interdependencies or transactions "seeing" each other before **commit**.

```
Lost updates

    T1 updates
    T2 updates
    T1 gets undone        T2's update disappears

Dirty read

    T1 updates
    T2 reads
    T1 aborts             T2 has seen something
                          he should not have seen
                          ("Dirty" data)

Unrepeatable read

    T1 reads
    T2 updates
    T1 reads again        T1 sees same record, with
                          different values

The following case

    T1 does +1
    T2 does +2
    T1 updates
    T2 updates            leaving +2, not +3
```

is an unrepeatable read (i.e., T2 overwrote something read by T1). There are then two distinct reasons for locking:

1. Lock inputs to guarantee consistency.
2. Lock outputs to mark them as dirty.

   Also known as

"read lock"		"shared lock"
and	or	and
"write lock"		"exclusive lock"

In the case of a read lock, the transaction needs to ensure that something will not change that (a) is being used by the transaction, but (b) will not be changed by it. Read locks will protect transactions against unrepeatable reads and dirty reads.

Write locks are used to prevent others from accessing something while a transaction is in the process of changing it. A write lock will prevent lost updates. It alone is not sufficient to prevent the other two cases. The locks are necessary on both ends, although it is possible to distinguish those who intend only to read from those who intend also to write.

This may be an important consideration where some particular data is being read a lot and only written to periodically. If everyone does write locks ("exclusive locks"), then all of the users of this piece of information will be effectively single-threaded on the database. If each transaction takes a substantial amount of time, this may have a considerable impact on the performance of the system.

Locking Protocol

Transaction T observes the consistency lock protocol if:

1. T sets an exclusive lock on any data it dirties.
2. T sets a share lock on any data it reads.
3. T holds all locks until the **end** transaction.

This protocol has clear implications for the way that a program must be structured. The program should appear as follows:

```
Begin
Boolean Procedure get_input;
    begin
    (*gets the next input to be processed          *)
    end;

While get_input do
    begin
    begin transaction;
    (*get locks and do updates                      *)
    if any_error
        abort
    else
        commit;
    (*abort and commit are assumed to free all locks*)
    end;
end;
```

One interesting aspect of the protocol is that all locks are held to the end of the transaction. This implies that some sort of currency has to be maintained on everything touched by the transaction, until **end** transaction, in order to be able to represent the lock. This, at least, will be the case where locks are represented explicitly, which is usual.

One way around this is to have some sort of structure lock. This implies the ability to lock a whole collection of records by simply touching one object. This could be provided by having the database management system allow an entire file to be locked. Or it could be provided by having all of the things that access the database adhere to a protocol. The protocol might, for example, require some particular record to be locked prior to accessing a related collection of records. In either event, *single-object locks* imply the overhead of keeping track of who has what locked; *structure locks* have the overhead of forcing single threading on the locked structure.

Another lock type that, in theory, seems very attractive but in practice has proven to be impractical is a *predicate lock*. Here, the user selects a collection of records by specifying a condition; any record that satisfies the condition is considered to be locked. The system performs the **lock** operation, not by keeping lists of locked things, but by keeping the predicate. If a user comes along and attempts to "register" a predicate that clashes with an already registered predicate, the user is made to wait. At the present time, a general algorithm to decide when two predicates clash has not been devised. If this problem is ever solved, it may provide the basis for a very fast, very cheap locking mechanism.

Predicate locks might solve something not addressed by locking mechanisms where explicit lock lists are kept: the problem of shadow locks. *Shadow locks* represent a sizable hole in the consistency lock protocol, and they arise in situations where a lock is implied by some operation but there is no object to lock; essentially what is being locked is the nonexistence of an object. If a transaction has to make a decision on the basis of the nonexistence of an object (if A does not exist, then create a B), there is nothing for the transaction to lock that will prevent some other process from making an A before the transaction can **commit**. The transaction cannot then be guaranteed to reprocess correctly. If the system aborts when the transaction is doing its **commit**, when the transaction is reprocessed after the system **abort**, it may produce a different result. A might be there.

Deadlocks

Deadlocks are the first major fly in the database programmer's ointment (the second is recovery). A *deadlock* is a situation where there are at least two transactions accessing the database, both of them performing locks, and each transaction manages to acquire a lock on something that the other transaction wants. The data management system software when someone requests a lock, forces the requester to wait if there is already a lock on the object. Therefore, using L (X,Y) to indicate that transaction X has a lock (L) on object Y, and R (X,Y) to indicate that transaction X has requested (R) a lock on object Y, deadlock will arise out of the following sequence of operations

```
L(T1,01)
L(T2,02)                        (Transaction 1)
R(T1,02)                        Here T1 will be suspended because
                                T2 already has the lock on object 02.
R(T2,01)                        Now T2 will be suspended because
                                T1 has the lock on object 01.
```

Neither T1 nor T2 can proceed. The only way to resolve the situation is for the data management system to pick on one of the users and arbitrarily free all of that user's locks. This leaves the transaction hopelessly compromised. Having involuntarily broken the aforementioned transaction protocol, the user must abort.

Any program that performs a sequence of updates against the database will have to allow for this situation. This, together with the requirements arising from the transaction processing protocol, implies a strict format for any program that interfaces to a database. The program must now look like this:

```
Begin
Boolean Procedure get_input;
    begin
    (*gets the next input to be processed              *)
    end;
Procedure do_accesses;
    begin
    do_access
    if deadlock
        begin
        abort;
        go reprocess;
        end;
    end;

While get_input do
    begin
reprocess:
    begin transaction;
    (*get locks and do updates                         *)
    for each access
        do_accesses;
    if any_error
        abort
    else
        commit;
    (* abort and commit are assumed to free all locks*)
    end;
end;
```

A lock type worth mentioning in connection with deadlocks is the *intentional lock.* So far, we have seen *write locks,* where a user is going to change something and wants to lock out all other accesses, and *read locks,* where no change is intended—others may access but not change.

Sometimes, it is desirable to be able to "upgrade" a lock from a read lock to a write lock; this may be done by waiting until all other read lockers have gone away. If, however, another process simultaneously tries to upgrade a lock on the same object, a deadlock will occur: Neither process will ever get the write lock because both are waiting while holding a read lock.

On certain types of database, it is desirable to allow lock upgrades, but this may lead to a substantial increase in the number of deadlocks. One way around this is to have an intentional lock. With an intentional lock (which must be system supported) there can be any number of read lockers for an object and no more than one intensional locker. Only intensional lockers can upgrade locks. If another intensional locker comes along, that user is made to wait. The intensional locker who has the lock can quite safely upgrade the lock to a write lock; it is guaranteed that there are no other processes trying to do the same, and there will be no deadlock on an upgrade.

User Interface Implications

For the moment, consider things from the point of view of the user. Typically, there are two things that the user is going to want to do, both of which are incompatible with the requirements of the transaction-processing protocols:

1. See something before he changes it. For example, the user may want to see an account balance before making a withdrawal, or see how many parts there are on hand before processing an order.

2. Make some changes and then change his mind. This is not so easy to illustrate with accounting applications; a better source of examples is a data dictionary. Assuming that the data dictionary has an on-line interface to it, and it allows databases to be described (who needs a DDL compiler anyway?), it may well be the case that a user will expect to be able to use an **undo** command, allowing some or all of his or her recent actions to be discarded, perhaps even **undo(3)**, undoing the last three commands.

Both of these have horrendous implications so far as the transaction processor is concerned. Looking at the change in account balance, from the program's point of view, this presumably consists of something like the following:

1. Get a request to process an account update
2. Lock current account and read balance
3. Display current account balance
4. Read balance change
5. Change balance and store
6. Next operation.

One question is, where are **begin** and **end** transaction? If **begin** is after Step 1 and **end** is after Step 5, what happens if the user goes out to lunch while the transaction is sitting on Step 4? The transaction may never terminate.

If there is a **begin** after Step 1, an **end** after Step 3, then another **begin** after Step 4, and an **end** after Step 5, then the balance may have changed because locks cannot be held across transactions (remember the transaction-processing protocol?). Various kludges have been devised to circumvent this sort of situation. Such things as keeping a time-stamp on the record, incorporating the time-stamp in the information displayed in Step 3 and the read back in Step 4, and checking the time-stamp before doing the update in Step 5. If the time-stamp has changed, the whole thing is rejected and the poor user has to start all over again.

The interface to the data dictionary, with the **undo** feature, labors under all of the same difficulties, only more so. Here, the interfacing program must deal with the possibility of things appearing and disappearing, and acquiring or losing relationships in an arbitrary manner. It is precisely this type of problem that an ad hoc query processor has to solve if it is to be used as anything more than an elaborate toy.

Transaction features necessary to support these types of systems include some support for *transaction nesting*, or allowing one transaction to take place inside another, allowing for transaction save points, and allowing for long transactions without crippling the database.

A final point: A transaction processor represents a resource so far as the system is concerned. However, it will almost certainly be the case that while the transaction processor is processing one transaction, it will not be able to process any others. Therefore, large or lengthy transactions (e.g., ones that require multiple interactions with the terminal) will tend to slow the system down.

PROGRAMMING: SOME BASIC TECHNIQUES

The capabilities required for the program to interface to the database are (1) the ability to declare the database, and (2) a set of operations that allow the database to be manipulated by the program. The set of operations necessary are the following:

- **open**
- **close**
- **restart**
- **create**
- **store**
- **delete**
- **find**
- **lock**
- **item update**
- exception handling
- **begin** transaction
- **commit**
- **abort**

The program works in an environment built and supported jointly by the database and by the operating system. The primary feature of this environment, from the program's point of view, is that the program itself will declare the data structures that will be treated as belonging to the program. It is the responsibility of the program to maintain and manipulate these data structures. In interfacing to the database, the program has a set of data structures present (as a result of the database declaration) that allow it to access data on the database, particularly to transfer data to and from the database, and to add and delete records on the database. These data structures are usually referred to as *cursors*.

CURSORS

Cursors have a number of universally applicable features:

- A cursor has a type, in the sense that it points at some particular class of objects—usually, though not necessarily, a record.
- Cursors may be moved, copied, or closed.
- A cursor has a currency; at any given moment in time, it points at some particular place.

Various operations are possible on a cursor:

- **Fetch** or **read**, allowing some information to be retrieved from the database (what is retrieved depends on what the cursor is pointing to at the time)
- **Insert** or **create**, adding a new record into the database
- **Update**, changing the contents of the current record
- **Delete**, which deletes whatever the cursor is pointing to
- **Move**, which repositions the cursor.

Cursors may be set to any of the following:

- Beginning of the file, prior to the first record in the file
- End of the file, after the last record in the file
- Next record in the file
- Prior record in the file
- Between two records (only after a **delete** operation)

Cursors may point to

- Structures (i.e., files or indexes)
- Embedded structures

EXCEPTION HANDLING

If recovery and deadlock are the flies in the programmer's ointment, exception handling is the fly in the user's ointment. The user is at the mercy of the way in which the program and the system handles exceptions. The user has to have enough information to sort things out when they go wrong. This is, perhaps, one of the major barriers to the use of ad hoc, free-format, query processors. The exceptions encountered are likely to take two forms:

1. Both the data management system and the programs that access it may encounter a wide variety of exception conditions that cannot be handled in advance. When such a situation arises, it is usually the case that either the system operator, or an application or system software specialist, will have to be called on to sort things out. These types of exception conditions are inherently beyond the competence of the average user; they should also be relatively rare.

2. When some action is performed that is possible, in principle, but not reasonable. Usually, the action is being used in an appropriate or illegal context, such as (a) doing a **delete** where only inquiries are allowed, (b) supplying values for height, age, or weight that are too large or too small, and so on. These kinds of errors are especially problematic for the user because they are likely to arise frequently if the system is used extensively.

The program that sees or generates the exception condition may be content with merely an error code, but the user needs a great deal more—at the very least the following:

- Someone who can explain the error
- Some short text indicating what the error means and which error it was
- Extensive documentation indicating what the error means and how it is possible to avoid making the error again
- The ability, built into the system, to try the operation again
- Clear identification of what entities in the database were involved in the error.

No single program can hope effectively to provide these kinds of features. Good error handling, as with so many other things, is a question of a consistent system wide approach, making the environment predictable and manageable so far as the user is concerned.

In a semantic database, the problem is particularly pressing. The database will catch a very wide range of errors, and the system is much more likely to be used by casual ad hoc users. As a result, it is much more likely that the user will see errors detected by the database itself, as opposed to errors that have been detected by some program that handles accesses to the database. The database must then be able to present an error to the user in a reasonably intelligible fashion.

In addition, a fundamental aspect of the semantic database is that the **verify** operations may encompass a number of different entities. Consider, for example, the following **verify**:

> No employee's salary may exceed the average for his or
> her department by more than 50%.

It is surprising the number of circumstances under which this can be triggered. For example:

- Someone gets too large an increase—this is the obvious one.

- Someone becomes semi-retired and takes a cut in salary; his or her salary does not violate the constraint, but someone else's might now do so.

- A new employee joins the department; her or his salary may be too low and make someone else's invalid, or the new salary may be too high.

- Someone leaves the department, so somebody else's salary becomes too high.

In all but the first case, it is not the entity being accessed that is invalid but some other quite unrelated entity. A major problem for exception reporting is the mechanism to be used in identifying, to the end user, which entities are implicated in an invalid update. In an ad hoc environment, there is the different but related issue of how the user is to resolve the invalid update.

Wherever possible, integrity should be enforced by the database. Wherever possible, error handling should be left to the database. Any deviation from these principles will lead to a reversion to the database model; this in turn will imply that the system is less flexible, more likely to become inconsistent, and less accessible to the ad hoc, casual user.

PROGRAM RECOVERY

From a programming point of view, there are two quite different types of recovery: batch and on-line recovery. *Batch recovery* is the case where the program runs against the database independently of any other systems. The batch program is responsible for its own recovery. *On-line recovery* is the case where the program is running under a message control system, or MCS (CICS in an IBM environment). The MCS is responsible for handling recovery.

Batch Program Recovery

One approach to batch programs centers on the idea that the program can reprocess input without having to worry about what occurred on the previous run. An example might be a program that goes through the database, deleting flagged records. All the program needs to know is where it stopped the previous time, and it can then just carry on from there.

This is actually a rather unrealistic assumption. It is usually the case that a batch program will be dealing with structures outside of the database (a print file for example) and will have to coordinate what happened on the database with what happened to the structures outside of the database, potentially a very difficult problem.

The program at least has to address the following questions:

- Is a restart necessary?
- If it is, what went unprocessed in the previous run?

The answer to the question "what went unprocessed on the previous run?" can only be obtained from the data management system itself. Assuming a **global undo**, anything can happen to the database from one run of the program to the next. Strategies here vary from one implementation to another, usually involving the program placing, in some special area visible to the data management software, enough information to allow the program to restart if necessary.

The real problem, so far as the system is concerned, is the fact that there may be any number of restart points. Assuming that the data management system supports a **global undo**, the restart information will have to be stored in the system's audit trail and retrieved as a part of the recovery process. The program will then have to have some nontrivial piece of logic to allow it to handle the information it gets back at restart time. Inevitably, there are complications. For example, what will the program see if it fails while restarting? Or what should the program do if it restarts and does not have any restart information? Or if it does not restart and there is some restart information?

Furthermore, if there are multiple batch programs running against the database, the result of the reprocessing is not guaranteed to be the same as the results of the original processing. If the programs happen to get restarted in a different order, and there are interactions among their updates, the interactions are likely to be sequence dependent, and so will change from one sequence to another.

One of the criteria for considering a program to be a batch program was the fact that it had exclusive use, at least of its part of the database. The reason for this requirement is the sequencing problem.

On-line Program Recovery

An on-line program is a special case of a batch program. With on-line programs, the structures outside of the database happen to be a data communications network, and there are multiple programs accessing the database simultaneously. The on-line program has to be able to ensure the following:

1. Messages are not lost
2. Messages are not processed twice
3. Responses are not lost
4. Responses are not processed twice
5. If messages have to be reprocessed, they are reprocessed in the order in which they were originally processed.

It is one of the primary functions of an MCS (or CICS in an IBM environment) to ensure that the first four conditions are met. The MCS will have an audit trail. The audit trail will be used, in combination with the database audit trail, to ensure that messages and responses are not lost or processed twice.

Basically, the MCS will pass a stream of messages to a transaction processor. If the system fails, the MCS will obtain information from the database indicating which was the last successfully processed message. The MCS will then reposition its audit trail and resume processing accordingly.

The MCS should also tackle the more difficult problem of not just reprocessing messages, but also reprocessing them in the order in which they were originally processed. In order to do this, the programs processing the messages supplied by the MCS will have to stick to a protocol known as a "two-phase transaction."

TWO-PHASE TRANSACTIONS

In a *two-phase transaction*, the portion of the program that processes transactions is divided into two parts. In the first part, which is after the **begin** point for the transaction, the program acquires locks. In the second part, which is after a point known as "midtransaction," the program may free read locks, but it may not acquire any locks (read locks or write locks). Hence, the program is divided into a growing phase and a shrinking phase.

Throughout the process, the program is allowed to do updates to the database, but the normal considerations apply, which are that a write lock must be acquired on anything that is to be changed, and read lock must be acquired on anything that is to be referenced but not altered. Also, write locks may not be freed at any time before the **end** transaction because the transaction can at any time be undone. A program that adheres to a two-phase transaction protocol will appear as follows:

```
Begin
Boolean Procedure get_input;
    begin
    (*gets the next input from the MCS                    *)
    end;
Procedure do_accesses;
    begin
    do_access
    if deadlock
        begin
        abort;
        go reprocess;
        end;
    end;

While get_input do
    begin
reprocess:
    begin transaction;
    (*get locks and do updates                           *)
    for each btr-acess
        do_accesses;
    Mid transaction;
    (*do updates and free read locks where
      appropriate*)
    for each mtr_access
        do_accesses;
    if any_error
        abort
    else
        commit;
    (*abort and commit are assumed to free all locks *)
    end;
end;
```

The point of it all is this: After the midtransaction point because the
program does not acquire any more locks, it is not possible for the
transaction to be affected by any other transactions running concurrently with it. On a restart, provided the transactions are reprocessed
in the same order as the order in which they executed midtransaction,
the result can be guaranteed to be the same as the result produced on

the original run. The MCS therefore keeps track of the order in which the transactions reached midtransaction, and it ensures that if transactions have to be reprocessed, they are reprocessed in the correct order.

The use of a two-phase transaction will have the effect of increasing the degree of concurrency of the transactions running in the system. The transactions hold their locks for the minimum possible time and are therefore less likely to have to wait for each other. This is a relatively minor consideration though.

LOGICAL INTEGRITY, STANDARDS, AND DATA DICTIONARIES

Any database system must have all of the levels of the database hierarchy (illustrated earlier in this chapter) present if it is to be usable. Level 1 may only exist as some individual's understanding of how the data in the database is to be interpreted. Nonetheless, the existence of this interpretation is crucial to the integrity of the database. Because the database's integrity can only be assessed and maintained in the light of the interpretation that represents Level 1, without the presence of this level, the database's integrity is undefined.

It is quite possible to put together an application where the functioning of the system is purely dependent on a proper understanding of the application by its users, in which there is no explicit statement of the Level 1 semantics of the application. The database management system does not enforce the semantics of the application. The Level 1 integrity of the application is entirely dependent on a consistent approach to the application by the user. Users may perform operations that are syntactically correct but semantically incorrect, and the database may become corrupt as a result of some user's misunderstanding.

In practice, most of the data held in databases is far too valuable to be left vulnerable to individual errors in this way. Programs are written specifically to provide at least some degree of enforcement of the Level 1 semantics of the application. Given that the database administrator is concerned with all aspects of database integrity, the database administrator must exercise considerable control over the programs allowed to access the databases. Apart from a full implementation of the SDM, there are three notable control mechanisms available: programming standards, logical integrity, and data dictionaries.

Programming Standards

The standards enforced by different data processing installations vary, depending on the circumstances applicable at the installation in question. Some obvious areas are worth mentioning:

- Standard approaches to recovery for both batch and on-line programs.
- Standard approaches to transaction processing—that is, all programs must be at least correct transaction processors, and other more complex restrictions may be applied (e.g., two-phase locking).
- Standard approaches to the implementation of relationships and the programmatic handling of relationships
- Locking protocols, particularly for database hot spots (that is, portions of the database for which there is very high contention).

Logical Integrity

There must be a common understanding, among individuals designing programs that access a given database, as to the meaning of the data in the database. At present, there is no better strategy than narrative descriptions of the meaning of different items in the database. Fortunately, with the advent of the SDM, it is beginning to be possible to specify much of the semantics of a system in an unambiguous fashion. Even the existence of these data models as a formal mechanism for describing the meaning of the database is a significant advance over the previous state of affairs, where the principal tools available were record-based systems.

Data Dictionaries

A data dictionary can be a powerful tool for controlling an entire data processing environment, not just a database. The data dictionary can give some guarantee that programs, at least so far as Level 3 of the database hierarchy is concerned, not only are accessing the database correctly, but also are using the data extracted from the database correctly.

The data dictionary provides the ability to share not only descriptions of data stored in databases, but also descriptions of files and of screens. The dictionary allows a single item to be used in various contexts. For example, it is possible to declare an "emp-name" item 30 characters long; the item may then be used in various classes, screens, and files; in all contexts, the dictionary will treat it as the same item and the system will guarantee that the appearance (if not the usage) of the item is consistent and correct.

Item usage may be checked manually using an "impact of change" report. This report will list all the screens, files, classes, and processes that use a given item. For example, a change in an item's size may be carried out in a controlled and systematic fashion.

DATABASE RECOVERY

Databases must be consistent. A database that reflects a partially completed transaction is not consistent. Because transactions result in multiple physical I/Os, it is possible (in fact, highly likely) that after a system crash of some sort, where a database has updates being processed against it, the database will be in an inconsistent state.

The mechanism used by the database to get itself back into a consistent state is the audit trail. The audit trail consists of a record of all the changes that are made to the database by any transactions processed against the database. The audit trail contains an image of what the database looked like before the transaction was processed (for other reasons, it also keeps a record of what the database looked like after the transaction was processed).

When the database needs to recover, it can **undo** any transactions that have only been partially processed against the database, thereby bringing the database to a consistent state.

Transaction Interactions

If transactions abide by a correct locking protocol, they will not interact, and so the fact that a given transaction has disappeared should not affect any transactions processed either concurrently with it or before it. Any transactions processed after the transaction completes will only see the results of the transaction as it unlocks its read locks, or when it commits and unlocks its write locks. Therefore, provided that the transaction is not lost once it has completed (or committed), there will be no adverse interaction between transactions.

Quiet Points

If some transaction is being processed against the database, the database, by definition is considered to be in an inconsistent state. This is inconvenient (though not an insuperable problem) when (a) recovering the database, (b) performing such operations as a dump, or (c) performing an analysis of the state of the database. A point at which no one is in a transaction state is known as a quiet point (described in Chapter 14); at such a point, the database may be guaranteed to be consistent. When the system does a **global undo**, it will take advantage of the existence of quiet points on the audit trail.

Control Points

Given that the audit trail contains a secure record of any updates to the database, the database buffers are only written out to disk on a demand basis. Other things being equal, it would be possible for a changed buffer to sit in memory indefinitely.

On a recovery, any such unsaved alterations will have to be reconstructed from the audit trail. On a recovery then, the data management system has to go back to the last point in the audit trail at which the database buffers have been written out—that is, flushed to disk. Transactions must be reprocessed (using afterimages) from the last point at which the buffers were written out, up to the end of the audit trail. As mentioned in Chapter 14, the point at which the database buffers are written out is known as a control point; its essential function is to limit the distance it is necessary to go back in the audit trail when reprocessing updates.

MEDIA RECOVERY

A rebuild operation, or **global redo**, may be used to recover from media failures. It will work by rebuilding the entire database, starting from some dump, and reapplying all afterimages up to the end of the audit or to some specified point. This approach works if there is a bad spot on a disk file, but it is not the most efficient approach.

It may well be the case that only a very small portion of the file is affected. In this case, it is likely to be far more effective to rebuild only the damaged portion of the database. The rest of the database may be assumed to be correct. The process of rebuilding a portion of the database is a **partial redo**.

If an image of the area to be fixed happens to be in the current audit file, the fix may be accomplished relatively rapidly. Otherwise, it will be necessary to go to the last dump, get the area to be fixed, and then read through the audit files from the last dump, picking up any alterations to the area to be fixed. The rows to be fixed will be locked out for the duration of the operation, but the rest of the database should remain accessible.

Physical Integrity

The main kinds of errors detected routinely by the system are normal I/O errors and errors picked up as a result of either block-level integrity checks or CHECKSUM. Using these gives a reasonable guarantee that the data returned to some program accessing the database is correct. If the data management system is a fairly stable system and (as a rule) consistently points an index at the correct record, excludes inapplicable entries in an automatic partial index, deletes a deleted record from an index, and so on, errors will generally be detected.

Perhaps the main problem here is databases that have records that are very infrequently accessed. Some verification may be performed as a part of the process of dumping the database. It is still conceivable that some errors might go undetected for long periods of time.

A database analysis function may be provided with this in mind. Extensive integrity checking may be done on the database files, ensuring that a wide variety of pointers and conditions are correct. Errors are always possible, but the possibility of errors (outside of program bugs) can be made to be very small.

Backup

The backing up of the database is intended to allow the database to be reestablished after any sort of system failure. Obviously, there will be some disruption. However, the amount of disruption is directly proportional to the frequency with which backups are performed.

What is involved in reestablishment after a system failure depends on the type of failure. It should be possible to reestablish the entire system from scratch, which will involve backing up more than just the files dumped by the normal database backup routines. The really lethal failures are those where a combination of failures happen together, such as where apparently unconnected parts of the system fail together because of some unrecognized or unavoidable common component that happens to develop a fault, electrical power systems and the operating system being the most common culprits.

A number of different things require backup:

To Be Backed Up	Effects of Loss
System time-stamps and system description files	Database cannot be reorganized, programs cannot be compiled; ultimately, database will be unusable; will have to fabricated time-stamps
Tailored files	Can be rebuilt from directory file
Data files	Rebuild from dump and audit files
On-line control files	Can be reestablished using the system directory
Audit file	If the database is intact, **immediately** take a database dump, and be sure not to lose it; otherwise, reprocess input.
User programs code and source	No good doing a rollback if the programs needed to reprocess data no longer exist.

Regular dumps of the database as a whole are the responsibility of the user. Some systems allow the database to be dumped while in use. If a recovery is done using a dump generated while the database was in use, the system will get the dump into a consistent state (if necessary) using the associated audit files before using the dump.

The system may maintain a dump directory, indicating which dumps have been performed and on which magnetic tape reels particular portions of the database are to be found (very useful if a **partial redo** has to be performed).

It is always desirable to coordinate database dumps with audit files, allowing a database and its associated audit files to be kept and, where necessary, used together.

Discontinuities

There are a variety of circumstances under which it is possible for discontinuities to arise in the audit. *Discontinuities* are points in the audit, past which it is not possible to recover. It is not possible to do **global redos** or **undos** through the discontinuity. This means that if there is a problem (e.g., a media fault) prior to the discontinuity, any dump prior to the discontinuity cannot be used to fix the database.

As a result, whenever an audit discontinuity is generated, the database must be dumped immediately after the discontinuity.

Discontinuities are likely to be caused by the following:

- File-format conversion reorganization
- Record-format conversion reorganization
- File initialization

It is also worth remembering that the loss of an audit file is effectively a discontinuity.

17

SapperDB (Stores and Parts Database)

INTRODUCTION

The chapter on integrity was mainly concerned with the process of ensuring that updates against a single database are performed correctly. With virtually all of the database operations considered so far, only a single database has been involved. This is a nice, comfortable assumption to make, but it is very unrealistic.

Normally, a program is not just dealing with a single, recoverable system, such as a particular database. Rather, it is usually called upon to deal with lots of different, quite uncoordinated things: a print file and a database, a database and a disk file or magnetic tape file, or perhaps two quite independent databases. How is locking, and particularly deadlocks, to be handled? How is recovery to be dealt with? How is the system to be updated in such a way that nothing is processed twice, everything is processed once, and everything is processed in the right order?

One example of a solution to this problem has already been encountered in the form of the message control system (MCS). Many of the paraphernalia and protocols surrounding MCSs are designed just to deal with this problem of recovering two otherwise uncoordinated things. The situation faced by an MCS involves a data communications network and a database.

This may sound hopeful; perhaps we can solve all our problems by just using lots of MCSs. But of course, things are by no means as simple as that. More protocols and formalisms are required, more tricks and devices must be used. Specifically, two major problems must be confronted:

1. How can two separately recoverable things be coordinated during recovery? The basic issue here is that of *distributed databases.*

2. How can information be moved from one database (or system) to another? This is the *import–export problem.*

For some reason, both of these issues tend to be relegated to the backwaters of database technology. But they are both very much a part of the everyday experience of the database programmer. These days, moving data from one database to another is a fairly common thing to have to do. Moving data from a database to a file or a workstation, or from a workstation back into a database is not merely common; it is the norm. All of these situations assume both the import–export problem and issues associated with distributed databases.

If you find yourself involved in any of the aforementioned activities, this chapter is of interest to you. The chapter begins with a discussion of an application in which databases are distributed all over the place, and data is imported and exported as an everyday occurrence. There follows a discussion both of some of the operations required by the application and of the rationale behind them.

STORES AND MANUFACTURING INVENTORY SYSTEM

This hypothetical application is used by a foreign subsidiary of a multinational manufacturing company. The subsidiary is concerned with the distribution and, in some cases, the assembly of appliances marketed by the parent company. The subsidiary also purchases some components locally. Therefore, the database system has two main elements:

1. *The parts description and manufacturing information system:* This pro-

vides information about the various parts used in the manufacturing process, particularly their origin, usage, and description.

2. *The parts supply system:* This is concerned with the supply of parts to various likely users of the parts. The various likely users of the parts are many licensed dealers, seven manufacturing locations, and several other subsidiaries. The system has to keep track of parts by location and type. It assumes that the origin, usage, and description are also available.

The system has to be able to represent the following:

- *Different parts:* Particular appliances may contain any number of parts (typically about 20,000–30,000); a particular part may be used in any number of different appliances.

- *Different versions of the same part:* Parts change in various ways. For example, the color, constituent material, heat dissipation characteristics, and assembly procedure may all vary within the same part. It is necessary to keep track of both the part and the versions of the part.

- *Parts in packages:* Parts are delivered by the parent company in packages, which may then be used in the assembly process, or in some cases, may be delivered to dealers. Parts may also be delivered individually. The system has to keep track of which parts are contained in which packages. The packages also come in versions. A particular package version consists of a particular configuration of part versions.

- *Packages used in appliances:* Which packages are used in which appliances has to be recorded.

- *Parts from local sources:* These have to be recorded as alternatives to particular versions of particular parts as manufactured by the parent company. One of the main objectives of the system is to allow locally sourced parts to be substituted for the parts manufactured by the parent company.

One of the main characteristics of the system is that it changes all the time:

- Not only are new parts being delivered all the time, but new appliances are being designed.

- New parts and new versions of parts for existing appliances are being produced all the time, either locally or by the parent company.
- And new packages are being configured whenever the manufacturing process is modified to accommodate changes and refinements.

Much of this information is supplied by the parent company in regular database releases. These provide information about any new appliances, packages, or parts that may be produced by the parent company.

Parts and packages arrive in shipments; the shipment will have a data tape associated with it, describing the parts and/or packages contained in the shipment. It is possible for a shipment to contain a part or package description that has not been seen previously; hence, it is necessary to process the shipment description before processing the shipment itself. If this is not done, the process of loading the description into the database may fail.

The system keeps track of *instances* of appliances. For any appliances handled or produced by the subsidiary, the parts supply system (a) records the origin and destination, and (b) keeps track of the current location. For locally sourced parts, information is kept about local suppliers and what they supply.

THE SCHEMA

The schema contains the following classes:

- Part
- Part version
- Package
- Package version
- Appliance

There is an ISA relationship between part and part version and between package and package version. This indicates, for example, that a particular part version is an *instance* of some part. Parts are used in packages, and packages are used in appliances. It is normally the case that an appliance can be manufactured from any configuration of packages; it is less likely that part versions may be mixed. Parts and packages have a relationship to the things for which they may be used as a replacement.

The schema may be outlined as follows:

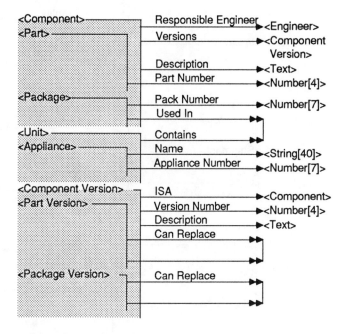

Some points about the schema:

- The component version actually stores instances of component.
- A part version can replace a part version that ISA different part.
- Package versions can replace a package version that ISA different package.

The stores schema is relatively simple and is designed for a completely separate database. This is justified on the grounds that although the stores applications need access to part and part version information, they will never be allowed to alter this information. What the stores applications will be concerned with is altering information about the location of instances of part versions (note that this is not part versions as instances of parts, but actual instances of versions of parts);

this is done mainly in the form of item counts rather than of individual items.

The stores schema:

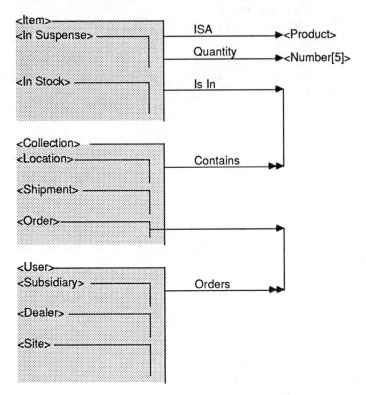

Updates to the parts description database will affect the stores database, but the effect is equivalent to the effect of a schema alteration. Note that both "location" and "order" are subclasses of "collection." For the purposes of the stores system, the principal relevant characteristic attribute of the two classes is that they are collections of products supplied by the company. Products may be parts, packages, or appliances, and the "products" class is actually just a mechanism allowing a relationship to be established between this database and the parts description database.

There are no relationship attributes. The class "items" reflects collections of instances of items. "Items" will obviously be of a particular type, however the item-type information is stored elsewhere.

The stores and description databases are both maintained by the subsidiary head office organization, but the description database is only maintained at the subsidiary head office. The stores database is maintained at all site locations (which includes the head office, which is a site) and at some distributors. The reconciliation process involved in receiving a part shipment has already been mentioned.

IMPORT–EXPORT

The movement of data from one database to another may be performed by using an export file. This is a file with two parts. One part is a description of the data contained in the file; the other is the data itself. This is logically equivalent to the schema and the data that make up a normal database.

When a shipment arrives from the parent company, it may contain parts that have not previously been seen by the subsidiary. When a shipment arrives, if there are any parts present on the tape that are not present in the parts description database, they have to be added in. Once the part descriptions have been added in, the new shipment may be added to the stores database. The subclass, "suspense of collection," is for items that are expected in a shipment. The information required to process the shipment is all contained in an import file.

When the import file is received by a site, it is processed by a program that reconciles the import–export schema and then reconciles the import–export entities and loads the data.

Schema Reconciliation

First, the schemas of the target database and the import file are reconciled. If there are any discrepancies, the process stops until such time as the discrepancies can be eliminated. This can only be done on the basis of some sort of programmer intervention. This intervention is itself automated to the extent that schema updates are usually precanned and applied in the form of release-level updates.

The schema reconciliation mechanism is extremely simple and merely consists of ensuring that the queries contained in the import file are valid (this validation is done by the DML parser). The import file will contain a number of queries that are there only for the purpose of determining the validity of the target database. These queries are themselves embedded in a program, the source for the program being present as a part of the import file.

The program is constructed (or rather extended) as a part of the process of designing an extension to the schema. Where an extension is made to the base schema, queries are added to the program that will detect the fact that the new parts of the schema are not present.

Reconciling Entities and Loading the Data

Each class in the database has a label attribute. It is the function of the label attribute to act as a qualified identifier for the entity. Qualification here has a similar interpretation to qualification in a programming language. In a block-structured programming language such as Pascal, an identifier only has to be unique within the scope of the environment that contains it; that is, it has to be unique by owner.

The label attribute is similarly defined to be unique by owner, the owner being an entity for which the labeled entity is a constituent. This concept is extremely useful in a variety of contexts. For example, in error reporting, the label attribute may be used to identify any entity involved in an error; in returning information about an entity where just a class or an EVA name has been specified, the label attribute may be used; and in the SDM diagrams, where no other indication is available, the class label attribute is used to identify entities (e.g., all of the items in angle brackets are label attribute values).

In the import–export context, it is important to know which entities are already present in the database and not to add them in a second time. For individual parts, it can safely be assumed that they are not present, but for part descriptions, it may be the case that they *are* present. Part descriptions get added as a by-product of the receipt of a shipment containing the parts of the type in question. Therefore, which parts are present depends on what happens to have been handled by the site in the past.

The algorithm for entity reconciliation goes like this:

```
For each part in the shipment

    If there is no part that both has the same name and
    has owners with the same names
```

> Load the part description, with all of its
> relationships, into the database

Otherwise

> Add the part to a duplicates list

For each part in the duplicates list

> For each relationship to another part in the
> shipment
>
> > If the relationship is not already in the
> > database
> >
> > > Add it in

All of this is by no means cheap, but there is absolutely no other way of achieving the same objective. It is essential not to duplicate entities and not to duplicate relationships.

It is worth emphasizing that two essential characteristics of the system make the import operation possible: (1) *the label attribute*, which acts like a surrogate that is valid across more than one database; (2) *the schema comparison operation*, which both depends on the ability to dynamically compile DML statements within the execution of a program and ascertains the result of the compilation. Some equivalent to these capabilities is essential to the viability of any import–export process.

In the case of the SapperDB system, the allocation of the label attribute values is the responsibility of the parent company. It can only be performed by a central agency, thereby ensuring that the label attributes are always both unique within their contexts and valid.

DISTRIBUTED DATABASES

The EVA ISA relationship from "item" to "product" is an interesting case. The case "item" is in the stores database, but the class "product" is in the descriptions database. In this case, there is then an EVA that apparently spans two different databases.

Granted that this is a design schema rather then an implementation schema, it may be reasonable to depict the situation in this way. A fair question though is this: In practice, can any sensible interpretation be applied to the ISA EVA? In a sense the answer has to be "No." A relationship cannot reasonably span two different databases—not, at any rate, a relationship as defined in the SDM. A relationship is defined in the model by establishing two EVAs as inverses of each other. The fact that "the EVA is in" is the inverse of "the EVA contains" implies that any update to the one is also reflected in the other. But if two database are involved—that is, if the EVA and its inverse are contained in two different databases—it is simply not possible to guarantee that this coordination of the two sides of the relationship will be performed correctly. The rules that define a database cannot be enforced, so the system cannot be a database. A database is defined by its rules; if they are unenforceable, it is not a database; it fails to meet its own definition.

The point about rules defining a database has been justifiably belabored because it has a very important corollary: Any system that does obey the rules of a database *is* a database. It does not all have to be in the same place; it could be scattered around on different machines. It does not all have to be accessible, so long as the rules are obeyed; whether it is possible to gain instant access to some particular data is immaterial. It does not all have to be in the same format; some of the data could be in an IMS database, some in an INGRES database, and some of it might not be in a database at all. Further, the data does not even have to be character-based data in the normal sense of the term; it might be graphics images, recorded sound, or anything else that might be describable by your data model. All is possible if the rules about the consistency of the data in the database can be enforced.

This, at least partially, is what distributed systems are all about. They are concerned with the business of enforcing rules across multiple systems. Unfortunately, this turns out to be very expensive. One obvious source of the cost of the system is the data transfer that has to take place among the various components of the distributed system. These are sometimes referred to as *hosts*. On each host is some part of the database, and any operations processed against the database may involve work being performed by one or more of the hosts. Having done its work, each host presumably collects some sort of result and returns it to the originating host.

Even assuming that very high speed links are available among all the hosts, the processing of even the simplest queries might take a very long time. But this is only a part of the problem.

It might seem reasonable to assume that an inquiry would be much more expensive than an update, because at least the update does not involve returning anything. All that has to happen is that the participating hosts be informed of the type of update for which each is responsible. This is not so. The explanation comes in the form of a problem described here as the idiots' problem:

A number of idiots each have charge of a group of imbeciles; it has been agreed that they shall all meet at a certain beach and have a party. It has been agreed that one group will bring some wood to do the cooking. The problem faced by the idiots is this: They have not determined the beach on which they will meet; the party is to be that very evening at four o'clock, and it is already three o'clock in the afternoon. It takes an imbecile at least 45 minutes to travel from one group to the other. Being imbeciles, they tend to get lost. How could the idiots arrange matters so that they all go to the same beach?

It would be possible to relax the conditions a little and merely say that they are going to meet at a beach at some time, and allow them to send imbeciles to each other until such time as some suitable arrangement has been arrived at. But even this has its problems! How is it to be guaranteed that the process will ever reach some satisfactory conclusion? They may just go on sending imbeciles to each other until everyone is lost. Of course, being idiots and imbeciles, no one thinks of using the telephone.

This has obvious connections with programming and programmers, but the real point is distributed systems. The beach party is a transaction, the idiots are hosts in a distributed database, and the imbeciles are messages. The message is "Is the party at beach X OK?" (or "Is this update to the database OK?"). The problem faced by the idiots is how to arrange the party; the analogous problem faced by the hosts is how to arrange the transaction. There is no solution to the problem that can be guaranteed to lead to a successful party.

One pragmatic solution is as follows: Pick one of the idiots and designate that person as the party organizer. All the idiots only send imbeciles to the party organizer, who says "Can you go to beach X?" When everyone says, "beach X is OK," the party organizer then says to everyone "OK, go!"

For the hosts, the same applies. One host is designated as the coordinator. All of the different hosts involved in the transaction, when they are ready to perform the transaction (i.e., when they reach **commit**), send a message to the coordinator saying, "OK, I can now commit." Note that they do not actually commit. They keep all locks, and the transaction does not yet become visible to other users of the system.

Once the coordinator has had an OK message from all of the hosts involved in the transaction, the coordinator sends out messages to all of the hosts, which says "OK, go!" It is up to the coordinator to keep track of which hosts were involved in the transaction and to make sure that all hosts say "OK" before giving the "OK, go!" It is also up to the coordinator to keep track of any hosts that do not respond to the "OK, go!" and ensure that all participants in the transaction complete the transaction. It must not be the case that an "OK, go!" message gets lost. The coordinator must keep saying "OK, go!" until the transaction has completely gone!

A transaction protocol that involves a coordinator in this fashion is known as a two-phase commit. The reason for the name should be fairly obvious: The transaction has two phases. In the first phase, the transaction gets to a stage where it is able to commit—that is, where it can be guaranteed that the transaction will not make any more changes to the database, and that no changes made so far are in any way illegal. In the second phase, the transaction lets the coordinator know that it can commit and, when told to do so, actually does commit.

It should now be quite apparent why update transactions need not be any cheaper than inquiry transactions, so far as the amount of work is concerned, and this is only half of it. Another major problem with distributed updates is deadlock detection across the network. Deadlocks may easily occur as a result of transaction X on Host 1 having a lock on something that transaction Y on Host 2 needs to lock in order to be able to continue and ultimately commit. Simultaneously, on Host 2, the reverse may be the case, with Y holding something required by X. If the system is to keep a global deadlock table, an enormous amount of information may have to be shunted from one host to another in order to maintain the table. There are a number of possible solutions to this (none of which is discussed here).

Note that if only one updater is assumed, deadlocks are not a problem. It is feasible to build a coordinator by using a normal database management system as a way of keeping lists of users who can **commit** and users who are ready to end the transaction. So, given some reasonably limited objectives, a distributed system is not too difficult to put together without these limitations, though it can represent a major problem.

Getting back to the EVA ISA relationship from "item" to "product," the relationship is given by the label attribute. The label attribute in turn is guaranteed to be valid because a single process administered by the parent company always ensures that label attributes are valid. So the system can be made to work in a reasonable fashion.

USES OF IMPORT–EXPORT

Import–export is a very useful concept in understanding a variety of situations. For example, a query will have two parts: (1) a condition indicating which entities are to be selected by the query, and (2) the attributes—extended, inherited, and immediate—that are to be retrieved. These can easily be seen as an export file—that is, a file that has both description and content associated with it. **Update** may similarly be viewed as an import operation.

Another place where import–export is useful is in understanding changes to a database schema. If radical changes are to be made to a database schema, and an import–export facility is available, if it is possible to export from the old schema to the new schema, the new schema can be considered a semantically meaningful evolution of the old.

With workstations running such things as spreadsheet applications that are using data extracted from a database, an essential operation is import–export. Import–export allows the workstation to extract data from the database and subsequently re-import it back into the database. Note that this allows the workstation to deal with data derived from the database without the workstation having to act as a host in a distributed database, with all of its attendant problems. The workstation can import the data, manipulate it, and then reapply it to the database without having to maintain locks or a transaction state on the original database. All that is required is for the workstation operator to be able to manage the entity reconciliation process required by the import of the data.

CONCLUSION

In some respects, SapperDB is a poor example of a distributed database. It is not a single database, in the sense of it being possible, with single DML statements, to manipulate data on different hosts. On the other hand, it does behave like a single database, inasmuch as (a) it has protocols that ensure that certain vital aspects of the corporation's data are kept secure and consistent, (b) it does not get lost, and (c) it does not get messed up.

SapperDB is representative, in the sense that it deals with a more general situation. A monolithic, distributed-database management system is only one special case. Any system that involves two independently recoverable units is also a distributed system and will have to solve the same problems.

18

Security and Control

INTRODUCTION

Security represents a special issue for the database designer. It is often, though not always, the case that commercial databases have to have some security associated with them. It is also often the case that the specification of security is not properly integrated either into the design of the database itself or into the design of the user interface.

This is largely a fault of the tools available for dealing with security. As has so often been the case elsewhere, there is a confusion of objectives. Security-related issues become embroiled with issues that should properly be dealt with as a part of the design of the database schema.

This discussion of security does not attempt to provide a comprehensive view of security, but rather it aims to clarify the relationship of security and security-related integrity concerns to the process of designing a database. This chapter begins with an overview of security and concludes with a discussion of security in the context of a database.

APPROACHES TO SECURITY

Security revolves around the idea of securing objects—that is, having an association between users and objects, which specifies which objects may be accessed by which users.

In practice, the term security tends to cover three distinct types of function:

The privacy function: This involves protection against unauthorized access. The privacy function is concerned with the process of preventing certain users from seeing certain data present on the system. The implication is that for all legal users of the system, and any object present on the system, it is possible to determine whether the user is allowed access to the object. It should also be possible for any user–object pair to determine what kinds of operations the user may perform on the object. On a large system, this could be a very large amount of information. It can be visualized as a matrix with objects down one axis, users down the other, and a checkmark on the intersection to indicate that a given user can access a given object. The matrix becomes three-dimensional if users, objects, and operations have to be taken into account.

The protective function: This involves the protection of the system against possible accidental damage. For example, initializing a disk unit or rebooting the system are unlikely to lead to compromising the system's privacy, but they may have disastrous effects all the same.

The secure function: This is aimed at protecting the system against malicious damage or hostile access. It is likely to be combined with the privacy and protective functions, but it is useful to distinguish it from these two. This is because the secure function is extremely difficult to provide in a reasonably watertight fashion, whereas it is possible for business data processing organizations to provide for privacy and protection in a quite satisfactory manner. Given sufficient resources and time, there is virtually no system in which the secure function cannot be subverted.

The protective and privacy functions must ultimately rely on the secure function for the protection of the mechanisms used to implement them. Given that they have to rely on the secure function, and that the function itself may not be very effective, the conclusion must be that often protection and privacy can be reasonably provided only where all users can be assumed to be neither malicious nor hostile. Once the characteristics of the secure function have been determined, providing for the integrity of the protective and privacy functions is relatively trivial.

A very important factor is the level of security required by the system. It is the assumption here that the level of security required is moderately high, but that after-the-fact detection of security violations is acceptable—that is, it is not necessary to be able to detect and prevent security violations in such a way that it is never possible for a user to see data he is unauthorized to see. This type of approach does require some portions of the system to be inaccessible all the time (especially for update purposes), but it permits a fairly liberal approach to the access mechanisms allowed to the end user.

The three components of security are then considered separately, but it should be borne in mind that, at least for privacy and protection, there is a clear trade-off between security and usability. The more secure the system becomes, the less usable it becomes.

SECURE SYSTEMS

Security, like truth, is absolute. If a system is to be secure, the secure function must be unbreakable. But absolute security, like absolute truth is rather hard to come by. There is only one way to guarantee the security of a system: Do not allow anyone to use it! This is obviously true on two counts:

1. The fact that the system can be used by someone inevitably implies that, accidentally or maliciously, it could be used by someone else who happens not to be authorized. There are so many possible circumstances where one individual may be mistaken for another that it is impossible to guard against all of them.

2. Any data processing system is inevitably going to be unmanageably complex when it comes to something like detecting a malicious or accidental leakage of information via some channel that, for whatever reason, is not being directly protected by the security system. Data communications lines, electromagnetic emissions, and waste paper all represent potential vehicles for information leakage.

But worst of all are the programs running on the system. Programs are remarkably unpredictable things, even a quite small program may have tens of thousands of possible outcomes for a limited set of data. The security function must encompass the entire operating system and has an unlimited possible set of data. A mainframe operating system may run to 1,000,000 lines of code in a high-level language or 4 to 5 times that much in an assembler language. There is no need here for malicious programmers or Trojan horses (described later). In an artifact that large and that complex, there are bound to be inconsistencies and errors.

An awareness of the problem, a limited and realistic set of objectives, and a realization of the cost both of securing a system and of not securing a system are all essential ingredients of a good system design.

Insecure Users

A system could be considered to be secure if only authorized users were allowed to use it. But the authorized users themselves are a major source of trouble. Two basic features are required to allow for multiple users to access the same system:

1. User identification—that is, a user code of some sort
2. User authentication—a password mechanism

The user code is used to identify the user and determine what operations he or she is allowed to perform and what objects he is allowed to access. The password is the mechanism that ensures that the user is indeed authorized to use that code, the assumption being that if the user knows the password associated with the user code, he is allowed to use it.

The passwords represent the real problem. It is important that an unauthorized user should not be able to guess someone else's password. But long, complicated passwords are difficult to remember, as are random passwords. As a consequence of this, people tend to use short passwords that are easy to remember, like date of birth, home town, home state, favorite football team, and so on. It is not difficult to write a program that runs through a few thousand obvious items attempting to use them as passwords. In the case of two- and three-character passwords, a few thousand items may even cover all possible combinations.

There are a number of things that can be done to improve matters so far as the security administrator is concerned. For example, people may be required to alter their passwords on a regular basis. People may be prevented from using some obvious passwords. Perhaps the most heinous offense is to allow the password to be identical to the user code. From the user's point of view, this is an excellent arrangement because if you can remember the user code, you can also remember the password.

Even if some control can be exercised over the choice of password, there will still be holes in the system: User-code–password combinations taped to the sides of terminals on which they may be used, terminals left logged on, passwords typed in while unauthorized users are watching, and so on. Without a reasonable degree of awareness on the part of the users of the system, security can never be completely assured. One method of accentuating user security awareness is by ensuring that all security violations are logged and reported. If there is an awareness that security is being monitored, casual misuse of the system is less likely to occur.

The same considerations apply to security design as to database design. A system for which the user has no responsibility and over which he has no control will be regarded as something to be circumvented and subverted, not used and improved.

Insecure Systems

A system that can be protected against unauthorized access via normal channels is relatively easy to produce. Protection against access via abnormal channels is extremely difficult. Access via abnormal channels come in several distinct types:

1. *Misuse of special functions* may occur. For example, system memory dumps may contain any amount of information that should not be seen outside of the installation. But dumps may have to be sent to the manufacturer or to a specialist support function for system software debugging purposes. The system diagnostic and maintenance functions are likely to allow access to absolute memory and disk addresses without any regard to the security applicable to the

objects being accessed. It may even be possible to run system diagnostic functions on the system when the operating system, with its attendant security mechanisms, is not even present.

2. There are likely to be *faults in the system* or side effects to normal system operation that can compromise the security of the system. For example disk scrubbing, which is the process of wiping out the contents of a disk area allocated to a file when the file is removed, may work ordinarily, but it is unlikely to work if the system fails while the file close operation is taking place. This may result in an "unscrubbed" file, a potential hole in the system security. There is a rather depressing observation attributed to E. A. Hauck to the effect that the more error-correction logic is built into a system, the more likely the system is to fail in an undetected fashion. It seems quite likely that a similar consideration applies to the process of attempting to ensure that a system will not fail in such a way that it will compromise the security of the system. Overt security breaches may become less frequent, but it may become more probable that undetected security breaches will occur. The observation is justified, if nothing else, by the fact that the system has all that extra code.

3. *Trojan horses* (i.e., programs or other objects introduced legitimately into the system, which have features deliberately hidden in them, which may subsequently be used to subvert the system's security) come in any number of disguises, the most obvious being compromised compilers and operating systems, but all sorts of other possibilities exist.

It is extremely difficult to guard effectively against all three sources of subversion. In a data processing environment with a normal number of features, the probability of finding something in Category 1 or 2 is extremely high. It is accepted as being almost impossible to guard against the third category. If a subversive feature has been built into either the compilers, the operating system, or perhaps the system's microcode, it is highly unlikely that the system can be configured in such a way that the system security could not be compromised before the Trojan horse was discovered.

A useful concept here is the idea of the trusted computing base or TCB. The TCB is the part of the system software that has to be trusted, that one has to assume to be correct and secure. The idea is this: In a system with a defined TCB, if there are any Trojan horses in the system, to be effective, they must be inside the TCB. If the TCB is secure and validated, the system can be taken to be secure.

The U.S. Department of Defense and the National Security Agency have defined various levels of security:

- Division D—Minimal Protection—The system does not meet any of the higher-division requirements.

- Division C—Discretionary Protection—The system supports access privileges controlled to the level of the group (or individual in Division C2). The system has a secure log-in and audit mechanism and forces all users to use this mechanism. The system ensures that individual objects (memory, files, etc.) are secure from unauthorized access.

- Division B—Mandatory Protection—The system supports access privileges to the level of the individual. Every object in the system (including physical devices) has a security label physically attached to it. These labels must be printed on any output produced using these objects. Separate operator and administrator modes should be supported. That is, it must be possible to establish both users that have privilege and users that can grant privilege. The system must demonstrably support the "reference monitor" concept of access control. The system security features must be extensively documented, and test routines must be provided for user use. At higher sublevels, the TCB must be formally proven to be correct. Covert channels must be identified and their usage logged.

- Division A—Verified Protection—Security at the level of Division B functionality must be supported, and the system must be extensively documented.

PROTECTED SYSTEMS

It is not usual to make a distinction between securing a system and protecting it. The distinction, however, is useful here, as it provides a method for describing the differences between types of systems—specifically, between large, multiuser mainframes and small, single-user, personal computers.

The users of a system may be arranged in a hierarchy from those most able to damage a system to those least able to damage a system:

1.   System programmers
2.   Operators
3.   Application programmers
4.   System administrators, people responsible for running particular applications and monitoring inputs and outputs
5.   Data entry clerks

A number of other individuals might be added (e.g., the security administrator, if there is one), but the aforementioned five suffice.

Each level requires access to an even higher level of privilege and, as a result, may accidentally or intentionally do more damage to the system than the preceding level. Systems may be rated, so far as protection is concerned, on the basis of the type of access required by the average user of the system.

When a system requires the average user to be able to do Level 2 things, the system has no protection. This is normally the case with personal computers. Most mainframes provide some differentiation among users, but many, for example, make no distinction between Levels 1 and 2, or between Levels 3 and 5. Particularly because of the lack of a distinction between Levels 3 and 5, it is common to find installations where the programmers are ordinarily not allowed to use the "production" machine. They are limited to a test machine. Protection has to be provided by physically isolating the potential offenders.

PRIVATE SYSTEMS

Privacy implies an association between objects and users. The owner of the object can decide who can access it and how. Objects here will always be either files or objects in a database.

Accesses may come in various forms. An access may be

- Read only (i.e., the user can look at the data but not change it)
- Read/write (i.e., the user can both access the data and change it).

Users may be (a) users as normally understood, (b) programs, or (c) terminals. Some systems do not provide the distinction between users on the one hand and programs and terminals on the other, but it is an extremely useful one. For example, if it is necessary for a user to perform a highly privileged function (removing some particular global file for example), the function can be provided in the form of a program capable of performing the function, but not capable of doing anything else. The program is nominally very privileged, but functionally not privileged at all. Similar considerations apply to terminals. The ability to disable certain types of input, regardless of the status of the user, is very useful if terminals have to be at insecure locations.

DATABASES AND SECURITY

Databases have to provide all types of security—that is, the database system must be secure, protected, and private wherever necessary.

In order to provide the functions needed to support the protection and privacy components, the database management system will almost certainly have to be part of the TCB. If nothing else, it will have the ability to see all of the data in the database, so it will be a superuser with respect to the data in the database.

Protection is provided by the database audit trail. There are at least two possibilities here:

1. Keep all of the changes made to the database in a separate file, the audit trail. The database itself just reflects the current state of affairs. If, at any time, it is necessary to know what change was made to an entity, this can be determined from the audit.

2. Never overwrite data. Instead, when some data item is modified, make a copy of the data, altering the affected item to reflect the change. The copied data is linked back to the original, and so it is always possible to determine what change was made when. This arrangement is typical of proposed implementations for temporal databases.

The second alternative does not make allowance for media failure, which is one of the essential functions of the audit trail mechanism. This function can be provided for in other ways. Media failure can be provided for by duplicating the database, doing identical I/Os to more than one disk for each write. This has already been mentioned in the chapter on performance.

There are also a number of utilities that might be used in protecting the data in the database. One of the most important is a static database analysis tool. There are a number of integrity constraints that can be checked automatically with respect to the lower levels of the database mapping hierarchy. It is easy enough to provide a utility as a part of the database management system that will ensure that these kinds of integrity constraints are not violated. The sort of things being considered here are either indexes containing dangling pointers or invalid available space chains. The **global** and **partial redo** operations were described in the chapter on integrity: they assume reapplying updates in order to reestablish a database that has become corrupt. Where corrupt data is discovered by the static database analysis tool, **a global** or **partial redo** may be used to reestablish the integrity of the data.

However, consider the following possibility. Record x in the accounting database gets touched once a year when doing the year end accounting function. In one particular year, a week after the year end, record x is corrupted by some unrelated process in a legitimate way; it might be altered or deleted. Twelve months later, the next year end is run; it encounters record x and fails. Record x has not been touched for 12 months. It is not possible to fix this by going back to the last dump, or through the previous audit trails. The only way to undo the damage, using the functions available within the database management system, is to go back 12 months and reprocess all of the data.

Clearly, protection against program error is very difficult to provide. This is particularly the case with a nonsemantic database. Very little of the semantics of the database can be inferred from the schema; the only possibility is to write a set of specialized programs that can periodically be run to check the integrity of the data.

With a semantic database, much of the semantics of the data will be enforced at run time. It is a simple matter to ensure that some relationship or record does not get deleted—simply make it required.

Privacy is where most of the security-related features of a database management system are to be found. The privacy-related security provided by a database will probably be tied to the model underlying the database management system. There are two generally recognized approaches: (1) the CODASYL schema and subschema approach and (2) the relational model view mechanism.

The CODASYL committee has defined security in terms of a subschema. The subschema is a subset of the total schema and may include or exclude fields, record types, or records. The idea is that a user may then be restricted to the use of a collection of subschemas that only allow access to data to which the user is authorized.

The *view* mechanism is similar, inasmuch as a user is restricted to a set of views that is presumed to be adequate to the demands she or he is likely to make on the database. The major difference is that whereas a subschema will not introduce new objects into the database (although things may be renamed), the content of a view can be derived from a query against the database. For example, a database containing the following relations

Employee

Employee Number	Employee Name	Employee Department
1234	I.Newton	1001
2341	B.Pascal	1001
4321	D.Mephisto	1002
3211	G.Leibniz	1000

Department

Department Number	Department Name
1001	Pragmatists
1000	Idealists
1002	Advocates

could be provided with a view made from a **join** of the employee and department records. In this case, the view would represent *which* employees worked for *which* departments. If, for some reason, an employee was allowed to see employee names but nothing else, he or she might be allowed access to the department–employee view.

Department–Employee

Department Name	Employee Name
Pragmatisits Pragmatists Advocates Idealists	I.Newton B.Pascal D.Mephisto G.Leibniz

For the SDM there is no mechanism defined similar to the relational view or to the CODASYL subschema mechanisms. There is a compelling argument as to why this should be so. To some extent for CODASYL systems, but especially for relational systems, a major by-product of the security mechanism is the introduction of additional semantics into the schema. For example, the department–employee view is nothing more than a statement of the fact that there is a multivalued relationship between departments and employees. Or if there was another view defined on employee, which only allowed employees to be seen if they happened to speak a block-structured language, the view would be the following:

Employee

Employee Number	Employee Name	Employee Department
2341 3211	B.Pascal G.Leibniz	1001 1000

Newton and Mephisto have been left out. Obviously, some semantics are being introduced, probably in this case a subclass.

Consider the implications of a similar capability in an SDM. Sub-classes and relationships are to be introduced into the schema as a by-product of the definition of the security space for the schema. This is absurd. It makes no sense at all to define subclasses as a part of the security; the subclasses must be a part of the schema.

Another argument that has been offered in support of the view mechanism is that it is desirable to have some way to simplify a complex schema. The argument supposes that it is necessary under some circumstances to be able to present an abbreviation of the schema that is easier to understand (one would hope) than the complete schema. This may be quite reasonable in the context of a relational model or a CODASYL system, but it is not clear that it applies to a semantic database.

We now return to the three system types described in the chapter on implementation: the file model, the database model, and the semantic model of a system. One of the main characteristics of the database model is that it is necessary to anticipate all of the requirements of all of the users that system is ever likely to have. Any user that is unfortunate enough not to have been anticipated will have to wait while somebody designs, codes, and tests a suitable program. This is the source of the application backlog.

One of the main advantages to be had from the use of the SDM is the possibility of building systems in which users do not have to wait for someone else to provide what they want; they can go and get it for themselves.

What are the implications of the introduction into a semantic database of ostensibly simplifying views? They are an attempt to anticipate, in advance, the requirements that the users are likely to have. They are a regression to the database model, and they would be a most undesirable feature, overlaying and hiding the semantics of the underlying system.

The ability to summarize and abbreviate the description of a complex system is essential to any reasonable interface. But it is unrealistic to assume that one person's summary would be suitable for use by everyone else, or that a summary will never change, or that a summary will always be used. Security should not be confused with interfacing issues. It is one of the more unfortunate characteristics of the relational model that it virtually obliges the designer of the system to confuse these issues.

The security mechanism for an SDM then should provide a reasonable level of privacy without introducing new semantics into the schema. The types of access restrictions available for a class may be expected to include the following:

- *No restrictions:* All of the attributes of the class may be accessed for both inquiry and update, and all entities are visible. There is an interesting corollary here; access to all of the class's attributes, unless otherwise qualified, could be taken to mean access to the entire database. It is very likely that there is a path from a given class to a substantial portion of the other entities in the database. All of their attributes are extended attributes of some entity in the class. Because all of the attributes of the class are to be accessible, any of the extended attributes may be accessed as well. This is clearly not a useful interpretation of "no restriction"; the interpretation intended here is no restriction on the access to the immediate attributes of the class.

- *No access:* This opposite extreme from no restriction applies equally to access to the entities in the class as extended attributes of some other class to which the user does have access.

- *Access to a limited set of entities within the class:* This is not really a subclass, although in some senses, it may be viewed as such. The set of entities is defined by a condition (grade > 14 or salary > 40,000 etc.) and so may be seen as a subclass in the same sense that a query result is a subclass.

- *Access to some attributes but not others.*

- *Allow or disallow modify, delete, or create.*

- *Statistical access:* This may allow users to touch entities in the evaluation of a statistical function (e.g., average) but not allow the user to look at the object directly. This is a rather unusual case and has all sorts of academically interesting implications, but it may be ignored for the most part.

These then are the types of privacy-related functions that may be expected from a semantic database system. It should be noted that none of them have semantic implications; they do not require or assume the introduction of additional semantics into the schema.

There are some cases missing here: notably, there is no concept of a security hierarchy with users owning entities and being able to grant access permissions to other users. All of the security establishment process takes place as a part of the schema declaration. This is inflexible, but at the present time probably unavoidable. The provision of the security functions described so far will tax the processing power of even the most efficient systems. Large amounts of data are implied by the very complex definition of the security space; the run-time security space search implications are considerable. At least for the time being, the preceding features are as much as is to be expected from a semantic database management system that is to provide a production level of performance.

On Progress

Mother's Market and Kitchen: *Dasd enters, looking for the others.*

Dasd. Now, where is everyone? Ah, there we are. Hello everybody. You're all looking hungry. Am I the last to arrive?

Meph. It's been sheer torture. Auth here has been regaling us with accounts of his wife's ancestors' cooking habits.

Auth. I've been reading up on my Hilda's. Where is it?

Auth opens the book.

HILDA'S
"WHERE IS IT?"
OF RECIPES

CONTAINING, AMONG OTHER PRACTICAL AND TRIED RECIPES,
MANY OLD

CAPE, INDIAN, AND MALAY DISHES AND PRESERVES:

ALSO

DIRECTIONS FOR POLISHING FURNITURE , CLEANING SILK , etc.

AND A

COLLECTION OF HOME REMEDIES IN CASE OF SICKNESS.

BY

HILDAGONDA J. DUCKITT

Dasd.	The latest thing in do-it-yourself Medicare!
Auth.	Not exactly, it was published in 1896. Its full of the most amazing things. For instance, Moss Bolletjes.
Meph.	What?
Auth.	Moss, like the stuff that grows on trees, Bollickies. Like Bullocks, only Bollicks. Means little balls, in this context, buns. Allow me to read you the recipe. It's rather a long one, but full of interest, and, as Hilda says, "very good." To get the real flavor of it, you have to hear it read in a good Afrikaans accent.

"MOSS BOLLETJES."

(An old Dutch Recipe. From Mrs. Moorries.)

Ingredients

2 lb of Raisins	1 1/2 lb. Butter
16 lb. Flour	1 lb. Fat

Dasd.   Sixteen pounds of flour! How many kids did this lady have?

Auth.   Let me finish. You don't make this recipe three times a week and twice on Sundays.

3 1/2 lb. Sugar	2 tablespoons of Aniseed
8 Eggs	2 Nutmegs grated

1 tablespoon Cinnamon, very finely pounded

"Moss Bolletje"—so called from "Moss," juice of the grape in its first stages of fermentation, and "Bolletje," a bun. During the wine-making season, the freshly fermented grape juice is commonly used instead of yeast by the country people at Stellenbosch, French Hoek, etc., and very nice buns, etc., are made of it. When grapes are not to be had we take raisins, as in following recipe, and put them in a jar which is previously seasoned by having had fermented raisins or grapes in it.

Ivle.   Hang on a minute. What are we having up this end of the table? We'll have the Oriental Stir Fry.

Dasd.   Spaghetti and Tomato Vegetable Soup.

Auth.   Tacos, please. Where was I? Here we go:

This jar is not *washed* with water, but generally dried in the sun and kept closely covered from dust, and only used for making the "moss," in as one is so much surer of its fermenting in a given time if made in a seasoned jar or calabash.

Cut the raisins or mince them, put them into a
jar or calabash with twelve cups of lukewarm
water, on the stove, or warmest part of your
kitchen for twenty-four hours, till they ferment.
Having ready the flour in which, after being well
mixed with the sugar, spices, etc., make a hole;
into this strain the fermented juice of the raisins.
Sprinkle some flour over the top and set to rise for
some hours in a warm place. Then melt the butter
and fat, warm the milk, whisk the eight eggs, yolks
and whites separately. Mix the whole well together
into a stiff dough, knead with the hand for quite
three-quarters of an hour, let it stand overnight to
rise. In the morning roll into buns, set in buttered
pans in a warm place, let them rise for half an
hour. Brush with the yolk of an egg, and some milk
and sugar. Bake for half an hour in an oven heated
as for bread. To dry, cut into two or three when
cold, and put into a cool oven overnight. *Very
good.*

So she says!

Dasd.   Three days to make aniseed balls! Thank heavens for instant
        mixes.

Auth.   They represent an improvement sometimes, I suppose, but
        prepackaged food seems to me to be the root of a great deal
        of the culinary evil in the world.

Ivle.   I'm very partial to microwave dinners myself.

Auth.   I don't know why you're eating here, then.

Ivle.   'Cause you recommended the place.

Auth.   I suppose I did. Well good whole-food restaurants are rather
        few and far between. I'm sure Hilda would have a terrible
        time finding somewhere to eat around here if it weren't for
        this place and one or two others like it.

Meph.   Hilda would be just as satisfied as the rest of us. Southern-fried
        chicken. Hamburgers and fast-food pizzas. I bet she
        wouldn't give a thought to her three-day grape juice buns.

Auth.   Maybe. But what about this then?

PUDDING (RICE)

(My Mother's Recipe)

Boil one cupful of rice in one and a half quarts of
new milk; when soft stir in a tablespoonful of
butter. When cold, whisk up three eggs, add some
cinnamon or Naartje

Dasd.   Narchie?

Auth.   Tangerine, Satsuma—

(Tangerine orange) peel, stir well together, and
bake for twenty minutes in a buttered pie-dish.
Very good.

She says again. The recipe is simplicity itself. Why does
anyone ever bother to buy tinned rice pudding?

Dasd.   Because of that "when cold" business. It takes a heck of a long
time to cool down one and a half quarts of milk.

Auth.   Quite so. It's not that it's difficult; it's just that you have to
know what you are going to be doing. You have to have an
objective in mind, boil up the rice and the milk in the
morning, so you can finish making it when you come home
in the evening. Nobody's likely to do that. Now the people
who make the pre-prepared muck take advantage of that.
They take advantage of the fact that we are like a bunch of
chickens with our heads chopped off, rushing from one
meal to the next, never giving any thought to the process
of eating beyond the pure mechanics of getting the stuff
hot, and shoveling it down our gullets in the minimum
possible time.

Dasd.   I think some people would be kind of insulted by that. I know
plenty of people who take a lot of trouble over some meals,
not all maybe, but certainly over some.

Auth.   Do they? No one these days would make Moss Bolletjes on
the grounds that it takes too long. Eating is an interruption.
Spending 3 days making some buns would be taken as
inconsistent with the objectives of the process, which is

"no fuss nutrition." I don't argue with the objectives. What I do think is wrong is the way that the "no fuss" bit has been allowed to completely dominate the way we buy and prepare food. We have no respect for the food itself. It has to be quick or decorative, not just plain good for you.

Meph.   It's a lost cause. The way we have to prepare food is dictated as much by the sheer number of mouths to feed as by our attitudes to the food itself.

Auth.   So that's why we use something like 30 calories of food to produce one calorie of beef, which we then stick in a hamburger?

Meph.   Nothing wrong with beef.

Auth.   If you can afford to throw twenty-nine calories in the bin for every one you eat. That, to my mind, is a real case of a lost cause, of losing sight of the cause behind eating. Anyway, you're wrong about the inevitability of beef. There are plenty of restaurants that have perfectly acceptable menus without having any meat on them. Mothers manage just fine without meat. The best food I've ever had came from a vegetarian restaurant, "Food for Friends."

Dasd.   Never heard of it.

Auth.   Likely you wouldn't. It's in Brighton, in the south of England. The bloke who runs it has produced a remarkable book, *The Reluctant Vegetarian*, explaining how he makes much of the food served in the place.

Dasd.   Why reluctant?

Auth.   He doesn't seem to be a vegetarian by conviction, but rather just from preference. He thinks vegetarian food is better: It tastes better, it's better for you, it's easier to prepare, and you can eat it with a reasonably clear conscience. The really striking thing about the book is that it doesn't just discard all the carnivorous ways of making food; nor does it just present a meatless version of the carnivorous recipes. It is something really new, a whole new way of looking at and preparing food that takes the best of what people used to do, and bends it to a new, and better, set of purposes.

Dasd.   What's his name?

Auth.   Simon Hope.

Meph.   Hope for a brave new world. Diet always seemed to me to be one of the weakest points about most utopias.

Ivle.   You obviously have not made much of a study of the subject. The socialist utopia outlined by Marx was the culmination of the historicist materialist process described in *Das Kapital*. Completely determined by everything that went before. Inevitable, given everything that went before it. Really, a description of the utopian state is superfluous. Anyone with a proper understanding of history could predict any desired characteristic of the state.

Dasd.   Oh boy.

Meph.   Bertrand Russell has some good things to say on the subject. He says there are three possible types of utopia; they are based on various possible types of individual. The individual as the common man, as the hero, or as the cog (or democracy, fascism, and communism), each of the last two having their own utopias—destruction and regeneration for fascism, and servitude for communism.

Ivle.   What could be more honorable than service?

Meph.   No. There is no honor for the servant, I'm afraid. Russell has a nice quote on the subject. The cog can only bow to the dictates of the machine. "In time men will come to pray to the machine: 'Almighty and most merciful Machine, we have erred and strayed from thy ways like lost screws; we have put in those nuts which we ought not to have put in, and we have left out those nuts which we ought to have put in and there is no cogginess in us'—and so on." The machine becomes an end in itself and not a means to what it produces. There is no honor in that.

Auth.   And there is honor in eating decent food. In not just being a slave to whatever we find on the supermarket shelves. It is a question of responsibility for what you do and who you are.

Ivle.   But how can you get where you are going if you don't know where you are going. Utopias are essential; we would be blind without them.

Auth.   All that attitude results in is the idea that "the end justifies the means." It doesn't matter how you get there as long as you arrive in the end. It doesn't matter what humiliation and suffering are inflicted, as long as the ultimate destination is never lost sight of.

This contrasts with the attitude that we can only judge what we can see. We must measure improvements in terms of the world we actually live in. Not to do so leads to the attitude that any action, any state of affairs is acceptable if it can be shown (and almost anything can be shown) to constitute a step toward the final solution.

Meph.   Why, you wax lyrical!

Auth.   What it amounts to is that we have to have goals that are distant enough to be a concrete improvement over our present state, but near enough and limited enough that they may be reached in, and controlled by, the lives which we ourselves lead.

Dasd.   Ultimate goals, I suppose, are like ultimate truth—something we must strive toward, but we should not hope to achieve?

Auth.   I never did feel too happy with the idea of a utopia. What could be more boring—life as an endless fishing trip—I don't even like fishing. The ideal has to be one of an ever-renewing goal.

Ivle.   It'll never work. Absolute purpose, like absolute truth, has to drive us all in the end. And anyway, who wants to be constantly looking for goals? People will get tired of it and relapse into orthodoxy. Either that or they will look for a great leader in whom they can trust, who will lead them to the millennium. People can't live by goals; they must have routines.

Auth.   Oh it doesn't really matter what sort of activity is being considered; the same applies. One way to guarantee failure is to take on goals that are not on a scale appropriate to the organization concerned. Goals that are too distant will only lead to fascism and the worship of the hero. The great man capable of achieving the unachievable. Either that, or the unachievable goal will lead to communism, where the great machine can be relied on to achieve the distant goals. Of course, neither the great man nor the great machine does anything of the sort. They may set themselves up as some sort of ultimate goal, but that is all.

Fascism or communism, on a small scale, is no less ugly for the people involved. If you take away from people the ability to control the world they live in, to set their own goals, or if you impose on them goals that they cannot realistically achieve; it doesn't really matter whether it is a clerical department in a commercial organization or an entire country that is involved, the result will be very much the same. If each cannot make his own utopia, take responsibility for his own goals in life, we are all the losers. Things must be managed so that it is possible for people to do just that.

Dasd.
You shouldn't smirk, Ivan. Consider the implications of the cog model as against the common man model. Unless the machine is going to be able to specify exactly how every cog is to behave under all circumstances, those cogs are going to have to spend an awful lot of time asking for, and waiting for, instructions. In the common man model, the individual is responsible for himself. He knows what he has to do because he decides for himself what is to be done. As long as all the individuals that make up a group have a common understanding of what it is they are trying to achieve, of what their goals are, the system has got to be the better of the two.

All you need is some reasonably clear way of letting everyone know where you are, where you would like to go, and how you would like to get there. A good data management system, perhaps . . .

Hey! the food. Boy, I'm starving!

Vanity

Be assured, the Dragon is not dead
But once more from the pools of peace
Shall rear his fabulous green head.

The flowers of innocence shall cease
And like a harp the wind shall roar
And the clouds shake an angry fleece.

'Here, here, is certitude,' you swore,
'Below this lightning-blasted tree.
Where once it struck, it strikes no more.

'Two lovers in one house agree.
The roof is tight, the walls unshaken.
As now, so must it always be.'

Such prophecies of joy awaken
The toad who dreams away the past
Under your hearth-stone, light forsaken,

Who knows that certitude at last
Must melt away in vanity—
No gate is fast, no door is fast—

That thunder bursts from the blue sky,
That gardens of the mind fall waste,
That fountains of the heart run dry.

Robert Graves

Glossary

Note: An asterisk [*] following a page number indicates a definition or an extended discussion regarding the nature of the topic in question.

a posteriori and a priori statements, 91*; *see also* statement types abort, 316*

absolute capacity, 353*

abstract types

 An *abstract type* is a type (or a domain) and an associated set of functions which accept that type as a parameter.

 implementing SDM, 232

 manipulating descriptions of, 141, 271

 and records, 68

abstraction, 23; *see also* aggregation; generalization

 Abstraction involves selectively attending to particular features of an object while ignoring other features. Abstraction is fundamental to *classification*, wherein some group of objects, sharing some particular feature, are taken to be a class.

ACA (ALGOL compiler written in ALGOL), 266–269

access, 239*

access time, *see* disk subsystem terminology

accuracy, 165, 168

ACM (Association for Computing Machinery) publications, 22–23 active and inactive dictionaries

An *inactive data dictionary* is one that is not required at all in order to run the system. Some dictionaries are described as being "compile-time active" dictionaries, implying that they have to be present at compile time, but they need not be present when the system is actually in use. An *active dictionary* is one in which the dictionary validates operations performed on the machine at execution time rather than at compile time.

ad hoc user, 153, 262, 382

Ad hoc means "for this case only." An *ad hoc user* is one whose requirements cannot be anticipated in advance, as they vary from case to case and from day to day.

aggregation, 23

Elements of a class are *aggregates*; that is, they are abstractions having heterogeneous components, and they may have elements of other classes as components. Components of aggregates may be collections of homogeneous values to represent, for example, multivalued associations among entities. Because of the unique representation of the elements of a class, any modification of an element is reflected everywhere that element appears as a component. The aggregated components that characterize an entity may be referred to as the "attributes of the entity."

ALGOL (algorithmic programming language), 268–269

alphabetic comparison, 141

analyst, 176

analytic statements, *see* statement types

angle brackets, 62*, 116

ANSI/SPARC system model (American National Standards Institute), 231–232

This model is typified by three layers: the *external layer*, providing tailored access on a by-user basis; the *conceptual layer*, roughly corresponding to the idea of a *schema* (which is the total logical structure of the database); and the *internal layer*, which is the physical nuts and bolts of the system in the form of files, records, indexes, and so on.

APL (a programming language—designed for working on matrices and algorithms), 237

appliance servicing system, 55–61

      An *audit trail* is a file containing a change history for a database.
      In first-order logic, it is possible to assert that individuals of a
      certain type share a certain property:

$$(\text{for all x}) \, (C(x) \rightarrow P(x))$$

That is, if x is a C, then x will have property P. This type of statement is essential to the formulation of a schema.

      The condition C is required by the *axiom schema of separation.*
This axiom says that it is not possible to assert a property without
also specifying the class of objects to have that property. You may
wonder where C came from. C is a property, and so it requires
another predicate:

$$(\text{for all x}) \, (C'(x) \rightarrow C(x))$$

As with self-reference, this requirement generally gets swept
under the carpet. The common approach is to say that C must be
a class defined only by extension—it must be a list of things. But
this approach severely limits the applicability of the language as a
whole. It means we can only speak of things when the things
involved are defined by a list. This, of course, is quite useless
because the things we want to speak about are precisely those we
do not have on our list. How else can we ever find out anything new
about the world? The axiom schema of separation says, "If it's not
on your list, you can't say anything at all about it!" So much for
logic.

slice, 307, 310
subclasses, 138
system components, 306
types, 138, 139
verifies, 158
as a type, 127
and types, 105
Classification, 195–197

> This is a process whereby any of the entities being modeled that share some common characteristics are gathered into classes. All elements of the class have the same class type. However, the entities of the class are represented uniquely—that is, the database must behave as though it contained only one copy of the entity.

closed systems, 10*
coarse table, 341*
COBOL (**com**mon **b**usiness **o**riented **l**anguage), 16, 104, 219
CODASYL (Conference on Data and System Languages), 77, 418–419
Codd, E. F., 23
command language, commands as data, 266–270
commit, 371; *see also* two-phase commit

> After a **commit**, it is not possible for a transaction to disappear without invalidating any transactions that came after it.

comparing descriptions, 171
compiler, 7, 24, 267–269
complex entities, *see* entity
composition of functions, 41
compound identifiers, *see* symbolic reference

> A *compound identifier* is a name, symbolic reference, or key that consists of more than one record item.

compound type, 126*
computer, 6–7*; *see also* microcomputers and performance
computer aided design (CAD), 198–201
conceptual layer, *see* ANSI/SPARC system model
conclusions in formal systems, 112
concurrency, 387

> The extent to which more than one process may access a database at the same time.

condition, *see* selection expression

Item A is said to be *dependent* on item B, if a given value in B implies some value in A. Therefore, name may be dependent on social security number if, given a valid social security number, there must be one, and only one, name associated with it.

A *designative entity* is an entity that represents a many-to-one relationship between other entities. Characteristic, associative, and kernel entities can all be designative as well.

A *directory* is a data structure used by the system to describe other data structures that are a part of the system.

disk subsystem terminology
>   A *cylinder* is a logical slice through the disk.
>   A *track* is the minimum physically addressable unit on the disk platter surface.
>   *Read heads* are the parts of the disk drive unit that actually either read the information from the surface of the disk or write the information onto the disk. Read heads are usually movable, with one read head per surface; some systems, however, have multiple moveable heads per surface. Earlier systems quite commonly included a "head-per-track disk," with one read head per track; for these systems, the read head did not have to be movable.
>   *Seek-time* is the time taken to move the disk read heads across the face of the disk so that the head is positioned over the track that contains the data to be read.
>   *Latency* is the time it takes the disk to rotate so that the data to be read from the track is actually under the read head.
>   *Transfer rate* is the amount of data per unit of time that can be transferred from the disk unit to the disk controller.
>   *Access time* is the time it takes to actually get at the data on the disk. With movable-head disks, this is the seek-time plus the latency; with head-per-track disks, there is no seek-time.

In first-order logic, it is possible to identify a particular function as the identity function, giving the following:

$$\text{(for all } x)\ F(x) = x$$

But in second-order logic, it is possible to assert the existence of the identity function, allowing the following:

$$(\text{there exists } u) \ (\text{for all } x) \ u(x) = x.$$

In second-order logic, it is possible to make a statement about statements (i.e., "metastatements"). This is akin to the idea of a language that can be used to describe a language—that is, a grammar, sometimes referred to as a "metalanguage." The prefix *meta* generally implies a higher-order object. In the same way that a metalanguage is a language in which it is possible to talk about language, metalogic is logic about logic, and metadata is data that describes data.

Elements of a class can be described in different ways by means of subclasses. Elements of a subclass also belong to their parent class. The type of the elements of a subclass is a subtype of the type of the elements of the parent class. The subclass mechanism includes the ISA hierarchy of semantic networks.

Hume argues that "even after the observation of the frequent constant conjunction of objects, we have no reason to draw any inference concerning any object beyond those of which we have had experience" (Treatise of Human Nature, 1739, Book I, Part III, Section VI). If any universal statement is to be proven or established from experience, some principle of induction must be invoked. However, "the principle of induction must be a universal statement in its turn. Thus if we try to regard its truth as known from experience, then the very same problem which occasioned its introduction will arise all over again" (Popper, 1968).

Experiment and observation may establish that some hypothesis is satisfiable, but it cannot be used to prove a hypothesis. In fact, inductive proof is a contradiction in terms.

infix notation, 41*

Infoexec, trademark of the Unisys corporation, 141

information concepts, 74–83

information content, 167, 174–175, 183–184*, 219–220
   cost, 186

inheritance, 203

inherited attribute, *see* attribute, inherited

initial value, *see* attribute, initial value

input/output (I/O), 299, 303, 312–313

insert, 149–150, 227, 256, 318

integer, 127, 128*

integrity, *see* consistency

intensional definition, 96–97*

intentional lock, *see* locking, intentional lock

interface, 259, 262–272, 358–362
   assessing an, 266, 270–272
   and integrity, 363–364
   and locking, 377–379

internal layer, *see* ANSI/SPARC system model

intersection class, *see* relationships, relationship attributes

intersection file, 249–251

inverse attribute, *see* attribute, inverse

inverse function, 41*
   in SDM, 146

I/O, *see* input/output

ISA (operator meaning "is a"), 146, 195, 196–197, 202, 205–206, 256, 304

join (relational model operator), 34*, 34–36; *see also* outer join
   as navigation, 143

Kanji, 129

Kent, W., 23

kernel entity, *see* RM/T

A *kernel entity* is an entity that is neither characteristic nor

> An *occurring item* is an item that can take more than one value, typically an array or a list.

> A join of table A to table B, retrieving attributes a1 and b1, matching attributes a2 and b2, will only return attribute a1 if there is a corresponding b1—that is, if a2 and b2 match. In the *outer join*, a1 is always returned, regardless of whether there is a corresponding b1. For example, in a simple join, a retrieval of the location address and employees based at the location would exclude any locations that had no employees based at them. To see all locations, the outer join would have to be used.

A database is said to exhibit *referential integrity* when all relation-ships present in the database are understood and properly maintained by the database management system. This encom-passes data-valued attributes, entity-valued attributes, depend-ent entities, and generalization hierarchies.

Codd's relational model/Tasmania, proposed in Codd (1979), imposes semantics onto a relational database by allowing entity relations of various types and by explicitly recognizing the existence of certain types of relationships.

The RM/T model is of some interest in a semantic database, as it may be used as a formalism for the description of the physical layer of the system.

The database schema (in the CODASYL sense of the term) is the explicit description of the database, providing the level of detail necessary for the description of the various levels of the information hierarchy.

subrange, *see* enumeration

subrole, 127, 129–130*, 198, 204–206

   representation, 254–256

   role modification, 150

subschema, 117; *see also* schema

> The idea of a schema is associated with that of a subschema. A *subschema* is a subset of the schema either (a) tailored for some particular application or (b) provided in order to add security. It corresponds to the idea of a logical database or, in relational terms, to a "set of views."

subscript, 64; *see also* PSL

subset, *see* subclass

subtype, *see* type, subtype

SUM (function), 145*

superclass, 101, 106; *see also* subclass

   ultimate superclass, 106

supervisor program, 303

surrogate, *see* entity identifier

SV, *see* attribute, single-valued; single-valued

syllogism

> A *syllogism* is an argument form consisting of a major premise, a minor premise, and a conclusion. Each part of the syllogism is a separate proposition. Syllogisms can only be analyzed within the predicate calculus.

   example, 27

   and Venn diagrams, 112

symbolic reference, 80–83; *see also* label attribute

> A *symbolic reference* is the technique used to establish a key for a record. The *key* is the symbol for the record and may be located in other records, indicating the existence of a relationship. The symbolic reference is also used outside of the system as a mechanism for indicating which objects are to be accessed within the system.

   and compound identifiers, 83*

   and simple identifiers, 80–83*

symbolic type, 127, 129*; *see also* PSL

syntax, 95

synthetic statements, *see* statement types

system development life cycle (SDLC), 12

system interface, *see* interface

            The classic example of *transitive closure* is a parts explosion. A *parts explosion* occurs when a part can be made up of parts and a query is to be formulated that retrieves all the subparts of a part, as well as retrieving each subpart of the subparts, and the process continues until parts are reached that do not have any subparts.

transitive function, 41
  in SDM, 146
Trojan horse, 414
trusted computing base (TCB), 414–415
truth, 174
truth table, 25
tuning, *see* performance
tuple

In the relational model, a *tuple* is an alternate name for a row.
Turing machine, 8

A *Turing machine* may be visualized as a railway line that extends to infinity in both directions. A single car, of a rather peculiar construction, is on the railway line. The car is small, has no floor, and completely encloses the sides and top of the operator of the car, who propels the car by walking between the railway lines.

The operator has a basic list of numbered instructions (e.g., [1] halt, [2] move one railway tie to the left, [3] move one place to the right, [4] write a symbol between the current railway ties). The stretch of track being operated displays a symbol— that is, an instruction identifier—between each of the railway ties. The operator moves the car up and down, as per instructions, continuing either indefinitely or until such time as a halt instruction becomes the current instruction.

two-phase commit, 406–407*; *see also* commit
two-phase lock, *see* locking
type, 105*, 234*
  compound, 125
  constructed type, 235, 236–237
  extensible types, 141
  implementation, 234–238
  primitive types, 235
  in SDM, 124, 125
  simple, 127–130*
  subtype, 106, 235

Bibliography

There is a very large and rapidly growing literature on the subject of database management systems. For example, the bibliography to Hull [1987] contains no fewer than 126 references, and this volume is only on applications and research issues. It is not practical or desirable to try to quote a range of articles from the technical journals as a part of a book such as this one. Therefore, the bibliography is presented in two parts: (1) an annotated reading list, which may be regarded as a starting point for anyone seeking information beyond that provided in the present book; (2) a list of references cited in the present text.

ANNOTATED READING LIST

ACM [1978] "Special issue on queueing network models of computer systems performance," ACM Computing Surveys, 10: 3.

Afsarmanesh, H., and D. Mcleod [1986] "A framework for semantic database models," G. Ariav and J. Clifford (Eds.), New Directions for Database Systems, Ablex.

Boolos, George S., and Richard C. Jeffrey [1985] Computability and Logic. New York: Cambridge University Press.

A complete and somewhat advanced text on subjects related to logic and computation.

Carnap, R. [1958] Introduction to Symbolic Logic and Its Applications. New York: Dover.

A clear, comprehensive, and rigorous introduction to symbolic logic.

Codd, E. F. [1970] "A relational model for large shared data banks," Comm ACM, 13:6, pp. 377–387.

This is the paper in which the relational model was first described.

Codd, E. F. [1979] "Extending the database relational model to capture more meaning," ACM TODS, 4:4, pp. 397–434.

A description of *RM/T*—a set of extensions to the relational model that provide the major components of the semantic data model.

Date, C. J. [1981] An Introduction to Data Base Systems—Vol. I and Vol. II, 3rd ed., Reading, MA: Addison-Wesley.

These two volumes are mainly oriented toward the relational model and the major IBM database management systems. Given this orientation, Volume I contains solid discussions of recovery, integrity, concurrency, and security. Volume II deals with more specialized aspects of the same topics.

Goldberg, A., and D. Robinson [1983] Smalltalk-80: The Language and Its Implementation: Reading, MA: Addison-Wesley.

Gray, J. N. [1978] "Notes on database operating systems," RJ2188. IBM, San Jose, CA. (Also in R. Bayer, R. M. Graham, and G. Seegmuller (Eds.) [1978] Operating Systems: An Advanced Course. New York: Springer-Verlag.)

Gray, P. M. D. [1984] Logic, Algebra and Databases. Chichester, England: Ellis Horwood.

An excellent text covering the relationship of logic and applicative programming to database theory.

Guck, R. L., B. L. Fritchman, D. Jagannathan, J. P. Thompson, and D. Tolbert [1988] "SIM: Implementation of a database management system based on a semantic data model," Quarterly Bulletin of the Comp. Soc. Tech. Committee on Data Engineering, pp. 23–32.

This, together with Jagannathan [1988], provides a good overview of an implemented, large-scale data management system based on the semantic data model.

Hammer, M., and D. Mcleod [1981] "Database description with SDM: A semantic database model," ACM TODS 6:3, pp. 351–386.

This is the paper in which the semantic data model was first described.

Hull, R., and R. King [1987} "Semantic database modeling: Survey, applications and research issues," ACM Computing Surveys, 19: 3, pp. 201–260.

Jagannathan, D., B. L. Fritchman, R. L. Guck, J. P. Thompson, and D. Tolbert [1988] "SIM: A database system based on the semantic data model," Proc. SIGMOD 88 Conf (Chicago), pp. 46–55.

Lazowska, Edward D., et al. [1984] Quantitative Systems Performance. Englewood Cliffs, NJ: Prentice-Hall.

Popper, K. R. [1962] Conjectures and Refutations: The Growth of Scientific Knowledge. London: Routledge and Kegan Paul.

Popper is best known for his book *The Logic of Scientific Discovery*. He made significant contributions in a number of fields. *Conjectures and Refutations* provides a good introduction to the broad sweep of his work.

REFERENCES

Backus, J. [1978] "Can programming be liberated from the Von Neumann style? A functional style and its algebra of programs," Comm ACM, 21, pp. 613–641.

Boole, G. [1958] An Investigation of the Laws of Thought on Which Are Founded the Mathematical Theories of Logic and Probabilities. New York: Dover.

Buneman, P., and R. E. Frankel [1979] "FQL—a functional query language," P. A. Bernstein (Ed.), Proc. SIGMOD 79 Conf., Boston, pp. 52–59.

Chen, P. P. [1976] "The entity relationship model: Toward a unified view of data," ACM TODS, 1:1, pp. 9–36.

CODASYL [1971] CODASYL Database Task Group, April '71 Report, New York: ACM.

Elmasri, R. and G. Wiederhold [1981] "GORDAS: A formal high-level query language for the entity–relationship model," Proceedings of the 2nd International Conference on Entity Relationship Approach, Washington DC, Oct. 1981.

Kent, W. [1979] "Limitations of record based information models," ACM TODS, 4:1, pp. 107–131.

Kent, W. [1983] "A simple guide to five normal forms in relational database theory," Comm. ACM, 26:2, pp. 120–125

Landin, P. J. [1966] "A lambda calculus approach," L. Fox (Ed.), Advances in Programming and Non-Numerical Computation. New York: Pergamon Press.

McCarthy, J. [1960] "Recursive functions of symbolic expressions and their computation by machine," Comm ACM, 3, pp. 184–195.

Popper, K. R. [1968] Logic of Scientific Discovery. London: Hutchinson and Company.

Shipman, D. [1979] "The functional data model and the data language DAPLEX," Proc. ACM SIGMOD '79 Conf., Boston; revised and printed in ACM TODS, 6, pp. 140–173.

Smith J. M., and D. C. P. Smith [1977] "Database Abstractions: Aggregation and Generalization," ACM TODS, 2:2, pp. 105–133.